Scripture Back
FOR THE Sunday Lectionary

A RESOURCE FOR HOMILISTS

YEAR C

Mary A. Ehle

Peg Ekerdt

Marielle Frigge, OSB

Jean Marie Hiesberger

Biagio Mazza

Mary M. McGlone, CSJ

Abbot Gregory J. Polan, OSB

Denise Simeone

George Smiga

Paul Turner

LITURGY
TRAINING
PUBLICATIONS

Nihil Obstat
Rev. Mr. Daniel G. Welter, JD
Chancellor
Archdiocese of Chicago
April 23, 2018

Imprimatur
Very Rev. Ronald A. Hicks
Vicar General
Archdiocese of Chicago
April 23, 2018

The *Nihil Obstat* and *Imprimatur* are declarations that the material is free from doctrinal or moral error, and thus is granted permission to publish in accordance with c. 827. No legal responsibility is assumed by the grant of this permission. No implication is contained herein that those who have granted the *Nihil Obstat* and *Imprimatur* agree with the content, opinions, or statements expressed.

SCRIPTURE BACKGROUNDS FOR THE SUNDAY LECTIONARY, YEAR C: A RESOURCE FOR HOMILISTS © 2018, Archdiocese of Chicago: Liturgy Training Publications, 3949 South Racine Avenue, Chicago, IL 60609; 800-933-1800; fax 800-933-7094; email: orders@ltp.org; website: www.LTP.org. All rights reserved.

This book was edited by Victoria M. Tufano. Kris Fankhouser was the production editor, and Kari Nicholls was the designer and production artist.

Cover and interior art by Steve Musgrave.

22 21 20 19 18   1 2 3 4 5

Printed in the United States of America

Library of Congress Control Number: 2018942586

ISBN 978-1-61671-434-5

SBSLC

For the Christian, Jesus' fulfillment of the Old Testament attributes the utmost importance to the truth of the Jewish Scriptures. Of course, the supreme reader of the Old Testament is Christ himself, who applied to his own life, Death, and Resurrection all that the Scriptures had promised (Luke 24:27). It is through this rich relationship between the Old and the New Testaments, in all of their various interrelated images and types, that the homilist is able to proclaim to the faithful the one supreme mystery of faith that is Jesus Christ.

Preaching the Mystery of Faith: The Sunday Homily
United States Conference of Catholic Bishops

Contents

ADVENT 1

CHRISTMAS TIME 13

LENT 33

THE SACRED PASCHAL TRIDUUM 49

EASTER TIME 73

ORDINARY TIME 95

HOLYDAYS, SOLEMNITIES, AND FEASTS 165

The Presentation of the Lord, February 2 166

The Most Holy Trinity, Sunday after Pentecost 168

The Most Holy Body and Blood of Christ
(Corpus Christi), Sunday after Trinity Sunday 170

The Nativity of St. John the Baptist, Vigil, June 23 172

The Nativity of St. John the Baptist, Day, June 24 174

Sts. Peter and Paul, Apostles, Vigil, June 28 176

Sts. Peter and Paul, Apostles, Day, June 29 178

The Transfiguration of the Lord, August 6 180

The Assumption of the Blessed Virgin Mary, Vigil, August 14 182

The Assumption of the Blessed Virgin Mary, Day, August 15 184

The Exaltation of the Holy Cross, September 14 186

All Saints, November 1 188

The Commemoration of All the Faithful Departed (All Souls), November 2 190

The Dedication of the Lateran Basilica, November 9 192

The Immaculate Conception of the Blessed Virgin Mary, December 8 194

KEY TO ABBREVIATIONS FOR CHURCH DOCUMENTS 197

Advent

Universal Norms on the Liturgical Year and the General Roman Calendar states the purpose of the Advent season:

> Advent has a twofold character, for it is a time of preparation for the Solemnities of Christmas, in which the First Coming of the Son of God to humanity is remembered, and likewise a time when, by remembrance of this, minds and hearts are led to look forward to Christ's Second Coming at the end of time. For these two reasons, Advent is a period of devout and expectant delight. (39)

Unlike its pre-Conciliar focus on penance and conversion, similar to Lent, the liturgical reforms of the Second Vatican Council shifted the focus of Advent to a time of devout, joyful, and hopeful expectation of Christ's past, present, and future coming. The four Sundays before December 25 encompass the Advent season with Gospel readings that reverse our usual sense of time. The Gospel for the First Sunday of Advent focuses on the future coming of Christ, with the Second and Third Sundays highlighting Christ's adult ministry, while the Fourth Sunday turns our attention to his infant birth.

FIRST READINGS

The First Readings for Advent for all liturgical cycles come from the prophets with the exception of a reading from 2 Samuel on the Fourth Sunday in Year B. Of the other eleven selections, seven are taken from Isaiah. This year, Year C, none come from Isaiah, but from four different prophets, Jeremiah, Baruch, Zephaniah, and Micah respectively. On the First Sunday Jeremiah speaks of God's promises being fulfilled through a "just shoot" from the house of David who will establish the people and the land, calling them "the Lord our justice." On the Second Sunday, Baruch promises that Jerusalem, now in mourning and misery, will be restored by God and will experience a better future filled with God's mercy and justice. The Third Sunday, known as Gaudete (or "Rejoice") Sunday, has Zephaniah call Israel to rejoice for the Lord will restore it to former glory and will choose to dwell in the midst of the people as a mighty savior and protector. The last Sunday has Micah speak of Bethlehem as the place out of which one will come to rule Israel, restore it, and shepherd it in love and peace.

RESPONSORIAL PSALMS

On the First Sunday, Psalm 25 has us asking God to teach and guide us in the paths that lead to life. Psalm 126 on the Second Sunday is a call to the Lord to restore us and make us joyful once more. The response for the Third Sunday is a canticle from Isaiah 12. It expresses confidence in God as our savior, strength, and courage. This God has chosen to live among us and so we can only be grateful and highly joyful. Psalm 80 on the last Sunday appeals to God for salvation, praying that we might experience the intimacy of God's presence and that in seeing God face to face, we will indeed be saved.

SECOND READINGS

The Second Readings come from 1 Thessalonians, Philippians, and Hebrews. The first three all exhort and instruct disciples in the way of the Lord. The readings offer instructions in living according to the modeling that Jesus offered. As we wait in joyful hope and expectation of Christ's Second Coming, we are called to live out virtues and a lifestyle consistent with God's desires for all humanity. Love in service of others in the style of Jesus' life is the cornerstone and sure path. Hebrews calls us to do God's will in the same manner that Jesus came among us to accomplish God's will.

GOSPEL READINGS

Lectionary Year C gives us Luke's account of the Gospel as our guide. All four Sundays proclaim a Lucan passage and begin in a reverse time frame scenario. The First Sunday highlights the signs that will inaugurate Christ's Second Coming. The Second and Third Sunday focus on John the Baptist, the precursor who inaugurates the adult ministry of Jesus, by announcing that God's kingdom is near and calling people to conversion and change of heart. The last Sunday focuses on Mary and Elizabeth, two pregnant women who have chosen to cooperate with God's plan and who will be instrumental in helping to bring about God's reign and salvation to all. At the Visitation scene, Elizabeth acknowledges Mary's child to be the Lord by referring to Mary as the "mother of my Lord" (1:43).

Vigilantly Awaiting the Day of the Lord

JEREMIAH 33:14–16

This brief passage presents in context a powerful expression of faith: the prophet Jeremiah, confined to the court of the guard, receives a promise of divine restoration. After a long period of corrupt government and unfaithful leadership, God assures the prophet that a Davidic ruler will come to restore justice and righteousness to the land. The decades-long threat of invasion and suppression by foreign nations will end; safety and security will be established. This act of divine intervention will demonstrate the power of God's Word and actions. The final line, "this is what they shall call her: 'The Lord our justice'" (33:14), asserts faith in a divine act of renewal, re-creation, and salvation. The people of Judah and Jerusalem shall bear God's name: "The Lord our justice." Divine justice constitutes their way of life; it is the mind and heart of the people, and it informs the structures that govern them. Though fulfillment remains distant, the promise comes from God, assuring that it will be accomplished in time.

PSALM 25:4–5, 8–9, 10, 14 (1B) For centuries, Psalm 25 has been known as the "Advent Psalm." As a Wisdom psalm, it includes instructional elements, but it also bears expressions of longing, waiting, and hoping for divine redemption. The psalmist pleads to be guided, taught, and shown the paths of divine truth. The language of the psalm gives voice to a longing for the communion with God that arises from the experience of divine deliverance. Once sin is wiped away by mercy and forgiveness, the sense of God's justice far exceeds any possible human offering. God's mercy exceeds all human expectations and forms the divine-human relationship as friendship.

1 THESSALONIANS 3:22—4:2 The earliest Christian traditions expected the Lord to return soon after his Resurrection. First Thessalonians is believed to be the earliest of Paul's letters; it voices this expectation of the imminent return of the Lord Jesus. It is in that spirit that Paul exhorts the community to live fully in accord with Jesus' command to love. Anyone who does this will be found blameless at the Lord's advent.

CONNECTIONS TO CHURCH TEACHING AND TRADITION

- "Each Gospel reading [for Advent] has a distinctive theme: the Lord's coming at the end of time (First Sunday of Advent), John the Baptist (Second and Third Sunday), and the events that prepared immediately for the Lord's birth (Fourth Sunday)" (LMI, 93).

- "We do not only preach that Christ comes once, but also a second time as well, even more glorious than the first. Our Savior, the Lord Jesus Christ will come from heaven at the end of the world, in glory on the last day. For there will be an end to this world of ours, and the created world will all be made new" (Cyril of Jerusalem, Catechetical Homily for Advent).

Paul affirms the importance of mutual support in finding the path to righteous living. The good example of others invites us to do likewise. For Paul, teaching by example is the principal form of instruction in the Christian Way. Elsewhere Paul asserts that such example brings the teaching of Jesus to life (see 1 Thessalonians 1:6; Philemon 1:3–10; 3:17; 1 Corinthians 11:1).

LUKE 21:25–28, 34–36 The Scriptures for this First Sunday of Advent offer varied perspectives on God's advents over the course of salvation history. In contrast to Jeremiah's promise of a future healing and St. Paul's invitation to "abound in love" (1 Thessalonians 3:12), this Lucan Gospel passage presents an apocalyptic vision of the return of the Son of Man, employing images of cosmic upheaval and national catastrophe. At the historic moment of Luke's composition of the Gospel, these elements of universal turmoil suggest that the powers of good and evil are vying for dominion. Their presence here brings into focus the fact that the Gospel faces enemies that want to stamp it out. This is nothing new. The prophets faced similar challenges as they proclaimed God's Word, and Luke may be borrowing their imagery to show that his message is rooted in God's revelatory Word.

Luke's classic Advent message is "be vigilant . . . and pray" (Luke 21:36), for it is in those two dispositions of the heart that one discovers the pathway of Christian living and readiness to meet God. The evangelist emphasizes that this assault of evil will come upon everyone; no one is exempt. We know not the day nor the hour when we will meet the Son of Man. Advent stirs the human heart to be watchful and ready in prayer, disposed to encounter the God who comes among us each day.

Deliverance Is Coming

BARUCH 5:1–9 Though we think of Isaiah as the prophet of Advent, it is interesting to note that his writings do not appear as the First Reading in any of the Advent Sundays of Year C. However, in this week's reading from Baruch, we find images similar to those of the Isaian corpus. In its scriptural context, this passage displays a hopeful message to those who have witnessed the destruction of Jerusalem, their capital and religious center, now taken over by foreign rulers. The devastation of the past is coming to an end. God's advent among this chosen people will be a gathering in of all who have been scattered, led by none other than God. The prophet's symbolic language describes God as overturning the very fixtures of creation—lofty mountains and deep gorges—to express the huge scope of the act of redemption about to take place for the once-devastated people of God. Salvation is near at hand.

PSALM 126:1–2, 2–3, 4–5, 6 (3) This beautiful psalm places on the lips of those who have been ransomed an account of their experience, a movement from captivity to rejoicing. It is one of the Psalms of Ascent, those hymns thought to have been sung by pilgrims on their way to Jerusalem for the three annual festivals, and again on ascending the steps of the Temple. This psalm serves to remind later generations of the experience of captivity and the subsequent release brought about by the mighty yet loving hand of God. Remembering the past is an important element of faith often expressed in the psalms, a reminder that God's salvation will be the final word.

The beauty of this psalm is in the surprise arising from God's marvelous act of deliverance: "we were like men dreaming" (126:1). So great was their surprise at seeing this decisive act of redemption unfold before them that the people could only laugh out loud in amazement and astonishment. The imagery is drawn from the rural agrarian experience of Israel, a verbal picture of the hard and sorrowful work of sowing that ultimately emerges in rejoicing at an abundant harvest. The contrasts of language and imagery in this psalm give fitting expression to the wonder and amazement of the chosen people at God's endless goodness to them.

CONNECTIONS TO CHURCH TEACHING AND TRADITION

- "In order to extend to all regions of the earth, [the Church] enters into human history, though it transcends at once all times and all boundaries between peoples" (LG, 9).

- "What is called for is an evangelization capable of shedding light on these new ways of relating to God, to others, and to the world around us, and inspiring essential values" (EG, 74).

- "In the modern era, the idea of the Last Judgment has faded into the background: Christian faith has been individualized and primarily oriented towards the salvation of the believer's own soul, while reflection on world history is largely dominated by the idea of progress. The fundamental content of awaiting a final Judgment, however, has not disappeared: it has simply taken on a totally different form" (SS, 42).

PHILIPPIANS 1:4–6, 8–11 St. Paul has a special friendship with the people of Philippi. Their fidelity to what they have been taught has endeared them to Paul. When he remembers them in prayer, his heart is filled with joy. He is confident that the grace of God at work in them will bear much fruit at the coming of Christ. Here, Paul uses the expression "the day of Christ Jesus" (Philippians 1:6), building on language familiar in the writings of the prophets: "on that day" when God's coming will reverse the powers of evil and bring a heavy judgment on those who have been unfaithful. As the Philippians have been trustworthy partners in spreading the Gospel, it will surely be a day of blessing for them.

The plan of God continues to unfold within their community as love grows ever stronger. In bearing the Gospel in their hearts, they know how to choose the path of righteousness, discerning what is of value in living the Christian life.

LUKE 3:1–6 In this Gospel passage, we hear echoes of our earlier reading from Baruch, which recalls the prophet Isaiah. Here, Luke quotes the majestic and wondrous language of the prophet to introduce John the Baptist, the great prophet of the final age. The opening description of John resembles the textual introductions of the Old Testament prophets. It includes data about the times and the rulers of the era and provides a clear sense that this call is from God ("the word of God came to John the son of Zechariah in the desert" [Luke 3:2]). As the prophetic voice that is to precede the Messiah, John's task is to prepare the hearts of the people for the advent of the God-man, Jesus Christ. This preparation includes a call to repentance for past failings, which then leads to the divine gift of forgiveness of sins. The central theological message is that John the Baptist announces the end time, the advent of God that was spoken of by all the earlier prophets. The final age is beginning.

The closing line of this passage rings with a message of hope: God's unfolding plan comes to fruition as "all flesh shall see the salvation of God" (Luke 3:6). The message is now not for the Hebrew people alone; all are invited to take their place among the chosen in accepting the message of the Gospel. Salvation is for all.

ZEPHANIAH 3:14–18A The Book of Zephaniah collects oracles or sermons preached in Jerusalem around 620 BC. The context for this reading is Zephaniah's declaration that God will save a remnant of the meek and humble in Israel. Zephaniah sounds a bit like Isaiah who was told to encourage the people and speak tenderly because their service had ended and their sin was pardoned. Zephaniah offered his people three compelling reasons for hope. First, the Lord had removed their guilt—what they could never repay was expiated. Second, the Lord was in their midst. Whatever they had heard of warning and of God's wrath had been overturned and God was rejoicing over them! Third, as a direct consequence of God's love, they had nothing to fear. Discouragement would be unthinkable for a people so aware of God's saving presence among them. The reading proclaims that God will "renew you in his love" (3:17d). That phrase could as well be translated as "God will quiet you," leaving us with the image of a parent who holds a child near until all fear disappears.

ISAIAH 12:2–3, 4, 5–6 (6) Today we sing a canticle from the prophet Isaiah, one of many examples of psalms and songs found throughout the Bible. We get the sense that at this point in his prophesying, simple prose had become insufficient. Isaiah's message seemingly had to overflow into a prayer of praise, not unlike St. Thomas Aquinas who quit theologizing about the mystery of the Eucharist to compose a hymn, *Pange Lingua,* the classic hymn of Eucharistic devotion. The canticle underlines the joyous theme of the day and bridges the First and Second Readings as it declares "[m]y strength and my courage is the Lord" (12:2). With the image of drawing water from the fountain of salvation it assures us that God's saving care is like a well that will never run dry; all we need to do is seek it out. The canticle invites us to meditate on our own salvation history, to remember when we have recognized God in our midst. The antiphon also reminds us that recognizing God's presence can transform everything.

CONNECTIONS TO CHURCH TEACHING AND TRADITION

- "The . . . Old Testament predicted that the joy of salvation would abound in messianic times. . . . Perhaps the most exciting invitation is that of the prophet Zephaniah, who presents God with his people in the midst of a celebration overflowing with the joy of salvation" (EG, 4).

- "God's presence accompanies the sincere efforts of individuals and groups to find encouragement and meaning in their lives. He dwells among them, fostering solidarity, fraternity, and the desire for goodness, truth and justice. . . . God does not hide himself from those who seek him with a sincere heart, even though they do so tentatively, in a vague and haphazard manner" (EG, 71).

- "We have come to believe in God's love: in these words the Christian can express the fundamental decision of his life. Being Christian is not the result of an ethical choice . . . but the encounter with . . . a person, which gives life a new horizon and a decisive direction" (DCE, 1).

PHILIPPIANS 4:4–7 This, the closing of Paul's Letter to the Philippians, serves to recap his major themes, and it underlines his invitation to rejoice. That message takes on depth as we recall that Paul wrote while a prisoner facing a probable death penalty and the Philippians themselves were facing persecution. The verse, "Your kindness should be known to all" (4:5), is centrally important to Paul and yet not easy to translate. Other words suggested for "kindness" include forbearance, patience, courtesy and mutual respect . . . to name a few. With this phrase Paul is encouraging the community to give public witness to their faith, not necessarily verbally, but by the way they live together. In that, it is not simply their relationships that matter, but their whole approach to life. In the midst of all that they are facing, Paul urges them to dismiss anxiety and thus live with a peace they can never explain, but only enjoy.

LUKE 3:10–18 John the Baptist always accompanies us on the Third Sunday of Advent. John had created great expectations and those who heard him wanted to know how to respond. His reply could hardly have been more direct and concrete. He called on ordinary folk to be intensely attentive to others. The extra "cloak" (3:11) they should offer to another was actually a kind of undergarment—one would have to pay careful attention to realize how someone might be hiding their poverty! So too, knowing that another lacks sufficient food requires more than casual awareness. The other two groups who asked for instruction, soldiers and tax collectors, figured among the most despised or feared of the populace. Luke highlights their willingness to change, demonstrating the transformative power of the Gospel. What John demands is simply that they act justly—a change in practice that could thoroughly alter social interactions. John's message here can be summed up by saying, "all you need to change is everything." Addressing those who wielded petty power, he demanded an end to injustice. For those who had little, he prescribed such an opening of eyes, closets and cupboards, that all would be prepared for the one coming after him. They would act like a people who found God in their midst.

Leap for Joy

MICAH 5:1–4A Micah's hometown experience in the village of Moresheth (about twenty miles from Jerusalem) had a profound effect on his ministry. The inhabitants of Moresheth were poor people who stood helpless as the Jerusalem government stole their land and Assyrian armies savagely persecuted them as they marched to Jerusalem. Micah found his prophetic voice as he spoke on behalf of justice and in defense of the poor. On the Fourth Sunday of Advent, the First Reading is taken from one of the "promise" chapters of Micah. The prophet is not threatening doom; rather, he is promising good things to come. He shifts the focus from Jerusalem and identifies Bethlehem as the birthplace of the one who is to shepherd and rule Israel. Doing so connects the promised savior with David, the great shepherd hero of Bethlehem. Micah promises that the greatness of this shepherd will reach to the ends of the earth. This savior will bring peace to the people long enslaved by war's victors.

PSALM 80:2–3, 15–16, 18–19 The psalm's repetition of the shepherd image is another reminder that shepherds were familiar figures to the people who would sing this psalm. Shepherds were known to care for their sheep with devotion. No sheep would ever be counted as lost, even one stray would be pursued. That image comforted a people who longed to be protected and brought safely home. Psalm 80 speaks of the "son of man." This term, when found in the Hebrew Scriptures, usually refers to the long-awaited messiah. On this Fourth Sunday of Advent, the psalmist expresses longing for the day when the son of man will come to save them ("May your help be with the man of your right hand" and "protect . . . the son of man whom you yourself made strong"). The one whose birth is anticipated in the Advent season is indeed the Anointed One, the Messiah. For Christians, Jesus, who calls himself the Son of Man, is the fulfillment of the Hebrew Scriptures.

HEBREWS 10:5–10 Hebrews is the New Testament letter with an Old Testament name, which can sometimes be confusing. Confusion diminishes once the author's message and mission are understood. The author of Hebrews wrote to early Jewish Christians who struggled with their

CONNECTIONS TO CHURCH TEACHING AND TRADITION

- "Mary most perfectly embodies the obedience of faith. By faith Mary welcomes the tidings and promise brought by the angel Gabriel" (CCC, 148).

- "[T]he more docile we are to the promptings of grace, the more we grow in inner freedom and confidence during trials. . . . [T]he Holy Spirit educates us in spiritual freedom in order to make us free collaborators in his work in the Church and in the world" (CCC, 1742).

- "The Son of God Jesus Christ, as man, in the ardent prayer of his Passion, enabled the Holy Spirit . . . to transform that humanity into a perfect sacrifice through the act of his death as the victim of love on the Cross" (DV, 40).

own suffering in order to encourage them and explain human suffering in a new context. Using the background of their common history, the author explains the Jewish Scriptures in light of the suffering, death, and Resurrection of Jesus. He also reminds his audience of the sacrifices of old, making them new by identifying Jesus as the high priest who offers himself as the perfect sacrifice. This once-for-all sacrifice makes all others unnecessary. Because of Jesus' sacrifice, sins are forgiven and eternal life is promised. In surrender, Jesus has showed all people the way to the Father.

LUKE 1:39–45 In this beloved account of the Visitation, two pregnant women come together to support one another in the midst of the unknown. Elizabeth is too old to be pregnant. Mary isn't married yet. They each could carry shame. They certainly could be overwhelmed and bewildered. Instead they are instruments of grace in God's unfolding plan. In surrender to God's will, they set the course of human history and redemption. Elizabeth is the first to conceive and she is the first to proclaim that salvation has arrived when she greets Mary, "blessed are you among women and blessed is the fruit of your womb." Elizabeth's child within leaps for joy; he, too, recognizes the mother and the Savior in her womb. It is a foreshadowing event, for John will announce the way of the Lord in the years to come. Elizabeth's final word of praise honors her beloved cousin, Mary, who "believed that what was spoken to you by the Lord would be fulfilled." With these words, Elizabeth identifies Mary as the model of faithful discipleship. The Holy Spirit is important in this passage of faith. It is the Spirit's movement in the lives of these two women that allows them to recognize and accept God's plan. In surrendering to the unexplained and unknown, they find joy, and so it is for us as well. God's Spirit promised long ago and with us still will give us what we need no matter what comes. In such surrender there is the inexplicable joy that only God can give.

Christmas Time

The focus of Christmas Time is on the Incarnation, the mystery of God becoming human in the person of Jesus, and on the manifestations or epiphanies of Jesus to the world, represented by revelations to both Jews and Gentiles. The two pillars of this season, which runs from the Christmas Vigil until the Feast of the Baptism of the Lord, are Christmas and Epiphany, with the Feast of the Holy Family, the Solemnity of Mary, the Holy Mother of God, and the Feast of the Baptism of the Lord as corollaries to these two key pillars. The entire season is almost exclusively composed of solemnities. The traditional three Christmas Masses celebrated during the night, at dawn, and during the day were augmented by the addition of a Vigil Mass during the liturgical reforms of the Second Vatican Council.

FIRST READINGS

As is true with most of Advent, the prophet Isaiah plays a key role in Christmas Time. The First Reading for all three Christmas Day Masses comes from Isaiah highlighting the news of great joy at the coming of the light that dispels the darkness in this child born to us, and now revealed and made known to all the nations. On the Feast of the Holy Family we hear from 1 Samuel of Hannah and Elkanah's great joy at the birth of their son Samuel and of the dedication of their child as God's servant. On January 1, the Solemnity of Mary, the Holy Mother of God, the Book of Numbers tells of God blessing the people through Aaron, Moses' brother. The Epiphany reading from Isaiah speaks of Jerusalem's light and splendor, due to the presence of her Lord in the midst of the people and of the nations coming to offer homage and to proclaim the Lord's praises. As the season closes with the Feast of the Baptism of the Lord, Isaiah proclaims that God has comforted the people by coming with power and glory to shepherd them and to shower love, care, and tenderness on all.

RESPONSORIAL PSALMS

The psalms for the season resound with great joy at the wonderful deeds that God has done for the people and all the nations. God's actions are at work today as they were in the past, and all nations are witnesses to it. Light in darkness, salvation for the lost and forsaken, and God's gift of peace run through the psalms, as well as that transformation that results from God's presence among us for all those who open themselves to God's saving power.

SECOND READINGS

The Second Readings, while not directly related to the Christmas narrative, attempt to explore the mystery of the Incarnation theologically, spelling out the significance and meaning of God among us in the person of Jesus. The focus is on both the salvation given to us by God in Jesus, and on who we now are and who we are called to be as a result of God's gift.

GOSPEL READINGS

The Gospel readings follow the narrative of Jesus' birth and conclude with his baptism as an adult poised to begin his public ministry. Along the way, we hear passages that attempt to reveal the theological significance of the Incarnation, especially the prologue in John's Gospel, which is proclaimed on Christmas Day. The narratives of the Nativity, adoration of the Magi, presentation in the Temple, rescue from Herod's rage, finding of Jesus in the Temple, and the baptism of Jesus constitute the familiar, yet eternally engaging, proclamation of God's dwelling among us in Christ. The manifestation of Jesus to poor shepherds, seekers of life's wisdom, his foster father, hopeful and prayerful elderly, teachers in the Temple, and an itinerant preacher, underscores all the peoples to whom God chooses to make himself manifest.

THE NATIVITY OF THE LORD (VIGIL)
Generations Have Waited

ISAIAH 62:1–5 Have you ever tried to hush a singing child or quiet a baby's loud babbling? Sometimes, it seems impossible. Such is the wonderful image of the first reading from Isaiah: I will not be silent, I will not be quiet. We hear this reading every year at the Christmas Vigil Mass. It is a wonderful beginning to a day on which we cannot contain our joy or hold back our praise. Like the generations that waited in hope for the coming of the Messiah, we are all one people as we celebrate on this vigil night the coming of our Savior.

We have heard the songs of Isaiah throughout most of Advent and will continue to proclaim them at all the Christmas Masses. His wonderfully poetic images are meant to allay anxieties and restore hope to a dejected and broken people. Indeed, in the reading for the vigil, the very names that have been used to refer to Israel such as "Forsaken" and "Desolate" will now be replaced with new names: "Espoused" and "My Delight." Israel has long waited for this moment, and Isaiah promises that the wait has not been in vain. Just as the fulfillment of God's promise of a Messiah casts a bright light on this night of darkness, so, too, does a new and loving image offer Israel and all of God's people the prospect of daylight and new life. Isaiah cannot contain his joy and will not be silenced. So, too, are all of God's people invited to join their voices in a grateful song of praise for God's goodness.

PSALM 89:4–5, 16–17, 27, 29 (2A) Do you hear the echo? We sang parts of this psalm just last week on the Fourth Sunday of Advent. The same refrain, "For ever I will sing the goodness of the Lord" (Psalm 89:2), echoes across the days. We do, indeed, sing out praise for God's faithful response to his people throughout all of history. God's fidelity can be seen in the covenant he made and fulfilled with his people. In light of the promised Messiah, we, too, can sing with all the ages. When we feel defeated, abandoned, disgraced, or alone, these are the times we can hold fast to God's promise made long ago and fulfilled across all the ages, even in our own lives. When we encounter others who feel alone, discouraged, lost, or disheartened, we can offer them the promise of a God who walks beside them, holding them tenderly and treating them with compassion.

CONNECTIONS TO CHURCH TEACHING AND TRADITION

- "Conversion is the change of our lives that comes about through the power of the Holy Spirit. All who accept the Gospel undergo change as we continually put on the mind of Christ by rejecting sin and becoming more faithful disciples in his Church. Unless we undergo conversion, we have not truly accepted the Gospel" (GMD, 12).

- "To bring the good news from city to city and especially to the poor, who are often better disposed to receive it, so that it might be proclaimed that the promises of the New Covenant made by God had been fulfilled, this was the special mission for the accomplishment of which Jesus declared that he had been sent by the Father" (EN, 6).

On this night of the Christmas Vigil we remember the promise and its fulfillment in Christ's birth, and we rejoice!

ACTS 13:16–17, 22–25 We began this Advent season hearing Jesus' words to his followers to be watchful and alert. It was a call to pay attention. Now, we hear that call to attention from Paul. In this reading from Acts, Paul calls out to followers of Christ to listen. We want to stay alert to his message. He reminds his listeners of their great link to the exodus event and the establishment of the obedient servant of God in King David, but he continues with the announcement of the new exodus by John the Baptist. The Baptist's mission is to point the way toward God's mission. Jesus Christ will proclaim the Good News of liberation to everyone, for there is no distinction because all people are one with God and therefore with one another. John the Baptist, like Paul, prepares the way. We, too, are called to prepare the way, bringing the Good News so the Messiah can come again and again into our very lives and circumstances. When the world sees those signs of God's Incarnation, the entire people of the world will proclaim the goodness of God.

MATTHEW 1:1–25 OR 1:18–25 At the Vigil Mass we hear three sections of many names, representing multiple generations each: from Abraham to David, from David to the Babylonian exile, and from the exile to Jesus. The genealogy contains the names of ancestors, men and women as well as followers and sinners. Imagine hearing a confident proclamation of these names and connections. Instead of letting our attention fade with the unfamiliar names, can we surface the images of the many times God has been active in salvation history? These stories of these faithful men and women are like our family history. We hear the story of how it came to be that the Messiah was conceived and protected. The Gospel ends with the story of both Mary's and Joseph's faithfulness and trust in the promises of old. But for their action, the long line would have been broken.

THE NATIVITY OF THE LORD (MIDNIGHT)
A Savior Is Born for Us

ISAIAH 9:1–6 Isaiah, the most famous of Old Testament prophets, lived in the eighth century BC at a time of enormous crisis for the Hebrew people. The northern tribes of Israel had been deported by the Assyrians. This exile shaped Isaiah's prophecy as he both rebuked his people for their fickle ways and encouraged their faithfulness to the Lord. This reading from Isaiah is a song of joy that describes the advent of a king. In Isaiah's day, the meaning of the hymn was filtered through the lens of the Assyrian oppression. The prophet foretold that the chains of slavery, the yoke and pole, would be destroyed with the birth of a child. The child would be from the family of David. This son given to them would become the king whose dominion would be vast and forever peaceful. Today, we as Christians hear and understand this reading through the lens of the joyful Christmas feast and our belief in Jesus as the Wonderful Counselor and Prince of Peace.

PSALM 96:1–2, 2–3, 11–12, 13 (LUKE 2:11) The joy of this psalm leaps from the page as it anticipates the elation of a freed people, for when the Lord comes he will save all people from oppression. Then they shall "exult before the Lord." Those who sing this psalm do not have the option of keeping silent. Rather, they receive an explicit set of instructions from the psalmist: Sing this new song for we have reason to rejoice. Trust this news and praise the Lord. Spread the word beyond the next village. Take this word, as missionaries would, to the entire world. Announce his salvation every day for all days to come, for the faithful and constant Lord comes to rule with justice. Finally, the psalm's refrain, "Today is born our Savior, Christ the Lord," is taken from the Gospel according to Luke. Its use with the psalm establishes that the child born in the city of David is both the melody and the lyric of the new song. He is the long-awaited Messiah, the one who will bring justice to all the earth.

CONNECTIONS TO CHURCH TEACHING AND TRADITION

- Jesus was born into a poor family in a stable and lowly shepherds were among the first to witness to his birth. "In this poverty heaven's glory was made manifest[1]" (CCC, 525).

- "The primary and immediate task of lay people is . . . to put to use every Christian and evangelical possibility latent but already present in the affairs of the world" (EN, 70).

- "[B]y his Incarnation, he, the son of God, in a certain way united himself with each man. He worked with human hands, he thought with a human mind. He acted with a human will, and with a human heart he loved" (RH, 8).

---

1. Cf. Luke 2:8–20.

TITUS 2:11–14 Titus is a short letter that bears the name of one of Paul's colleagues. After a brief stay (Acts 27:12–15) in Crete, Paul entrusted the formation of the new faith community to Titus. This was a fledgling community without structure or leadership, so the letter is filled with directions about qualifications for leadership as well as behavioral codes for the entire community. The letter works out of the belief that faithful living begins with belief in Christ, whose coming as man has made God present in the world through the power of the Holy Spirit in a new and definitive way. In coming to live among us, Jesus modeled a way of life that to this day challenges presumptions of power and success. In his very person and life, he demonstrates that the things of this world will not satisfy human hearts. Only this will satisfy: "live temperately, justly, and devoutly." On this solemnity, these words still invite us to the real power of faith in Jesus Christ—God-with-us, the Savior of the world.

LUKE 2:1–14 Ours is a culture that has made Christmas into an iconic celebration. The secular world has defined Christmas in a way that stands in stark contrast to the message of the Gospel. As the Lucan narrative of Christmas teaches us, the birth of Christ is characterized by simplicity and faith. Luke positions the birth of the Lord in the reign of Caesar Augustus. The historical dates are slightly off, but that is a reminder that his account is not meant primarily as historical fact; it is a Gospel narrative of faith. In this instance, Luke's reference to local government establishes the point that the real Savior of the world is not a human ruler like Augustus. Rather, the Savior came as a child of humble birth and gave his life for the salvation of the world. In Luke's account of the Gospel, it is not the famous, powerful, or wealthy who first hear the Good News. Rather, Luke intentionally writes that the simple shepherds at work in the fields are the first to hear the angels' news. This stands as the evangelist's clear signal that the poor are first in God's favor. As we embrace the work of faith, the work of announcing salvation, we do so not just on Christmas Day, but on all days.

The Nativity of the Lord (Dawn)
The Light Shines

ISAIAH 62:11–12 Often when people were changed by an encounter with God, they were given a new name. So, too, Isaiah says the city of Zion will be given a new name. Her reputation of being forsaken and desolate will be gone, and instead she will be called "frequented" (62:12). Third Isaiah (55—66), from which this passage is taken, imagines a new dawning of creation. "Lo, I am about to create new heavens / and a new earth; / The things of the past shall not be remembered / or come to mind" (65:17). These passages, most likely written by disciples of Isaiah who carried on his work, speak of the beginning of a new place that welcomes strangers and foreigners. This new city will be frequented and sought out because of her own salvation and willingness to offer that gift to all.

PSALM 97:1, 6, 11–12 Psalm 97 proclaims God as a mighty king triumphantly coming to Mount Zion. The psalm effectively captures the emotion of Isaiah's hope for God's city and Paul's image of Baptism in the First and Second Readings. In this message of light, gladness, and thanksgiving, we can almost hear the shepherds in the Gospel reading: "Light dawns for the just; / and gladness, for the upright of heart. / Be glad in the Lord, you just, / and give thanks to his holy name" (97:11–12).

TITUS 3:4–7 This passage from Paul to Titus may have been used in the early Church's baptismal rites. The reference to the "bath of rebirth and renewal by the Holy Spirit" (3:5) reminded Titus that he was saved through Christ. Verse 3, the verse immediately before the beginning of the Second Reading, speaks of old vices, while verse 4, which begins the reading, tells of the generosity of God's kindness and love. At the end of this passage, Paul refers to two theological insights that are characteristic of his writing: we are justified by the grace of God and we are heirs who await the promise of eternal life.

CONNECTIONS TO CHURCH TEACHING AND TRADITION

- "No one . . . can approach God . . . except by kneeling before the manger . . . and adoring him hidden in the weakness of a new-born child" (CCC, 563).

- "Listening to the cry of those who suffer violence and are oppressed by unjust systems and structures, and hearing the appeal of a world that by its perversity contradicts the plan of its Creator, we have shared our awareness of the Church's vocation to be present in the heart of the world by proclaiming the Good News to the poor, freedom to the oppressed, and joy to the afflicted" (CU, 5).

- "Christ is the light of nations and consequently this holy Synod . . . ardently desires to bring all humanity that light of Christ . . . by proclaiming his Gospel to every creature¹" (LG, 1).

---

1. Cf. Mark 16:15.

LUKE 2:15–20 When we hear this passage from Luke, we step into the narrative at the point of the shepherds' response. This scene is the third annunciation story in Luke. The first story is Zechariah's (1:5–10), who, in protesting the possibility of a child, is struck speechless after his son John is born. The second is Mary's, who responds with an act of faith (1:26–38). The third precedes the passage we hear at this liturgy and is made by angels to the shepherds (2:8–14). The shepherds' response to the angels' announcement is immediate: "Let us go, then, to Bethlehem to see this thing that has taken place, which the Lord has made known to us" (2:15).

It is significant that the angels chose shepherds, who were seen as unclean, to be the first recipients of the Good News of Jesus' birth. This reinforces one of the main underlying themes of the Lucan narrative, in which the lowly are frequently singled out as recipients of God's blessings and favor. This announcement to the shepherds is in keeping with Mary's Magnificat in the previous chapter: "He has thrown down the rulers from their thrones / but lifted up the lowly. / The hungry he has filled with good things; / the rich he has sent away empty" (1:52–53).

Choosing the shepherds as the first recipients of the angels' message is not just significant because of their lowliness, it also relates symbolically to many other scripture passages. Many other Gospel stories and parables relate to the role of the shepherd. Some examples include the story of the shepherd who loses something precious, the story of the woman and the lost coin, and the story of the prodigal son and forgiving father. John images Jesus as the Good Shepherd, willing to lay down his life for his flock (10:11–15) and David, when he was called by Samuel before he came king, was tending sheep. In the Gospel for the Nativity Mass at Dawn, there is a major role for the shepherds who, after hearing the angels' message, go and see the child and then make the message known to the amazement of all who hear it. In fact, the shepherds never stop proclaiming the Good News and glorifying and praising God (2:17–18, 20). Theirs is a wonderful example of living Christmas for us to learn from.

Sing Joyfully to the Lord!

ISAIAH 52:7–10 Right at the beginning of the Isaiah reading, we hear a wonderful image of what it means to spread glad tidings. Stand upon the mountain and cry out! Announce salvation, good news, and peace! Sing for joy! God has come to his people to comfort and redeem them. In the face of Jerusalem's destruction and disgrace, God has come with new hope for his people. The writings of the prophet Isaiah were promulgated after the Babylonian exile in the sixth century BC. Some Israelites found themselves in a strange land, driven far from their homeland without any rights or freedoms. Yet some had been left behind. It appears that it is these sentinels or the watchers who now see the restoration of Zion before their very eyes. Those in exile are returning. They understand this joy of salvation and have raised the cry for all nations and all the ends of the earth to hear about their God who has begun this work. This is glad tidings!

PSALM 98:1, 2–3, 3–4, 5–6 (3C) Perhaps we have experienced the joy of breaking into song (or even excited speech with our words tripping over each other) when something wonderful has happened. The Responsorial Psalm we sing on Christmas Day could be sung by those we heard about in the First Reading, who were being joyfully reunited after exile. In fact, the image of singing and proclaiming to the ends of the earth is contained in both readings. Psalm 98, considered an enthronement psalm, celebrates God as king over everything. The psalm calls attention to God's victory in saving his people. The deeds of God and the faithfulness of the covenant can be seen by all. These flowing verses heard on Christmas seem to bring to a crescendo all that can praise God: songs, harps, trumpets, horns, voices, lands—break into song! We can add our joy, for a Savior who will witness to a life of justice and peace has been born. As we hear in the Gospel, into the darkness a light has come. The light of salvation has dawned, and the rays of that light will reach to the ends of the earth.

CONNECTIONS TO CHURCH TEACHING AND TRADITION

- "Every disciple of the Lord Jesus shares in this mission. To do their part, adult Catholics must be mature in faith and well equipped to share the Gospel, promoting it in every family circle, in every church gathering, in every place of work, and in every public forum. They must be women and men of prayer whose faith is alive and vital, grounded in a deep commitment to the person and message of Jesus" (OHWB, 2).

- "You have received the Spirit of Christ Jesus, which brings salvation and hope; your lives are a witness of faith" (GMD, 6).

- In Baptism, we are born into new life in Christ (CCC, 1277).

HEBREWS 1:1–6 If we ever wanted to do a theological reflection about Christ, these opening verses from Hebrews would be a good place to start. God has disclosed himself in his Son, Jesus, who is the Word of God. Christ is divine—one with and equal to God. In the past, the prophets revealed God in various but incomplete ways. Our ancestors and the prophets saw fragments or pieces, but now the Son has made God's salvation known again, as we have heard in the previous two readings, to all the ends of the earth. We hear two images for Jesus that are not very common: Jesus is the refulgence of God's glory and the very imprint of God's being. Jesus, the Son of God, is the bright and brilliant light of God, and he is the mark or indication of God's presence. The world has been changed because the Savior has come. It seems an appropriate expression to worship the Messiah along with the angels on this joyful Christmas Day as we proclaim the glad tidings of the Savior's birth.

JOHN 1:1–18 OR 1:1–5, 9–14 The Alleluia verse for the Mass for Christmas Day reads: "A holy day has dawned upon us. Come, you nations, and adore the Lord. For today a great light has come upon the earth." It seems a wonderful segue into these opening verses, also known as the prologue, from John's Gospel. Its opening phrase, "In the beginning," reminds us of similar biblical words rooted in Genesis 1:1. The light has emerged and been recognized, and the darkness has been overcome and banished. In rich baptismal imagery, we hear that we can be born again. The great light that has come into the world is God's Word, God's only Son, who came to offer us the chance to be born again as children of God by accepting and believing in his name. The evangelist John weaves together the identity of the Son and the testimony and proclamation of John the Baptist to that identity. This is who he was sent to serve, the one who was greater than himself and who revealed the face of God to the world: "The only Son, God, who is at the Father's side, has revealed him" (1:14). Like John the Baptist, we add our testimony to this witness. The Savior has been born!

The Holy Family of Jesus, Mary, and Joseph
We Are All God's Children

1 SAMUEL 1:20–22, 24–28 Samuel's birth story focuses on Hannah, his mother, one of two wives of Elkanah. We learn that Hannah was best loved, but barren, and thus the butt of scornful taunting. Hannah prayed fervently and was granted a son, Samuel. Although Hannah takes center stage, God is the primary actor in this drama: Hannah's pregnancy was a gift from God; she promised her son to God; and the major movements of the story take place around the Temple. In biblical terms, Hannah is a model Israelite. She prayed with great persistence for a child and dedicated that child to God. Dreadful as it sounds to modern ears, it was a great privilege for a child to be brought up in the Temple. Samuel grew under the care of Eli and was allowed to sleep "where the ark of God was" (3:3). Samuel was first presented at the Temple accompanied by a great sacrifice and Hannah continued to care for him (see 2:18). It was his presence in the Temple that allowed him to hear God's call and to make his own commitment, saying, "Speak, for your servant is listening" (3:10).

PSALM 84:2–3, 5–6, 9–10 (SEE 5A) This psalm, probably composed as a song for pilgrims going to the Temple, provides a perfect reflection on the life of both the boy Samuel given to the Temple and the boy Jesus who chose to remain there when his family caravan left for home. Somehow those two children felt lured by God and could pray, "Blessed are they who dwell in your house, O Lord" (antiphon). The first line of the psalm may well reflect the awed reaction of pilgrims who got their first glimpse of Jerusalem and the Temple, an exceptionally impressive work of architecture in a land where most people dwelt in simple adobe style houses rarely exceeding two stories, in towns that averaged four hundred in population.

We should note that the psalmist does not rest with the physical attributes of God's dwelling. The real yearning of the faithful is to dwell with God, to allow God to be their strength and shield, the one who hears their prayer. Then, wherever they are, they dwell in God's house as God's own children.

1 JOHN 3:1–2, 21–24 The word *love* makes up two percent of the total words in the First Letter of John, using it more

CONNECTIONS TO CHURCH TEACHING AND TRADITION

- "The sacredness of the human person cannot be obliterated, no matter how often it is devalued and violated because it has its unshakable foundation in God as Creator and Father. The sacredness of the person always keeps returning, again and again. "The sense of the dignity of the human person must be pondered and reaffirmed in stronger terms" (CL, 5).

- "There is a Marian 'style' to the Church's work of evangelization. Whenever we look to Mary, we come to believe once again in the revolutionary nature of love and tenderness . . . we realize that she who praised God for 'bringing down the mighty from their thrones' . . . is also the one who brings a homely warmth to our pursuit of justice. She . . . carefully keeps 'all these things, pondering them in her heart' (Lk 2:19). Mary is able to recognize the traces of God's Spirit in events great and small" (EG, 288).

than any other book of the New Testament. The point is not just the frequency with which the author uses the word, but love's effects. God's love makes people "children of God" (3:1) in the sense that they belong to God and share in God's life as surely as natural children belong to their parents. In truth, this sharing in God's life is deeper than natural because it is God's own choice. Not only a "choice," but we could say a divine project. This belonging does not happen spontaneously; God has been offering grace continually through the centuries and reaches out to each person in their own time and place.

That idea leads immediately into the world's rejection of God's children. According to this reading, the world seeks life in ways that have nothing to do with God (competition, dominance, materialism) and therefore cannot comprehend the children of God whose anchor and goal is Christ.

LUKE 2:41–52 In this reading, popularly called "The Finding in the Temple," we hear Jesus' voice for the first time in the Gospel accounts. Before we hear from Jesus, we learn that Joseph was pious enough to bring his whole family to the feast. We also learn how deeply disturbed he and Mary were at not knowing where Jesus was: the word describing their "anxiety" (2:48) is also used for the "torment" of the rich man in Luke 16!

The heart of the incident comes with Jesus in the Temple. First, we hear that his perceptive questions astounded the teachers. Then he informs his parents that he must be about the things of his Father. The translation of his words is difficult because it is obscure in the original that says, "[I]n my Father's . . ." (2:49). Most translations choose either "house" or something that indicates the "affairs" of his Father. What we learn here is that Jesus found himself drawn to the study of his tradition, and that his perception astounded the teachers, but his time had not yet come. Luke's introduction of Jesus has also prefigured all that is to come. In this incident we hear the Paschal themes of fearing that Jesus was lost in Jerusalem, of finding him after three days, all along with the motif that runs through all the Gospel accounts, that the shape of his entire life had to do with his mission from the Father.

NUMBERS 6:22–27 In our own time, the words "blessed are you" evoke an image of Mary, the Mother of God. Formed by frequent prayer of the Hail Mary, we can hardly say the words and think of anyone else. All four readings on this feast of the solemnity, however, speak of God's blessing made manifest among humanity. The First Reading from the Book of Numbers is itself a blessing for the people of Israel. The Lord gives Moses precise instructions to pass on to Aaron and his sons. They alone will be allowed to speak the name of God in blessing the people of Israel. The blessing is intended to fill the people with hope and confidence that the Lord is indeed in their midst and dwells among them. The Lord will shine his face (smile) upon them. He will not turn from them but will remain ever faithful. The sign of his blessing will be peace—peace more broadly understood than the absence of conflict or the resolution of division, but peace that will bring prosperity and well-being among the people.

PSALM 67:2–3, 5, 6, 8 (2A) Psalm 67 is a song of thanksgiving that expresses a community's gratitude for a successful harvest. However, the verse that makes that most clear, "The earth has yielded its harvest" (67:7), is omitted from today's psalm response. Thus, today the words of the psalmist draw us more deeply into a people's yearning for God's blessing and mercy. The psalm echoes the priestly blessing of the reading from Numbers (6:24) and expands the prayer to include requests for God's mercy and continued blessings. In the collective mind of this biblical people, God's blessings were tangible (the fruits of the harvest) and visible for all to see. The bounty of the harvest then would be a sign and bear witness so that "your way be known upon earth; / among all nations, your salvation" (67:3). Blessed as a people, they saw themselves as ambassadors of God's presence and power alive in the world.

GALATIANS 4:4–7 If one studies history, it is often the case that rules and regulations are imposed or waived in response to some prior event or challenge. Today's reading from the Letter to the Galatians should be understood in this context. The people of Galatia were Paul's converts from paganism. In Paul's subsequent absence, disingenuous

CONNECTIONS TO CHURCH TEACHING AND TRADITION

- "Blessed art thou among women and blessed is the fruit of thy womb, Jesus. After the angel's greeting, we make Elizabeth's greeting our own. 'Filled with the Holy Spirit,' Elizabeth is the first in the long succession of generations who have called Mary 'blessed.'[1] 'Blessed is she who believed. . . .'[2] Mary is 'blessed among women' because she believed in the fulfillment of the Lord's word" (CCC, 2676).

- "The perfect fulfillment of the Law could be the work of none but the divine legislator, born subject to the Law in the person of the Son.[3] In Jesus, the Law no longer appears engraved on tables of stone but 'upon the heart' of the Servant who becomes 'a covenant to the people,' because he will 'faithfully bring forth justice.'[4] Jesus fulfills the Law to the point of taking upon himself 'the curse of the Law' incurred by those who do not 'abide by the things written in the book of the Law, and do

1. Luke 1:41, 48.
2. Luke 1:45.
3. Cf. Galatians 4:4.
4. Jeremiah 31:33; Isaiah 42:3, 6.

missionaries moved into Galatia and challenged Paul's teaching that faith alone was sufficient for salvation. These wayward missionaries insisted that the new converts must also observe Jewish law and custom (that is, circumcision) in order to be saved. Thus, parts of the Letter to the Galatians include Paul's response to this outside interference. Paul establishes that Jesus took on the human condition in order to achieve the mission of salvation. He writes that God sent his Son who became human to "ransom those under the law" (4:5). Through the power of the Spirit all are now sons (men and women are both included in this term) and thus are freed. So, the new converts are no longer slaves to the old law, and thus those ritual practices are no longer binding.

them,' for his death took place to redeem them 'from the transgressions under the first covenant'[5]" (CCC, 580).

- "Because you are sons, God has sent the Spirit of his Son into our hearts, crying, 'Abba! Father!'"[6] (CCC, 742).

LUKE 2:16–21 It helps to read the preceding verses in Luke chapter 2 in order to get a better sense of the message of today's Gospel. In those earlier verses, we read that an angel of the Lord appeared to shepherds keeping evening watch in the fields. The angel announced that the birth of the Messiah had taken place that day in the city of David. When the angel left them, the shepherds set out for Bethlehem where they indeed found Mary, Joseph, and the baby. When they arrived, the shepherds, the first outside witnesses to the Incarnation, told Mary and Joseph the good news the angels had brought to them: this newborn baby is the Savior who will restore wholeness among God's people and peace to the earth.

Filled with amazement—incredulity, we can presume—Mary held all these things in her heart, to savor and reflect upon them. It is Luke's way of telling us that Mary, who we know as blessed among all people, came to a gradual understanding of the meaning of this birth and the life of her son. She is thus a model for all believers who ponder in faith that which is difficult to understand. She is the sign of hope and promise that God's Spirit remains ever with us, to lead and to guide us in the ways of the Lord, in the ways of peace.

---

5. Galatians 3:13; 3:10; Hebrews 9:15.
6. Galatians 4:6.

THE EPIPHANY OF THE LORD
Darkness Dispelled

ISAIAH 60:1–6 This passage from the last section of Isaiah is a high point in the story of the people of Israel. The exile is over and anticipation abounds. The prophet jubilantly proclaims that the light of the Lord shines on this newly freed people. Like moths to light, other nations gather and come to Jerusalem, not only to rebuild the city, but to pay homage to the Chosen People. This is perhaps the sweetest balm for the people of Israel. Long oppressed and enslaved, they now find themselves at the center of attention, as the prophet announces that "Nations shall walk by your light / and . . . wealth of nations shall be brought to you" (Isaiah 60:3a, 5d). Because they have been denied power and recognition for so long, it is natural to presume that this is at long last vindication for the suffering of the exile. And it is. However, it is the Lord's light that shines upon them and that is the light of truth and justice, not the light of wealth and riches. Thus, the city of Jerusalem shall be the light to all nations and radiance to all kings, not because of its wealth, but because of its relationship with the Lord, the Lord whose light shines forth calling all to justice for the earth.

PSALM 72: 1–2, 7–8, 10–11, 12–13 (SEE 11) The psalm's refrain establishes the majesty of the Lord: "Lord, every nation on earth will adore you." This refrain and the subsequent verses affirm the theme of the First Reading that the Light of the Lord is intended for all nations and all people throughout the earth. However, this enthronement psalm provides a markedly different take on the characteristics of a royal kingdom. Wealth is not the measure of success; rather, the psalmist describes an ideal kingdom where the Lord instructs the king to care for the poor, the lowly and the afflicted. In language worthy of the most eloquent of poets, we sing the psalmist's song that only then "justice shall flower in his days, / and profound peace, till the moon be no more" (72:5). On this Solemnity of the Epiphany of the Lord, when we celebrate the birth of a child who seems no match in power for Herod the king, the psalm reminds us that this is a birth that challenges those of us who think wealth and power are signs of divine favor. It is an invitation to remember, as the psalmist did so long ago, that true power is found in weakness and true peace in caring for the least among us.

EPHESIANS 3:2–3A, 5–6 In this epistle to the early Christian communities, we hear that God's plan of salvation, once a mystery, is now made clear. On this solemnity that celebrates the journey of Gentile Magi, come from afar to honor this newborn king, the true epiphany is the news that "the Gentiles are coheirs, members of the same body, and copartners in the promise in Christ Jesus" (Ephesians 3:6). It is radical news, that salvation is for all people, and more, Gentiles are to be full participants in the life of the nascent Christian community. We who are Christian today, modern Gentiles if you will, have a difficult time understanding that in the early Church there was a dispute about the role of foreigners in the life of the community. There were strong feelings and opposing factions as discussions raged about who could belong and what they would have to do in order to belong. Today's reading is indeed a revelation, consistent in the Pauline tradition, that all people are members of the same Body, made one in Christ Jesus.

MATTHEW 2:1–12 Matthew portrays the Magi as astrologers who followed a star as they searched for the newborn king of the Jews. Along the way, they came to the attention of King Herod and therein the plot thickens. Herod intercepts the Magi (Matthew does not say how many there are) and instructs them to report back so that he too may pay homage to this new king. The Magi continue to follow the star and they do find the babe and his mother. Like Joseph before them, however, they pay attention to a dream and skip the visit with Herod on the return journey. This Gospel account gives us two kings—one who is barely born and one who is wrapped in fear and suspicion. Fearful that he will lose power and riches, Herod is threatened by the newborn child. The child whose birth dispels the darkness, his kingdom is not of this world. He is no threat to Herod and yet of course he is. For as long as Herod, and any of us, cling to power and wealth as the source of peace and happiness, we miss the point that true freedom is found in surrender to the one who is Light to all.

THE BAPTISM OF THE LORD
Here Is Your God!

ISAIAH 40:1–5, 9–11 Imagine the joy of a people who know they are nearing the end of years of oppressive exile. Finally, they might have said, God has come to lead us home. In today's Isaiah reading, the sixth century prophet describes this anticipated journey out of Babylon. The merciful God can and will restore the people to their land. The words that figuratively illustrate how that will happen are familiar: every valley shall be filled in, mountains will be made low, the glory of the Lord shall be revealed, and all people shall see it together. This poetry of Deutero-Isaiah (chapters 40—55) still stirs human hearts and lifts human spirits as the joy of new freedom is proclaimed. God, powerful and merciful, will tenderly care for his needy sheep. Thus, the prophet can tell his people: Do not be afraid. The end of the painful time of exile is at hand. Here is your God!

PSALM 104:1B–2, 3–4, 24–25, 27–28, 29–30 (1) The psalm is an apt response to Isaiah's proclamation of the power and mercy of God. For this psalm is a song of glorious praise that extols God's wisdom and majesty. With words that paint pictures—"You spread out the heavens like a tent" (104:2), "you make the clouds your chariot" (104:3), "you make the winds your messengers" (104:4)—the psalmist makes clear that God is in charge. God is the Creator of all and is responsible for the very breath of humans and the constant renewal of the earth. So here is your God, people of Israel. Centuries later, God remains ever present, ever faithful, and ever merciful. God is the source of all breath and all life. The psalm calls us to a deeper awareness of the presence and power of God in all creation and mandates our care and preservation of the earth. For God is here, within, surrounding us and among us. When we root ourselves in God, when we open our hearts and hands, God will fill us with good things. When we look with eyes of faith, we will see that God's manifold works surround us. Then we cannot help but to protect the earth.

TITUS 2:11–14; 3:4–7 We sometimes forget that the early believers' nascent faith communities had no clear rules for establishing leadership nor any real rules for how to behave. In addition, there often was confusion and discord about the role of Jewish customs and laws (1:10) in the lives of the

CONNECTIONS TO CHURCH TEACHING AND TRADITION

- "The baptism of Jesus is on his part the acceptance and inauguration of his mission. . . . The Father's voice responds to the Son's acceptance, proclaiming his entire delight in his Son.[1] The Spirit whom Jesus possessed in fullness from his conception comes to 'rest on him.'[2] Jesus will be the source of the Spirit for all mankind" (CCC, 536).

- "While water signifies birth and the fruitfulness of life given in the Holy Spirit, fire symbolizes the transforming energy of the Holy Spirit's actions" (CCC, 696).

- "That which during the theophany at the Jordan came so to speak 'from outside,' from on high, here comes 'from within,' that is to say from the depths of who Jesus is. It is another revelation of the Father and the Son, united in the Holy Spirit" (DVI, 21).

1. Cf. Luke 3:22; Isaiah 42:1.

2. John 1:32–33; cf. Isaiah 11:2.

new communities. In the pastoral letters written to individual members of the early communities, Paul is at work establishing details of household codes, offering expected models of behavior, and providing criteria for the behavior and selection of bishops. Today's Second Reading is an excerpt from one such letter, in which Paul writes to Titus with directions for the early Christian community at Crete. The reading presents another glimpse of Paul's theology as he writes that the grace of God has appeared in the person of Jesus Christ. Now, as Jesus' followers wait in hope for his return, they are to reject the godless ways of their pagan past and live temperately and justly. With a quote from what is probably a preexistent hymn, Paul writes that through the "kindness and generous love of God / . . . he saved us through the bath of rebirth and renewal by the Holy Spirit" (3:4, 5). The baptized are freed from sin. No longer slaves, they now have hope for eternal life. Most significant, perhaps, is the emphasis on the Holy Spirit, the Spirit who will guide and renew the faithful as they wait in hope for the return of the Lord. So it is that our God remains ever with us.

> "Luke emphasizes the action of the Holy Spirit and the meaning of prayer in Christ's ministry. Jesus prays before the decisive moments of his mission" (CCC, 2600).

LUKE 3:15–16, 21–22 Luke takes great pains throughout his account of the Gospel to present Jesus as a person of prayer. Jesus ends his ministry in prayer and today in this Gospel account, Jesus begins his ministry with prayer. It is presumed that it is John who baptized Jesus, although Luke doesn't say that explicitly. Once baptized, Jesus turns to prayer. One might ask what Jesus would have to say in prayer. He was God, after all, but he was also fully human, and thus his need and desire to pray should never be overlooked. It doesn't say how he prayed or what words he used. Whether he used the prayers of his Jewish tradition, or engaged in an honest conversation with the Father, the point is that Jesus somehow rooted himself in the presence of the eternal God. It is perhaps how he, and he alone, seems to have heard the Father's voice, "You are my beloved Son" (3:22). We are called to learn to pray as Jesus did so that we can hear God's voice in the insights and murmurings that occur deep within us. This helps us to keep God near in our lives.

Lent

Overview of Lent

Lent runs from Ash Wednesday up to the Evening Mass of the Lord's Supper on Holy Thursday. With this Mass we begin the three solemn days, the Triduum of Holy Thursday, Good Friday, and the Easter Vigil. The readings of Lent focus on key Lenten themes centered on the Paschal Mystery—Christ's life, passion, death, and Resurrection. The six Sundays of Lent, including Palm Sunday of the Lord's Passion, have a definite structure with each Lectionary cycle highlighting a different aspect of the richness of the Paschal Mystery.

FIRST READINGS

The First Readings in all three cycles follow the same pattern presenting a brief outline of the story of salvation from creation to end-time fulfillment. In Year C, the First Reading on the First Sunday recounts God's mighty deeds on behalf of the people and their confession of faith in God during ritual offering and celebration. The Second Sunday recounts Abraham's sacrifice of Isaac, his only son, prefiguring Jesus' sacrificial death. The Third Sunday is Moses' burning bush experience, which reveals not only God's attentive care and concern for the people, but also the intimate revelation of God's name. The Fourth Sunday describes the first celebration of Passover in the land where they ate of the produce of the land and no longer manna. The Fifth Sunday has Isaiah pronounce the return from Exile, an event like a new Exodus leading to the creation of a renewed people. Palm Sunday focuses on Isaiah's Suffering Servant, who prefigures Christ in his desire to give of self for others.

RESPONSORIAL PSALMS

The Responsorial Psalms for the First and Second Sunday invite us to place our trust and confidence in the Lord who hears and responds to our call, especially when in need. The refrains from those Sundays, "Be with me, Lord, when I am in trouble" and "The Lord is my light and my salvation," richly express that necessary trust and confidence in God. The Third and Fourth Sundays have thanksgiving psalms, offering gratitude to God for the love, care, and concern expressed toward the people. On the Third Sunday, we are invited into the Lord's presence with thanksgiving, while the Fourth Sunday asks us to "taste and see the goodness of the Lord." The Fifth Sunday call us back to confidence and trust in God by proclaiming that "the Lord has done great things for us; we are filled with joy." Finally, on Palm Sunday, the introduction to Holy Week resounds as the psalm shifts to the lament refrain from Psalm 22: "My God, my God, why have you abandoned me?"

SECOND READINGS

The Second Readings, all from Paul's letters, are typically exhortatory in nature as they proclaim the marvelous work that God has done for us in Christ. In response to such great love manifested on our behalf, Paul encourages all disciples to believe in that great love and to live and act always attuned to the salvation accomplished on our behalf by Christ.

GOSPEL READINGS

The First and Second Sundays recount the temptations and the Transfiguration according to Luke. The temptations affirm Jesus' humanity along with the perennial struggle that he must have experienced during his life and ministry. Fidelity to the values and lifestyle here professed led to his sacrificial death on behalf of the whole world. The Transfiguration manifests God's glory present in and with Christ, which will be fully manifested in the Resurrection. Each Sunday highlights a key component of the Paschal Mystery, of Christ's suffering and death leading to Resurrection. The Third, Fourth, and Fifth Sundays stress the need for penance and conversion if the Paschal Mystery is ever to become a reality in the lives of disciples. The Third Sunday focuses on the need to be prepared for death by living as God desires, for one knows not the time or place. The story of the prodigal son is proclaimed on the Fourth Sunday, reminding all of God's great joy and pleasure in the return of the lost, those who humble themselves by acknowledging their sinfulness and throw themselves into God's loving arms. The Fifth Sunday recounts John's Gospel story of the woman caught in adultery, and Jesus' exhortation to go and "do not sin any more" (John 8:11). Palm Sunday proclaims the passion according to Luke, in which Jesus, the innocent one, willingly offers himself for others while forgiving his persecutors.

DEUTERONOMY 26:4–10 When the ancient Israelites talked about God, they recounted what God had done for them. They told about God's call to their ancestor Abraham and of their deliverance from Egypt. Both signified God's grace, power, and faithfulness to the covenant. The Israelites reminded themselves of God's presence by giving offerings and regularly reciting God's mighty deeds in history.

The harvest ritual described in this passage bridges the border between the Hebrews' experience in the wilderness and their experience as a settled people. The offering of the firstfruits of the harvest links with a recitation about where they came from. Always remembering their former lives as slaves and wanderers, our ancestors celebrated the gift of a sustaining land in which to live. Like all celebrations of God's saving activities, thanksgiving to God and generosity to others mark the ritual.

PSALM 91:1–2, 10–15 It is easier to enter new territory or situations when we know God is with us. The psalmist intimately knows God's saving presence. God is the one who saves, protects, and rescues.

In this week's Gospel, the devil quotes this psalm to Jesus during his time in the wilderness. He urges Jesus to test whether God truly protects him. Like the psalmist, however, Jesus knows a relationship with God is not about avoiding difficulty but about trusting God in the midst of difficulty.

ROMANS 10:8–13 The early Church found itself entering unexpected territory. Some Jews and a large number of Gentiles were willing to follow Jesus as God's Christ. If all of the early converts were Jews, it would have been simple to welcome them into the community. How to include Gentile believers who were not first converts to Judaism was more difficult. By what basic standard of belief would they judge conversion? The early confessional statement, "Jesus is Lord," was an essential one. It meant giving allegiance to Jesus rather than to Caesar. It meant believing that God, who raised Jesus from death, continued to work in the lives of all believers. On that basis, Jews and Gentiles could work together to create a new community in which

CONNECTIONS TO CHURCH TEACHING AND TRADITION

- God provides for our needs and frees us from oppression (CCC, 301–307).

- God is with us always, even in times of troubles (CCC, 2848).

- Jesus was tempted but did not sin (CCC, 538, Glossary).

- Like Jesus, we are tempted to put pleasure, possessions, and power before God (CCC, 540).

- Salvation comes through Jesus (CCC, 430).

race, nation, gender, and economic status mattered less than one's confession of faith.

LUKE 4:1–13 The story of Jesus' temptations in the wilderness is always told on this First Sunday of Lent. This year is Luke's turn to tell the story. Luke's temptation story follows Jesus' baptism.

Jesus goes into the wilderness led by the Spirit, whom Jesus experienced so vividly in his baptism. Jesus experiences trials like those his ancestors faced in their forty years in the wilderness. They, too, struggled to remain faithful to God when faced with hunger, the gods of other nations, and risky situations.

It is important to recognize the temptations as real options that Jesus could reasonably have accepted. The devil tempts Jesus with good things. It is good to eat when you are hungry. It is good to have the authority to bring about change. It is good to be protected from danger. Yet for Jesus to accept these good things from the devil would mean giving up his allegiance to God and abusing God's promise to care for him. Because he was grounded in Jewish faith and Scripture, Jesus had the resources to meet these temptations with integrity and confidence. He refuses to doubt or test his relationship with God, refuses to bypass the cross.

Lent is a perfect time for questioning, sorting our priorities, and recommitting ourselves to God. We remember that temptations are not aberrations or glitches in the Christian life. As in Jesus' case, temptations are part of that life, forcing us to focus on what is truly important.

Covenant Ritual

GENESIS 15:5–12, 17–18 The invitation to follow God's call breaks into the life of Abraham, whom God asks to give up everything—land and family. In return, God promises that Abraham will receive the land of Canaan and descendants "as numerous as the stars of heaven and as the sand that is on the seashore" (22:17). Abraham asks what good God's promises are because his wife, Sarah, is barren and beyond the age of childbearing. God renews the promise, showing Abraham the vast array of stars in the sky, saying to him, "So shall your descendants be" (15:5). The sign that the promise would be fulfilled is seen in an ancient ceremony. The parties entering the covenant (from the Hebrew word *berit*, meaning "to cut") took animals and birds and cut them in two. Then they walked between the pieces, saying in effect, "May this be done to you and me if the covenant is broken." In the covenant with Abraham, God takes the initiative to confirm the agreement. In the darkness, a flaming brazier and torch representing God's presence passes between the halved sacrifice. Nothing is required of Abraham but to accept and trust in God's promises.

PSALM 27:1, 7–9,13–14 Psalm 27 may have been two psalms joined into one. It is both a song of confidence in God (vv. 1–6) and a song of lament (vv. 7–14). The psalmist apparently faces a life-threatening situation and feels surrounded by the enemy, who accuses him of wrongdoing. Feeling separated from God's loving care, the psalmist trusts that God will come to his assistance. Even in darkness, the psalmist is unafraid and prays, "The LORD is my light and my salvation; whom shall I fear?" (v. 1). However, the psalmist does not take God's protection for granted. He desires to learn God's ways that lead to a life of integrity. The psalm ends with the exhortation, "Wait for the Lord; be strong, and let your heart take courage; wait for the Lord!" (v. 14).

PHILIPPIANS 3:17—4:1 Writing from prison, Paul cautions the Church of Philippi, "Beware of the dogs, beware of the evil workers" (3:2). These "evil workers" were certain traveling preachers who claimed they were wiser than others, especially Paul, who regards them as "enemies of the cross of Christ" (v. 18). Their insistence in wanting Gentile converts to obey Jewish dietary laws and circumcision as a way

CONNECTIONS TO CHURCH TEACHING AND TRADITION

- Jesus Christ is truly God and truly human (NCO, 89), the clearest expression of human meaning and destiny (NCO, 91).

- Jesus discloses his divinity to the three apostles during the transfiguration and begins preparation for his suffering in Jerusalem (CCC, 554).

- The images of cloud and light reoccur throughout the Scriptures as a veil for the glory of the living and saving God. This begins with Abraham and the covenant ritual, Moses on Mount Sinai, the transfiguration scene, and follows through the Ascension (CCC, 697).

to salvation denies the power of Christ's atoning death. Paul emphasizes that their behavior is not to be imitated. Human rituals and practices are not the focus of Christ's followers. Christ alone is the example to follow. Because Paul so closely aligned his own life with Christ by suffering for the sake of the Gospel, he can say, "Join in imitating me" (v. 17). As citizens of heaven, Christ's followers will be conformed to Christ's glorified body.

LUKE 9:28B–36 The first and second prediction of Jesus' passion in chapter 9 (vv. 22 and 44–45) bracket Luke's account of the transfiguration. As Jesus is about to set out to Jerusalem and the cross, he gives his disciples a glimpse of his glory. In comparing Luke's narrative with those of Mark and Matthew, only Luke says the transfiguration occurred "eight days" after his prediction of the passion. For Luke, the transfiguration is the beginning of a new creation. Only Luke says the event occurred while Jesus was at prayer (vv. 28–29), a major theme throughout his Gospel. Several details of the transfiguration recall the Sinai experience: Moses, the mountaintop, the cloud (Exodus 24:9–18), and Moses' changed countenance when he beheld the glory of the Lord (34:35). On the mountain of transfiguration, two figures appear alongside Jesus: Moses the great lawgiver and Elijah the great prophet. Some of Jesus' followers thought of him as Moses who provided bread in the wilderness (Luke 9: 10–17) or that he was Elijah risen from the dead (v. 19). Luke alone says Moses and Elijah spoke to Jesus about his "exodus," his passage from death to life. God's voice from heaven acknowledges Jesus as the Son and urges, "Listen to him!" (v. 35). Jesus reinforces this command in his second prediction of his passion: "Let these words sink into your ears" (v. 44; the Greek literally says, "Store these words in your ears"). Jesus' followers would do well to pay attention to his message of suffering as the path to glory. From this point to the end of the Gospel, Jesus will resolutely "set his face to go to Jerusalem" (v. 51) and his passion.

Forgiven, Healed, and Redeemed

EXODUS 3:1–8A, 13–15 We might be surprised too to see something extraordinary and remarkable in the ordinary moments that surround our daytime tasks. We do not expect holy mystery to cross our path and yet upon reflection we might concur that every moment of life really is a mystery. Moses, in an ordinary moment, encounters a God who reminds him of all that has been done for Moses' own people. God is not unaware of the suffering that has happened to the chosen people and offers them rescue and safety in a rich and spacious land.

In this dialogue with God, Moses wants to know how he is to speak about this experience. He is given the revelation of a new name for God, one that is personal and speaks of the ongoing and everlasting relationship that God will carry through all generations with the Chosen People. God will journey with these people and Moses as they seek the Promised Land. On that journey their God will be faithful always providing for them despite their fickleness and sinful ways. In a unique theological twist in his Letter to the Corinthians, Paul suggests that Christ was there with the Israelites in their spiritual baptism, their spiritual food and drink, and the spiritual rock that followed them. The similarities are strong—the Israelites' journey in the wilderness, the journey of the Church members of Corinth and our journey today—all involve a relationship with a God who offers loving-kindness, mercy, and faithfulness. Just like our ancestors on their journey, we are never alone but always accompanied by a loving God who wanted no more than that we show the fruit of our faithful response.

PSALM 103:1–2, 3–4, 6–7, 8, 11 (8A) "The Lord is kind and merciful" (103:8) seems like such a simple phrase, yet the second stanza of the psalm unpacks the abundant breadth of it. The Lord forgives all sin, heals all ills, and redeems our lives from destruction. The summons to bless the Lord at the beginning of this psalm is an apt way to offer praise and gratitude. The God praised in this psalm is astonishing and generous. The psalmist names the qualities and actions done by this God: abounding in kindness, compassion, mercy, securing justice, gracious, slow to anger. All this and God crowns us with kindness and compassion too. This is the God of the covenant, committed to the Chosen People

CONNECTIONS TO CHURCH TEACHING AND TRADITION

- "In his great love God intended the salvation of the entire human race. In preparation for this, in a special undertaking, he chose for himself a people to whom he would entrust his promises" (DV, 14).

- "The Church which 'goes forth' is a community of missionary disciples who take the first step, who are involved and supportive, who bear fruit and rejoice. An evangelizing community knows that the Lord has taken the initiative, he has loved us first (cf. 1 John 4:19), and therefore we can move forward, boldly take the initiative, go out to others, seek those who have fallen away, stand at the crossroads and welcome the outcast. Such a community has an endless desire to show mercy, the fruit of its own experience of the power of the Father's infinite mercy" (EG, 24).

- "The seed which is the word of God grows out of good soil watered by the divine dew, it absorbs moisture, transforms it, and makes it part of itself, so that eventually it bears much fruit" (AG, 22).

with a faithful love that defies the imagination. We sing this hymn of deep gratitude from the depths of our soul and very being because we can do little else confronted with this much loving-kindness. Yet the Gospel offers believers a lesson about turning our gratitude and praise into action by bearing fruit for God's reign.

1 CORINTHIANS 10:1–6, 10–12 We have all probably moaned or complained from time to time, but Paul's clear message to the Corinthians to avoiding grumbling goes much deeper than complaint. Do not follow the same path as your unfaithful ancestors who turned their backs on God. Pay attention to the example of what happened to them; this Church too could lose God's favor. We remember each day during this Lenten journey that we must demonstrate fidelity to God again and again at the depths of our being.

LUKE 13:1–9 As a devout Jew, Jesus knew the prayers and stories of his people. We often hear him quoting words of the prophets or the psalms as he taught his followers. The words of this psalm seem to echo in his lesson to his listeners in the Gospel account. Someone recounts the story of people who died terrible deaths. In the beliefs of the time they would have suspected these people had sinned and therefore suffered a deserving fate, yet Jesus dismisses this and offers a different lesson. See how quickly and unexpectedly death can come! Are you prepared and ready for that? In the parable Jesus offers, we can sense the vineyard owner's frustration keeping a tree that has not produced fruit for three years. A barren tree takes time, energy, and space. Better to cut one's losses and plant a new one, but the gardener intercedes asking for a little longer time to nurture it before it meets its fate. In the parable Jesus reminds us that we do not know what lies ahead, but we must participate in the chance that we are offered. God is both like the owner and the gardener. God wants us to bear fruit now rather than biding our time, and yet out of the loving kindness God offers mercy and more time. As the psalm reminds us, God has forgiven, healed, and redeemed us. What are we waiting for? The time of harvest is near.

The Everlasting Possibility of Repentance

JOSHUA 5:9A, 10–12 The First Readings of the Sundays in Lent, when taken as a series, tell significant moments from salvation history. They offer the Christian community a short lesson about the marvelous deeds that God worked for its ancestors from one generation to another. The themes of this reading do not connect with the other readings for this Sunday. They relate to the other First Readings of the Sundays in Lent.

This week the history continues with ancient Israel celebrating its first Passover in the Promised Land. Formerly enslaved in Egypt, the Israelites had been given their freedom, but they had to escape the pursuing enemy forces through the Red Sea. As today's reading opens, these expatriates have completed their long journey through the desert, and now they have reached their own land. While crossing the desert, they fed on manna, miraculously provided from the sky for their sustenance. Entering now their new homeland, the manna ceased. Instead, they ate richly and gratefully from the abundant produce of their property. Positioned on the Fourth Sunday of Lent, this episode seems to foreshadow the journey that faithful Christians make each Lent. They go through a time in a spiritual desert, Forty Days of fast and abstinence, knowing that a new day awaits them at the end of their wanderings. When they arrive at Easter Day, they will feast on the Good News of the Resurrection of Christ, who conquered sin and death. Passover marks the beginning and the end of Israel's journey. The Israelites fled their homes in Egypt on the first Passover. They settle into their new homes on a much later Passover. Passover was also the occasion for the Last Supper, and it remains the starting point for every Eucharist—as well as its destiny.

PSALM 34:2–3, 4–5, 6–7 (9A) The reasons for praising God are many, and Psalm 34 creates a litany of them. In Hebrew, this is an alphabetical psalm—the first letter of each verse spells out all the letters of the Hebrew alphabet in sequence. Therefore, the psalm does not develop a particular argument or tell a story. It presents variations on a theme.

The community sings the opening verses on this weekend perhaps because of the last strophe about God answering the distress call of the poor. As God remained faithful

CONNECTIONS TO CHURCH TEACHING AND TRADITION

- "Those who approach the sacrament of Penance obtain pardon through God's mercy for the offense committed against him, and are, at the same time, reconciled with the church which they have wounded by their sins and which by charity, by example and by prayer labors for their conversion" (LG, 11).

- "Followers of Christ who have sinned but who, by the prompting of the Holy Spirit, come to the sacrament of penance should above all be wholeheartedly converted to God. This inner conversion embraces sorrow for sin and the intent to lead a new life. . . . God grants pardon for sin through the Church, which works by the ministry of priests" (RP, 6).

- "For in the most blessed Eucharist is contained the entire spiritual wealth of the church, namely Christ himself our Pasch and our living bread, who gives life to people through his flesh—that flesh which is given life and gives life by the holy Spirit" (PO, 5).

to the covenant and ultimately provided a home for Israel wandering in the desert, so God continues to help the needy. However, the main reason for singing Psalm 34 this weekend is the refrain taken from verse 9. It is easy to imagine Israel singing this at the first Passover in its new home: they could taste and see that the Lord is good.

1 CORINTHIANS 5:17–21 Paul tells the Corinthians that new things are replacing old ones. In spite of their past sins, God is reconciling the world to himself and even entrusting the ministry of reconciliation to followers such as the Christians of Corinth. Paul urges his readers to be reconciled with God and to embrace the role of ambassadors of reconciliation.

The Second Readings of the Sundays in Lent generally take up a theme from either the First Reading or the Gospel of the day. In this case, the Second Reading looks forward. It prepares the community to hear about the profound forgiveness that one father offers his prodigal son.

LUKE 15:1–3, 11–32 Gathered around Jesus to hear what would become one his most celebrated parables were tax collectors, sinners, scribes, and Pharisees, a group who, even by association, would need to hear a message of forgiveness. The well-known story strikes familiar chords in the lives of nearly every person today: the temptation to squander a future on the passions of the present, the sad repercussions of bad choices, plotting a way out of trouble, the longing that parents feel even for children who fail, jealousy within families, the conflicts that can arise even between good values, the need for celebration, and the everlasting possibility of repentance.

The Lenten Gospel readings for Year C pertain more to the faithful Christian community than to the elect preparing for their Baptism. Lent has two purposes—one for each of these groups. One is preparing to accept Christ for the first time, while the other is working on its recommitment. This reading fits more with the group that is already baptized, yearning for repentance and renewal.

Do Not Condemn

ISAIAH 43:16–21 God's declaration to Israel, "I love you" (v. 4a), is central to Israel's entire history. God will act because the people are precious to God. God gives "nations in exchange" (v. 4b) for the salvation of the people of Israel. Writing during the Exile, Isaiah recalls the Exodus of God's people from slavery when God opened a way through the sea for the Hebrew people to allow them safe passage to the Promised Land. God will also allow the exiles to depart Babylon and return to their homeland. The Egyptian armies were destroyed when a flood engulfed them. So, too, Babylon will be "quenched like a wick" (v. 17b), never to flare up again. Isaiah sees the Exile as a "new exodus" that will surpass the old in glory: "Do not remember the former things, or consider the things of old" (v. 18). God is about to do something altogether new. The wild beasts will be tamed, and deserts will spring forth like a river to give drink to God's chosen people. God will wipe out the sins of the people and they will give praise to the God who loves them.

PSALM 126:1–6 This Psalm of Ascent was sung by the pilgrims on their approach to the Temple in Jerusalem. It was also a hymn celebrating an abundant harvest. The farmers have planted "the seed for sowing," and now the harvesters come "carrying their sheaves" (v. 6), the fruit of a plentiful crop. The psalm is also a remembrance of the release of the captives from Babylon and their return to Zion, the Temple mount. When the exiles returned to their homeland, they wept to see it in ruins, but the God who brought them safely home will restore their fortunes. When the Temple is restored, all nations will see their dreams become a reality. Those who toil in tears will one day rejoice as at a festival.

PHILIPPIANS 3:8–14 Paul lashes out at certain itinerant preachers who try to impose Jewish dietary laws and circumcision on Gentile converts. They espoused such practices as a way of attaining spiritual maturity, which Paul knows, can only come in God's eternal presence. Paul humbly states that he has a long way to go to reach the goal, but says, "I press on to make it my own, because Christ Jesus has made me his own" (v. 12). Paul looks back at his own efforts to reach perfection as a Pharisaic Jew. He considers it all as "rubbish" when compared to the "surpassing value of

CONNECTIONS TO CHURCH TEACHING AND TRADITION

- The remnant live in the hope of the "consolation of Israel" and "the redemption of Jerusalem" (CCC, 711).

- Those who die in Christ will live in Christ (CCC, 1006). Jesus' consent to death on the cross transforms death into new life for us through Baptism (CCC, 1009–1010).

- God alone forgives sin (CCC, 1441).

- It is through the sacrament of penance that the baptized can be reconciled with God and with the church (CCC, 980). The whole power of the Sacrament of Penance consists in restoring us to God's grace, joining us with him in an intimate friendship (CCC, 1468).

- Inspired by God's boundless mercy, we are expected to mirror that mercy to others (CCC, 1829, 2447).

knowing Christ Jesus" (v. 8). Paul forgets "what lies behind" in his old life as he strains "forward to what lies ahead" (v. 13) in the Risen Lord. Paul has no need to possess the prize others hold so dearly; Paul is already possessed by Christ.

JOHN 8:1–11 In John's Gospel the crowds were divided about the identity of Jesus as the Messiah. Some wanted to arrest him, but the Pharisee Nicodemus declared, "Our law does not judge people without first giving them a hearing" (John 7:51). Later Jesus said, "You judge by human standards; I judge no one" (8:15). Jesus' refusal to condemn anyone lies at the heart of the story of the adulterous woman.

While Jesus taught in the Temple, the religious leaders brought a woman to him and accused her of adultery. Hoping to catch Jesus in a contradiction of the Mosaic law, they ask him whether she should be put to death as commanded by Moses (Leviticus 20:10). Jesus was in a dilemma: Roman law prohibited Jews from administering capital punishment. Furthermore, if he agreed that the woman should be stoned, he contradicted his teaching on mercy and forgiveness. Silently, Jesus stoops down and writes in the sand—perhaps the sin of each accuser. Jesus may be performing a prophetic action, such as Jeremiah did when he wrote that those who rebel against God shall be "put to shame," literally, "written on the earth" (Jeremiah 17:13). When the woman's accusers demand an answer, Jesus says that the one without sin should cast the first stone. One by one, the accusers depart, and Jesus is left alone with the woman. He has not come to judge her but to save her.

LUKE 19:28–40 In the Gospel according to Luke, the entry of Jesus into Jerusalem is the culmination of the evangelist's travelogue motif. Jesus had set his face toward the city of his destiny, where he will complete God's will. When Jesus had set out on his way toward Jerusalem, he was rejected at the outset by the Samaritans (Luke 9:52–53). Now, as he enters Jerusalem, the Pharisees contest his jubilant reception (19:39–40), but the joy will soon give way to rejection.

ISAIAH 50:4–7 This is the third of the texts often called Servant Songs of Second Isaiah. (The others are Isaiah 42:1–4; 49:1–6; and 52:13—53:12.) Each of these songs paints a different portrait of what God's servant is to do and to become. Here we see the servant as the model disciple, with ears open to the daily instruction coming to him from God. In a special way, the closing line of this reading, "I have set my face like flint," anticipates Luke's portrait of Jesus. From this turning point in Luke's account of the Gospel (9:51), Jesus cannot be deterred from carrying out the will of the Father.

PSALM 22:8–9, 17–18, 19–20, 23–24 Psalm 22 is a lament, well known for its opening words, which are placed on the lips of Jesus in the crucifixion scene in Matthew's narrative. A part of this psalm often overlooked is the final stanzas. Commonly, the literary form of the lament concludes with an expression of trust, confidence, and even praise of God, just as we find in the closing lines of the verses chosen for this Responsorial Psalm. It displays the Resurrection motif of this lament, a hope beyond present suffering.

PHILIPPIANS 2:6–11 This selection from Saint Paul contains the text of an early hymn of the Christian Church proclaiming the Paschal Mystery to which Jesus has given witness. By emptying himself, Jesus is exalted and given the divine name by which he is known to us as Lord. It is for us to follow his example. By emptying ourselves, we are lifted up and given new life.

CONNECTIONS TO CHURCH TEACHING AND TRADITION

- Isaiah's third Song of the Servant depicts Jesus as the model Suffering Servant. His humility is a model for those who follow him (CCC, 520–521).

- By seeing our suffering in the light of faith, we find redemption in the struggles and pain of life (CCC, 164–165).

- Jesus' entry into Jerusalem on Palm Sunday is a messianic action. He comes as a Messiah who is humble and poor (CCC, 559–560).

- Understanding the trial of Jesus as described in the accounts of the Gospel in the context of his day and age enables us to comprehend his passion with greater clarity (CCC, 574–576).

- The death of Jesus cannot be blamed upon all the Jews of that time, nor upon Jews of our own day. The Church deplores all acts of anti-Semitism (NA, 4).

LUKE 22:14—23:56 Luke makes five points that differ from the other passion accounts.

1) The Last Supper. Luke's account of the Last Supper carries a farewell discourse not found in Mark or Matthew. After Jesus has spoken to his disciples about his coming death, the conversation takes an ironic turn. The disciples begin disputing among themselves who is the greatest among them. Jesus intervenes, reminding them that discipleship is about service, not honor or privilege.

2) The Garden of Gethsemane. In the accounts of the other evangelists, Jesus goes off to pray accompanied by Peter, James, and John. In the Lucan account, however, Jesus goes off to pray by himself. Jesus is portrayed in this scene as fulfilling the prayer that he taught to his disciples: "not my will but yours be done." Little do the sleeping disciples realize they are about to be led into the great temptation to which the "Our Father" refers when it says, "Lead us not into temptation."

3) The Trial before Pilate and Herod. Jesus is questioned three times: first by Pontius Pilate, who then sends him to Herod (which appears only in the Lucan account), after which Herod sends him back to Pilate. In all three cases, Jesus' innocence is the point that the evangelist clearly wants to present. Luke uses a special term to describe Pilate's final act of handing Jesus over to the people; the Greek word is *paredoken,* which means "being delivered up." This term carries the sense of being delivered up for the sins of the many in accord with the will of God for the Messiah.

4) Simon of Cyrene. Luke uses a particular expression to describe the manner in which Simon of Cyrene helps Jesus carry his cross. Luke writes that "they made him carry it [the cross] *behind Jesus*" (Luke 23:26, italics added). This echoes Jesus' earlier words, "Whoever does not carry his own cross and come *after me* cannot be my disciple" (14:27, italics added), which reflect the demands of discipleship.

5) The Death of Jesus. Two expressions on the lips of Jesus show that he is the Suffering Servant. First, Jesus offers forgiveness to those who are killing him, saying, "Father, forgive them, they know not what they do" (23:34). His dying words are, "Father, into your hands I commend my spirit," taken from Psalm 31:6, which highlight the intimate and loving relationship of Jesus with his Father.

The Sacred Paschal Triduum

Overview of the Sacred Paschal Triduum

The Triduum begins with the celebration of the Evening Mass of the Lord's Supper on Holy Thursday. The Scriptures address the heart of our faith: that Jesus gave himself as bread and wine to his disciples and commanded them to eat and drink in remembrance of him, and that when we do this in the Eucharist he is truly present among us under the appearance of bread and wine. We are also called to engage in service to our neighbor, following Jesus' example of washing the disciples' feet.

On Good Friday, we journey with the Lord, the innocent servant of God, who has taken our sins upon himself as he walks the path to Calvary. At the end, Jesus says, "It is finished," meaning "it is accomplished," or "it is perfected." He has completed the task he was given. He hands over his spirit.

On that most sacred night after dark on Holy Saturday, we gather at the Easter Vigil to rejoice in the Good News of Christ's Resurrection. All of Lent has led to this pivotal night of the entire liturgical year; even Advent and Christmas prepared us for this night. Everything we celebrate for the next fifty days until Pentecost results from our belief that Jesus is risen from the dead. Easter Sunday resounds with the joy of this night until the day, and the Triduum ends with Evening Prayer.

FIRST READINGS

On Holy Thursday, the First Reading from Exodus is the remembrance of the Passover meal preceding the Exodus, and on Good Friday, the First Reading is from another of the Servant Songs in Isaiah. At the Easter Vigil, there are seven Old Testament readings. Their proclamation makes the saving works of God throughout history present and real to us. On Easter Sunday, Peter summarizes the mission, death, and Resurrection of Jesus.

RESPONSORIAL PSALMS

The psalms of Triduum are suitable to each of the three days. On Holy Thursday, the antiphon used with Psalm 110 comes from the First Letter of Paul to the Corinthians; it speaks of the blessing cup as participation in the Blood of Christ. Good Friday's Responsorial Psalm is Psalm 22; its antiphon contains the words spoken by Jesus as he hangs on the cross: "Father, into your hands I commend my spirit," according to Luke

23:46. The seven Responsorial Psalms of the Easter Vigil, which correspond with the seven Old Testament readings, abound with themes of the glorious nature of the earth and the Lord himself, the Lord's faithfulness to his people, the salvation the Lord offers, and the joyful nourishment that comes from following the Lord and his word. Easter Sunday we pray from Psalm 118 for the first of three times (also on the Second and Fourth Sundays of Easter), repeating its Paschal acclamation: "The stone which the builders rejected / has become the cornerstone" (118:22).

SECOND READINGS

On Holy Thursday, the Second Reading from Paul's First Letter to the Corinthians gives the oldest written account of the Eucharist; it reminds us of what we celebrate each time we gather to pray the Eucharistic liturgy. On Good Friday, the Second Reading is from the Letter to the Hebrews. The letter speaks of the high priesthood of Jesus Christ. In particular, Good Friday's passage emphasizes the sacrifice of the High Priest's own life as an offering for sin. At the Easter Vigil, the Letter to the Romans points to the relationship of Christ's death and Resurrection to our own, through Baptism. On Easter Sunday morning, the Letter to the Colossians directs us to keep our minds on where Christ has gone and where we shall be; the First Letter to the Corinthian's hearkens back to the Passover roots of our Easter celebration.

GOSPEL READINGS

The Gospel readings present Jesus' example in his washing the feet of his disciples on Holy Thursday; John's account of the passion, emphasizing Jesus as Isaiah's servant of the Lord who is the one High Priest, on Good Friday; and Mark's account of the women at the empty tomb and their encounter with the angel, on the Easter Vigil. On Easter Sunday morning, we journey once again with Mary and then Peter and the disciple to the inexplicably empty tomb, reminding us that even for those of us who know how the events progressed, Easter calls us to contemplate mystery.

Evening Mass of the Lord's Supper (Holy Thursday)
Jesus Gives a Model

EXODUS 12:1–8, 11–14 This description of the first Passover meal represents centuries of reflection on the meaning of Israel's Exodus and the rituals that developed to celebrate it. The account appears within the Pentateuch, in Hebrew called the Torah, comprising the five most important books of the Old Testament. The final editors, writing with centuries of hindsight, placed the account after the Lord pronounces the tenth and decisive plague upon Egypt; the death of the firstborn will finally convince Pharaoh to release God's people from slavery. Long after Israel's passage from Egyptian captivity to a new life of freedom, the Lord's people continued to observe a religious festival in remembrance of this foundational event, as Jews do to this day.

As described in the Book of Exodus, the Passover meal appears as a meal-sacrifice, a ritual intended to strengthen bonds of unity between the Hebrew people and God, and among members of the community as well. In Israelite culture, a fellowship meal was a significant way to express and create mutual bonds and mutual commitment. As the ritual developed over centuries, participants told the story of God's deliverance as an act of remembrance. In biblical thought, to "remember" does not merely mean to call to mind past events; recounting of events makes an ancient reality real, present, and active here and now.

The narrative intersperses description of the impending plague and Israel's escape with elements of the ritual meal. The Passover supper, a family celebration, required an unblemished offering to the Lord; here the lamb's blood marks Hebrew homes so that the plague will "pass over" them but strike the Egyptians with divine judgment. This dramatic event leads to the second and deepest meaning of "Passover": with the Lord leading them, the Chosen People will pass from slavery to freedom. Hence, the author stipulates a perpetual celebration of this meal, to "remember" the saving acts of God.

PSALM 116:12–13, 15–16BC, 17–18 (SEE 1 CORINTHIANS 10:16) Several verses from a psalm of thanksgiving supply the Responsorial Psalm. The overall purpose of this psalm is to give thanks to God, but the Lectionary designates these verses because they especially fit the themes of Holy Thursday. The psalmist gives thanks by taking up "the cup

CONNECTIONS TO CHURCH TEACHING AND TRADITION

- "At the last supper, on the night he was betrayed, our Savior instituted the eucharistic sacrifice of his body and blood" (SC, 47).

- "Moreover, the wondrous mystery of the real presence of the Lord under the Eucharistic species . . . is proclaimed in the celebration of the Mass" (GIRM, 3).

- "In order to make society more human, more worthy of the human person, love in social life—political, economic, and cultural—must be given renewed value, becoming the constant and highest norm for all activity" (CSDC, 582).

of salvation" (v. 13). The psalm proclaims, "Precious in the eyes of the Lord / is the death of his faithful ones" (v. 15). These verses foreshadow the Eucharistic cup that Jesus shared at the Last Supper, as well as his own death looming on Good Friday.

The antiphon is taken from the same epistle that gives us the Second Reading. As Christians experiencing anew the last days of Jesus, and familiar with the meal traditions of our ancestors in faith, we sing, "Our blessing-cup is a communion with the Blood of Christ." Normally, the Responsorial Psalm echoes a theme from the First Reading or the Gospel. This is a rare instance when it pertains to the Second Reading, which has not yet been proclaimed.

1 CORINTHIANS 11:23–26 This oldest written account of the Lord's Supper was incorporated into Paul's letter less than thirty years after the death and Resurrection of Jesus. However, the Apostle's use of particular terms for handing on authentic Christian tradition indicates that it dates from an even earlier time. Paul appeals to the original core of faith and practice to correct the Corinthian community, a community still struggling to shed its social and cultural divisions. Distinctions based on status, wealth, and even the minister from whom they learned of Christ have plagued the community. Most disturbing to Paul, divisions have appeared among members who gather to celebrate the Lord's Supper, the meal meant to unite believers to Christ and to one another.

Referring to the earliest faith proclamation, the Apostle links the supper to Jesus' meal with disciples before his passion. This ancient tradition strove to communicate not simply Jesus' actions, but their meaning. The broken bread and outpoured wine recall and make present the very person of the Crucified and Risen Christ, who gave his entire person and life itself "for you." In New Testament times, "body and blood" signified the whole person as a unity. It is this complete self-sacrifice for the good of the other that the community celebrating the Lord's Supper must carry out "in remembrance" (see the First Reading). To "proclaim the death of the Lord" means to make present and active here and now his gift of life for others, without exception.

JOHN 13:1–15 Like the other evangelists, John places the death of Jesus near the time of the Jewish Passover, indicating that his passage through death to new life represents God's new and final act of deliverance. However, John's account of Jesus' last meal with his disciples before his execution differs from the synoptic Gospel accounts (Matthew, Mark, and Luke) in significant ways. Lacking an institution account, John instead presents a major aspect of his Eucharistic theology through Jesus' deeply symbolic teaching act at the supper. Like the entire Gospel account, this passage often carries multiple meanings.

In an earlier chapter, John presented Jesus as the Good Shepherd who would lay down his life for the sheep (John 10:1–18). At the supper, this supreme act of self-sacrificing love approaches, and it is here that disciples are commanded and strengthened to follow his example. The hour has come for Jesus to manifest love for his own "to the end"; in Greek the phrase can mean "to the utmost" or "to the point of death," and surely John intends both. In recounting Jesus laying aside his outer garment, the writer uses the same verb used to describe the Good Shepherd laying down life itself for the sheep. As John signaled at the very beginning of his Gospel account, some recognize who Jesus is and what he does, while some reject him. Both, however, share in the supper.

Assuming the role of a slave, Jesus demonstrates the depth of sharing in his life and mission that partaking in this meal implies, and begins to wash their feet. Resisting this astonishing role reversal, Peter protests, addressing Jesus as *kyrie*, "master" or "lord." Word and act present an astounding juxtaposition, especially in contemporary culture. A lord owned slaves, but most assuredly would never lower himself to behave like one, taking on a most demeaning task. Jesus replies that refusal to participate in this action will mean having no part with Jesus. Typically impetuous, Peter then demands a more complete cleansing. Jesus responds that those who have bathed need no further washing, though not everyone present is clean. On the surface, John points to the presence of the betrayer, Judas. However, the dialogue may also refer to the cleansing of Baptism, since John emphasizes that some accept life offered by Jesus, while others do not. A decision is required.

Lest the disciples miss the meaning of his symbolic act, Jesus teaches it again by word: the foot washing is a model for followers. By the standards of the prevailing culture, one could lower himself no further in serving another than to do so as a slave, as one owned by the other. By all human standards, one can give nothing more than life itself. Jesus is about to give his whole self, and life itself, for those he loves—an act that those who share his supper "should also do."

FRIDAY OF THE PASSION OF THE LORD (GOOD FRIDAY)
Jesus Dies for Us

ISAIAH 52:13—53:12 The beginning of the reading seems to anticipate its ending, describing a complete reversal of the servant's fortunes brought about by God. Though the servant grew up under the divine gaze, by human standards there was nothing remarkable about him. In fact, as a person accustomed to suffering, he was avoided by others, because Jewish belief assumed that various human sorrows resulted from sin.

Though mistreated, oppressed, and condemned, the servant bears all in silence, and though he is innocent, the view that suffering implies guilt prevails, and the servant is designated for burial among the wicked.

Like a psalm of thanksgiving, the poem shifts from lament to giving praise and thanks for divine reversal of the sufferer's plight, even before the fact. The prophet describes the most important effect of the servant's sacrificial suffering: the people will be justified, restored to right relationships with God and with all things. The servant who trusted in God's saving might is not disappointed: God purifies, renews, and justifies the people, and the servant himself is vindicated.

PSALM 31:2, 6, 12–13, 15–16, 17, 25 (LUKE 23:46) Psalm 31 appeals to God for rescue. The psalmist is desperate, but the psalm does not dwell in despair. It trusts that God will redeem the one in distress. This singer is so convinced of salvation that the psalm concludes with an exhortation to the hearer: "Take courage and be stouthearted, / all you who hope in the Lord" (v. 25). The antiphon, "Father, into your hands I commend my spirit," (v. 6) was spoken by Jesus on the cross as he breathes his last (Luke 23:46).

HEBREWS 4:14–16; 5:7–9 More a sermon than a letter, Hebrews is designated as a "word of exhortation" (13:22). The author interweaves a call to persevere in faith and mutual love with his interpretation of Christ as both perfect high priest and the atonement sacrifice itself. As divine Son of God, Jesus is capable of bringing about atonement. However, Christians called to imitate him should be reassured that their high priest is fully human, able to understand our weakness because he "has similarly been tested in every way."

CONNECTIONS TO CHURCH TEACHING AND TRADITION

- "The crucified Jesus has overcome divisions, re-establishing peace and reconciliation, precisely through the cross, 'thereby bringing the hostility to an end'[1] and bringing the salvation of the Resurrection to mankind" (CSDC, 493).

- "'The Church celebrates the redemptive death of Christ on Good Friday. The Church meditates on the Lord's Passion in the afternoon liturgical action, in which she prays for the salvation of the world, adores the Cross and commemorates her very origin in the sacred wound in Christ's side (cf. John 19:34)'"[2] (DPPL, 142).

- "On this day, when 'Christ, our passover was sacrificed,'[3] the church meditates on the Passion of her Lord and Spouse, adores the cross, commemorates her origin from the side of Christ asleep on the cross and intercedes for the salvation of the whole world" (PS, 58).

1. Ephesians 2:16.
2. Cf. SC, 5; St. Augustine, *Ennaratio in Psalmum,* 138, 2; CCL, 40; Turnholti, 1956, p. 1991.
3. 1 Corinthians 5:7.

The writer refers to Christ's days "in the flesh," emphasizing his complete identification with humanity. The Greek word here translated "flesh" is *sarx*, which indicates the entire human being as susceptible to weakness, suffering, and death. Fully experiencing "the flesh," Jesus called upon divine help in reverent submission to God. Jesus' action and attitude provides the model for Christian imitation, for he "learned obedience" through his own suffering. It is difficult to capture in translation the full meaning of the phrase rendered "when he was made perfect." It seems that the author wishes to reassure his readers that when God's plan reached its completion through Christ's death and Resurrection, he became the source of God's own saving life for all who, like him, learn obedience in trusting surrender to God.

JOHN 18:1—19:42 John presents Jesus' passion and death as the final and definitive self-revelation of God in Jesus, the divine Word made flesh. For John, Jesus freely chooses to lay down his life for those he loves, so that they may have fullness of life. In his passion and death, the Word Jesus himself spoke to "the Jews" (John 10:10–18) becomes a Word made flesh, a Word enacted. In John's account, Jesus appears to be the one in charge of all proceedings of his passion, from arrest through his last breath.

Unlike the synoptic accounts in which Jesus is seized, in John he steps forward to meet those who will lead him to death, with clear knowledge of what is about to happen. Taking an active role in his own capture, he asks those who confront him who they are looking for. To their reply, "Jesus the Nazorean," he responds three times, with dual meaning, "I AM." In Greek, his answer (*ego eimi*) can simply mean "It is I" or "I am the one." However, the Greek Old Testament translated the revealed name of God, often rendered "I AM" or "I am who am," with the same words. John again indicates that the true character of the divine Word made flesh will soon be fully revealed, and it will be manifest in Jesus' chosen act of laying down life itself for those he loves. Preventing Peter from doing violence to ward off Jesus' arrest, Jesus does not ask the Father to let the cup of suffering pass, as in the synoptic accounts. Instead, he freely embraces it, again proclaiming his identity as divine Word made flesh.

Alone among the canonical Gospels accounts, John states that Jesus carries the cross himself; the Word of God who is one with the Father relies only on divine assistance.

Only John speaks of Jesus providing for mutual care of his mother and the beloved disciple. Various interpretations of this act have been given; some believe it points to Jesus' care for those who belong to him to the end, and others see an indication that Jesus will soon hand over his work to those who do believe in him.

Jesus approaches the end of his earthly life and the work the Father has given him, aware that both are reaching completion. The evangelist portrays Jesus as fully conscious that his total self-gift will end his life in "the flesh" as it brings God's plan to its desired goal. John interprets Jesus' words "I thirst" as fulfilling Scripture; the author may be referring to Psalm 22:16 or Psalm 69:22. Both prayers present a faithful sufferer crying out to God in lament while still expressing hope in ultimate divine deliverance.

Finally, Jesus himself proclaims what the evangelist has stated, "It is finished." At this moment, Jesus "handed over the spirit." Yet again, John employs dual meaning. On one hand, he simply states that Jesus has died, returning the life-breath of God to the one who first created his life in the flesh (see Genesis 2:7). More profoundly, the evangelist proclaims that in ending his earthly life, Jesus fulfills his promise to send "the Advocate" upon returning to the Father (John 16:1–15). John uses the Greek word *parakletos*, variously translated but indicating the Holy Spirit; at root, the word designates someone who can be counted upon to stand at the side of another.

Christ Risen from the Dead

GENESIS 1:1—2:2 OR 1:1, 26–31A God creates humanity only after providing a sustainable world for it. The writer uses the word *adam*, meaning humankind, indicating that God formed humanity as a whole, male and female, in the divine image. This is God's purpose for *adam*; this creature alone can, and is meant to, reflect the Creator in the world. The author underscores the idea that God alone is the source of life for the human creature by using a specific verb meaning "to create"; this Hebrew word (*bara*) is used only of something formed by God. God instructs this unique creature, humankind, to "have dominion" over the other creatures. To avoid misunderstanding, this statement must be understood in Old Testament context. In the view of ancient Israel, the one true King was the Lord, and any human king was his representative. Hence, human rulers were expected to rule as God does, ensuring just and peaceful relationships among all people and things.

PSALM 104:1–2, 5–6, 10, 12, 13–14, 24, 35 (30) It would be enough if this psalm praised God for the wonders of nature, but it does something more. It praises God for the way nature is renewed each year and from one generation to the next. This quality of creation, its inherent ability to renew, makes this psalm a perfect choice for the Easter Vigil.

PSALM 33:4–5, 6–7, 12–13, 20, 22 (5B) As an alternative to Psalm 104, Psalm 33 may follow the First Reading. It, too, praises God for the wonders of nature. This psalm envisions that the waters of the ocean are contained as in a flask, confined as though in cellars in the deep. Notably, Psalm 33 includes morality among God's creations. God's Word is "upright," all God's works are "trustworthy," God loves "justice and right," and the earth is full of God's "kindness." Here is echoed the belief from the First Reading that what God made is good. We praise God not just for the things that are, but for the goodness of things that are.

GENESIS 22:1–18 OR 22:1–2, 9A, 10–13, 15–18 While this story often arouses revulsion in modern hearers, it has root in ancient cultures that practiced child sacrifice to express the willingness to return everything, even one's most precious object of love, to the god or gods from whom it came.

CONNECTIONS TO CHURCH TEACHING AND TRADITION

- "According to a most ancient tradition, this night is 'one of vigil for the Lord,'[1] and the vigil celebrated during it to commemorate that holy night when the Lord rose from the dead is regarded as the 'mother of all holy vigils.'[2] For in the night the church keeps vigil, waiting for the resurrection of the Lord, and celebrates the sacraments of Christian initiation"[3] (PS, 77).

- "The Passover vigil, in which the Hebrews kept watch for the Lord's Passover, which was to free them from slavery to pharaoh, is an annual commemoration. It prefigured the true Pasch of Christ that was to come, the night that is of true liberation, in which 'destroying the bonds of death, Christ rose as victor from the depths'[4]" (PS, 79).

---

1. Cf. Exodus 12:42.
2. St. Augustine, Sermon 219, PL 38, 1088.
3. CE, 332.
4. *The Roman Missal*, The Easter Vigil, 19, Easter Proclamation.

The writer makes clear from the outset that the story recounts a testing of Abraham, a divine inquiry into the degree of Abraham's trusting faith (Genesis 15:1–6).

Several poignant details underscore the cost of following God's terrible command. Abraham is told to take "your son . . . your only one, whom you love" and offer him as a holocaust—an offering burned in its entirety to signify holding back nothing whatsoever from God. On the way up the mountain, the child himself carries the wood upon which he is to be sacrificed. Addressing Abraham as "Father," Isaac innocently notes that they have brought wood and fire for a holocaust, but no sheep for sacrifice. His father's initial response already begins to emphasize his attitude of trust as he assures the boy that "God himself will provide" for the offering.

After arriving at the place of holocaust and preparing for the sacrifice, Abraham is prevented by a divine messenger from completing the sacrifice of his son. Unlike God's first call to Abraham, here the Lord's messenger calls his name twice. In the Old Testament, calling someone by name twice indicates a closeness of relationship between the speaker and the one addressed. God first speaks to protect Isaac, then assures Abraham that his actions bespeak complete reverence for God. Abraham's trusting obedience not only would have cost his beloved son but dashed any hope of fulfilling the divine promise of countless offspring. However, Abraham had told Isaac that God would provide a sacrificial offering, and his faith proves well-founded; the patriarch sees a ram nearby, which ensures a holocaust offering.

Abraham meets his testing with the same unshakeable trust in divine promises that he has shown earlier. In response, God again assures Abraham that the two great promises will be fulfilled: God will give him innumerable descendants, and through the offspring of Abraham, man of obedient faith, all other peoples shall be blessed.

PSALM 16:5, 8, 9–10, 11 (1) When things go wrong, we turn to God for assistance. Sometimes we demand help; often we hope against hope for it. However, Psalm 16 airs an aroma of confidence: "with [the Lord] at my right hand I shall not be disturbed." This psalm flows naturally from the story of Abraham and Isaac. Abraham, too, possessed

- "From the very outset, the church has celebrated that annual Pasch, which is the solemnity of solemnities, above all by means of a night vigil" (PS, 80).

- "As proclaimed in the prayers for the blessing of the water, baptism is a cleansing water of rebirth[5] that makes us God's children born from on high" (CI, 5).

- The words of the prophet Isaiah: "For the mountains may depart and the hills be removed, but my steadfast love shall not depart from you"[6] show the everlasting nature of God's love (cf. CCC, 220).

- "Nowhere is the deep spiritual bond between Judaism and Christianity more apparent than in the liturgy" (GMEF, 2).

- "Christ in his boundless love freely underwent his passion and death because of the sins of all so that all might attain salvation" (NA, 4).

- "By its very nature water cannot be treated as just another commodity among many, and it must be used rationally and in solidarity with others" (CSDC, 485).

---

5. Cf. Titus 3:5.
6. Isaiah 54:10; cf. 54:8.

the charism of confidence. He believed that, even in the most difficult circumstances, God would be faithful to the covenant.

EXODUS 14:15—15:1 As the reading begins, the Hebrews fleeing enslavement have reached the edge of the sea, only to find themselves seemingly at the mercy of Pharaoh's army. Moses appears doubtful that their escape will be complete, but God commands him to raise his staff and split the sea so that the Israelites may continue their journey to freedom.

As the Lord predicted, the pursuing Egyptians follow them, until God, in the form of a cloud of fire, throws them "into a panic" and clogs their chariot wheels. At this, Pharaoh's army sounds the retreat. The pursuers know they have been defeated because the God of the Hebrews, who has already proved to outrank all the gods of Egypt, fights "for them against the Egyptians." Awed by this mighty act of power, the Israelites affirm their belief in the Lord and in Moses as God's instrument.

EXODUS 15:1–2, 3–4, 5–6, 17–18 (1B) The Responsorial is the very song that Israel sings upon reaching the dry shores beyond the Red Sea. It retells the events of this Passover night. Throughout the song, the people give praise to God for freeing them from slavery.

ISAIAH 54:5–14 This passage from Isaiah most likely dates from the Babylonian captivity, probably near its end as God continued to speak words of return and renewal through the prophets. Earlier prophets had likened the relationship between the Lord and the Chosen People to that of faithful and unfaithful spouses. The destruction that befell God's people, was compared to the steadfast husband divorcing his wife for her repeated infidelity. As prophets like Isaiah turned toward messages of hope for the future, they continued to describe a restored relationship with spousal language and images.

Isaiah envisions an imminent and astounding reversal of the people's current state. With boundless fidelity, the Lord, Creator, and Redeemer of Israel will restore her as his beloved wife. The Hebrew words with which God speaks of

- "All evangelizing activity is understood as promoting union with Jesus Christ. Starting with the 'initial'[7] conversion of a person to the Lord, moved by the Holy Spirit through the primary proclamation of the Gospel, catechesis seeks to solidify and mature this first adherence" (GDC, 80).

- "He who makes the profession of faith takes on responsibilities that not infrequently provoke persecution" (GDC, 83).

- "Baptism is, therefore, above all, the sacrament of that faith by which, enlightened by the grace of the Holy Spirit, we respond to the Gospel of Christ" (CI, 3).

- "Baptism, the cleansing with water by the power of the living word,[8] washes away every stain of sin, original and personal, makes us sharers in God's own life[9] and his adopted children"[10] (CI, 5).

---

7. AG, 13b.
8. Cf. Ephesians 5:26.
9. Cf. 2 Peter 1:4.
10. Cf. Romans 8:15; Galatians 4:5.

restoring Israel express both the loyalty demanded by covenant relationship ("enduring love") and deeply felt tenderness ("pity"). God reminds the captive people that he has demonstrated fidelity to covenant promises in the past, as in the case of his covenant with Noah. Israel may turn from God, but God will never abandon his beloved Israel.

Isaiah now turns to address the devastated city, Jerusalem, speaking God's Word to her; she will be rebuilt with even greater glory than before. The Hebrew words translated as "justice" and "peace" connote wholeness and completeness, a state of being in which all live in righteous relationship to God and to one another.

PSALM 30:2, 4, 5–6, 11–12, 13 (2A) This psalm takes up the main theme of the Easter Vigil: the triumphant passion of our Lord Jesus Christ. He could have sung this psalm himself: "O Lord, you brought me up from the netherworld . . . / At nightfall, weeping enters in, / but with the dawn, rejoicing" (vv. 4, 6). With Christ, we are all brought up from the netherworld on this night that shines more brightly than the dawn.

ISAIAH 55:1–11 Chapters 40—55 of Isaiah are often called the "Book of Consolation," believed to date from near the end of the Babylonian exile. This part of the lengthy prophecy looks toward God's impending act of liberation from captivity (a captivity the people likened to their ancestors' time in Egypt).

Addressing the poor and hungry captive people, the prophet calls them to a rich and fulfilling banquet. In the centuries following Isaiah, an overflowing banquet came to symbolize God's definitive act of salvation. For Isaiah the image of a banquet carries overtones of renewing unity among partakers of the plentiful meal, since Israelite culture understood shared food as a sharing of life and mutual commitment. Through the prophet, God calls the people to listen and so have life. Despite the people's failure to hear, obey, and love God above all, his forgiveness now offers to renew the ancient covenant, not only with David but with "you," the entire Chosen People. Through the new Exodus of a restored people, all nations will turn toward their God.

- "It is desirable that the liturgy of Lent and Paschal time should be restored in such a way that it will serve to prepare the hearts of the catechumens for the celebration of the Paschal Mystery, at whose solemn ceremonies they are reborn to Christ in baptism" (AG, 14).

- "The readings from Sacred Scripture constitute the second part of the vigil. They give an account of the outstanding deeds of the history of salvation, which the faithful are helped to meditate calmly upon by the singing of the responsorial psalm, by a silent pause and by the celebrant's prayer" (PS, 85).

- "To accomplish so great a work Christ is always present in his church, especially in liturgical celebrations. . . . He is present in his word since it is he himself who speaks when the holy scriptures are read in church" (SC, 7).

- "Finally the resurrection of the Lord is proclaimed from the Gospel as the high point of the whole Liturgy of the Word" (PS, 87).

While the phrase, "seek the Lord," was often used by priests to invite worshippers to the sanctuary of the Temple, Isaiah broadens its meaning. He seems to ask the people to find God near at hand. Turning toward God's presence, however, calls for repentance, a change of heart and action. The prophet reassures the people that their ever-faithful God will meet them with forgiving mercy. The Hebrew word rendered "mercy" carries overtones of the tender love a woman bears for a child of her womb.

Isaiah begins a kind of conclusion to the entire "Book of Consolation" by recalling the core reason for his confidence that return, renewal, and restoration will certainly come to pass: God's Word, which carries the very presence of God. It bears divine power and will not fail to accomplish the divine will, which always desires human healing, wholeness, and deliverance.

ISAIAH 12:2–3, 4, 5–6 (3) The Lectionary offers us this passage to follow the previous reading because of the similarity in the way it applies the image of water, and because it comes from the same biblical book.

The canticle rings forth with praise of God. The singer proclaims, "I am confident and unafraid" (v. 2). God is the source of salvation, just as a fountain is the source of life-giving water. As we prepare for the celebration of Baptism, we are reminded of all that God promises, and how confidently we stand in faith.

BARUCH 3:9–15, 32—4:4 This reading comes from a portion of the Book of Baruch patterned after wisdom literature, and virtually equates wisdom with the divine teaching given in the Law. The importance of the message in this section of Baruch is evident in its language. "Hear O Israel" was the beginning of a prayer that Jews recited daily. It calls the covenant people to hear and obey the Lord alone, and to love their one and only God above all else (Deuteronomy 6:4–5). The author poses a rhetorical question to the captive people, asking how it came to be that they find themselves in exile. The obvious answer follows: they have forsaken God's teaching, source of all wisdom.

The author calls the people to rediscover wisdom so that they may endure and once again find life and peace.

Wisdom, typically personified as a feminine figure, comes from God, Creator of all things. Once again echoing Deuteronomy, the author stresses that those who follow her by observing God's teaching will have life, while those who leave the path of wisdom will perish.

The reading closes with an exhortation to repentance, which the prophets often expressed as a call to "turn" or "return." True repentance requires a dual action: turning from the way of evil, and turning toward God and divine wisdom given in the Mosaic law. God's people have been given a great gift: what pleases God is the way of wisdom, revealed in the Torah.

PSALM 19:8, 9, 10, 11 (JOHN 6:68C) These verses of Psalm 19 build upon the theme of wisdom from the previous reading. We come to know God through meditation on his decrees. God revealed these to us in the covenant, so they detail the wisdom that exudes from the very being of God.

The Lectionary gives us a refrain taken from the Gospel according to John. The verse is spoken by Peter after Jesus has given the discourse on the Bread of Life. Many of those who heard him speak these words, however, turned away. Jesus looked fearfully at his closest followers and asked if they, too, were going to leave him now. Peter said no, adding, "Lord, you have the words of everlasting life" (John 6:68c). That statement of faith becomes the refrain we sing to a psalm that praises the wisdom of God. It also foreshadows the initiation of those who will share Holy Communion for the first time at this Mass.

EZEKIEL 36:16–17A, 18–28 Ezekiel, a prophet and priest of the Jerusalem Temple, arrived in Babylon among the first deportees from Judah, and continued to prophesy in the land of exile. The destruction of both the city of Jerusalem and the Temple represented an unimaginable blow to the Chosen People reasons for their desolation and God's promises of renewal.

In verses immediately preceding those in this reading, God directed the prophet to address the mountains and hills of ancient Canaan. Ezekiel announced divine assurance that the land itself would be renewed, once again producing fruits of the earth, and that upon the Promised

Land, both cities and people would be rebuilt. This reading begins with another statement of reasons for devastation and loss of the land: its people, the elect people of the Lord, despoiled it themselves by their conduct. They not only shed innocent blood, even blood of their own people, but repeatedly turned to idols instead of the God who chose them. They were chosen for a purpose: to make their covenant God known to all other nations and peoples by serving the Lord alone. In Hebrew, one word means both to serve and to worship, and their worship of the Lord was to include both communal ritual and a way of life. Ezekiel proclaims that their own repeated wandering from the ways of worship have brought divine judgment upon them.

Speaking through the prophet, God confronts the exiles with another reality: their fate has dishonored God's own name. In biblical thought, a name conveys the very essence of what is named; it represents the entire history and reputation of a person named. Nations that witnessed the fall and destruction of the Israelites questioned whether they were in fact the people of the Lord, thus profaning the "name" of the Lord. The promised restoration, therefore, will take place not for the sake of those whom God has rightly judged, but for the sake of the Lord's own good name as the one who remains forever faithful to Israel.

God then details the renewal that will once again demonstrate that the Lord is a God of covenant faithfulness and enduring love to Israel, despite her numerous infidelities. Not only will the captive people return to a renewed land; God will cleanse them of their sin and the root of their sinfulness. In ancient Israel, the heart represented the core of a human being; a stony heart meant a person closed to God and the divine life within. With the recreating gift of a new, "natural" heart, God's people will become what they were intended to be: a community breathing together with God's own life, guided by divine teaching.

PSALM 42:3, 5; 43:3, 4 (42:2) The Lectionary offers three possible responsories to the Ezekiel reading. The first, from Psalm 42, is sung whenever Baptism will be celebrated at the Easter Vigil. The psalm asks God for the gift of God's light and fidelity, so that those who receive it may approach the dwelling place of God, and specifically the altar of God.

These verses eloquently prophesy the journey of the cate-chumens, who thirst for the waters of Baptism, and attain it through the light and fidelity that God extends to new believers through the covenant.

ISAIAH 12:2–3, 4BCD, 5–6 (3) In this song of praise, we thank God for all that he has accomplished. This response follows the Fifth Reading and is offered again as one of the alternatives following the Seventh Reading. In practice, it could logically be sung here whenever the seven readings are abbreviated and the Fifth Reading has been eliminated, but the Responsory may be used twice on the same night.

Here, the English Lectionary recommends it as one of the options if Baptism is not celebrated during the Easter Vigil. This may seem puzzling because the image of water is so strong at the beginning of these verses. In fact, the liturgical books are not consistent on this point. The *Ordo Lectionum Missae* recommends this psalm, not the previ-ous one, when Baptism is to be celebrated.

PSALM 51:12–13, 14–15, 18–19 (12A) Tradition calls seven of the 150 psalms "penitential." This one is perhaps the greatest of them. It expresses the remorse we feel after sin-ning and our cries for forgiveness. These particular verses, coming at the end of the psalm, focus on renewal. They work well after the passage from Ezekiel, which employs a similar image—a new heart. In reestablishing the covenant with us, God remakes us. We reenter the covenant not as the same people, but as those who have known sin, repented of it, received forgiveness, and resolved not to sin again. This psalm is recommended for an Easter Vigil that does not include Baptism. It more nearly suits the faithful Christians coming for renewal after observing a rigorous Lent.

ROMANS 6:3–11 Paul wrote the Letter to the Romans, actually more of a treatise than a letter, near the end of his life, about thirty years after the death and Resurrection of Christ. From its earliest days, the Church understood Baptism as immersion in Christ, shedding one's former way of life and taking on a way of life patterned according to his passage through death to greater life.

In the previous chapter, Paul stressed the depth of God's love revealed in Christ, who died for those who were still sinners. In today's reading, Paul explains that in Baptism, Christians enter into Christ's manner of dying: death as self-giving love that leads to greater life. In Baptism the believer is buried "with him" and grows in oneness with him "through a death like his." It is this likeness to Christ and union with him that brings transformed life, a sharing in his Resurrection. Paul's view of Baptism calls for nothing less than a complete change of the whole person, a transformation wrought by the interaction of divine power and human choice. For anyone who embraces Baptism as a way of being "baptized into [Christ's] death," the former self or person enslaved to sin is "done away with." The "sinful body" (Greek *soma*) does not signify physical flesh alone, but rather the human being as a whole, with all its perceptions, attitudes, and behaviors when it is dominated by sinful influences. One who, in Baptism, dies with Christ, is freed from that power and lives in him as a new person, "for God."

PSALM 118:1–2, 16–17, 22–23 (ALLELUIA) We give thanks to God, whose mercy endures forever. This psalm gives many reasons for thanksgiving. It opens with the simple assertion that the Lord is good, and that "his mercy endures forever" (v. 1). It then announces the power and deeds of God's right hand. You can imagine Jesus singing this psalm: "I shall not die, but live, / and declare the works of the Lord" (v. 17). Christians can affirm, "The stone which the builders rejected / has become the cornerstone" (v. 22).

LUKE 24:1–12 Luke's description of the early Church indicates important ministries of women in the growth of Christian faith and life, and today's Gospel portrays them as first witnesses to the Resurrection.

The previous chapter ends with Jesus' burial, observed by women disciples who then prepared to anoint his body after the Sabbath. They come to the tomb at daybreak, indicating a shift from the darkness of Jesus' torture and Crucifixion to the dawn of new life. Nearing the tomb, the women discover the first sign that something out of the ordinary has happened. Tombs in the ancient world were often caves or abandoned quarries used for burial, sealed with a wheel-shaped rock in a groove before the opening. It would normally require several men to move such a stone, but the women find that it has been moved aside. Upon entering the tomb, they do not see the body of the "Lord Jesus." Luke's use of "Lord," a title of authority and divinity, may already signal that the power of God lies behind the inexplicable reality before them.

As the women struggle to understand, heavenly visitors, identified by shining garments, make their appearance. They deliver the astonishing message that the women seek in vain for the dead, for God has raised Jesus from death. (Like many New Testament authors, Luke uses the formulaic "divine passive": "has been raised.") The angelic message continues, pointing out that what Jesus promised earlier has in fact occurred (Luke 9:22). Their call to "remember" means much more than a simple recall of the past. In biblical thought, to remember involves bringing to bear in the present, with deepened insight and understanding, previous words and events of salvation history. The women do remember, and so they return to other disciples to announce what they have heard: he has been raised. The translation "announce" carries much of the meaning of the Greek word used here; the women are not merely reporting, they are making a proclamation of faith. However, that faith will need to grow, even in the Eleven, for they discount the women's announcement as nonsense. Peter goes to investigate for himself, to find only burial cloths. Luke says that Peter marvels at the sight, but he does not yet claim that he believes. That growth in faith will happen only through his own experience of the Risen One.

Set Your Heart on Higher Things

ACTS 10:34A, 37–43 Here, Peter's speech abruptly ends as he is interrupted by the Holy Spirit. It is a very significant moment in the history of the early Church as Peter is dealing with the challenge of accepting non-Jews as full sisters and brothers in the faith.

As Luke sets the scene, Peter is making a formal speech. In it, he summarizes what he assumes is common knowledge about Jesus of Nazareth—although almost everything he assumes that others "know" is an interpretation that springs from his faith. In reality, the only reason for Peter to be making a speech is to give witness to his faith.

Peter summarizes the life, death, and Resurrection of Jesus as a victorious confrontation with the devil, evil, and suffering. In the context of the Acts of the Apostles, Peter is preaching his first homily to Gentiles, fulfilling his commission to testify that Jesus of Nazareth was sent by God and vindicated by God. In the midst of his proclamation that Jesus is the one promised in the Scriptures and the one who gives forgiveness of sins, the Holy Spirit takes over and Peter baptizes the listeners, thereby commissioning them also to give witness.

PSALM 118:1–2, 16–17, 22–23 (24) This is the last song of the Hallel collection (Psalms 113–118), the songs sung at Passover. A song of thanksgiving, it recalls the Exodus and the return from Exile. With those salvific events in the background, it is a perfect song of joy for the celebration of Easter. As we cry out with joy that "this is the day the Lord has made" (antiphon) we are invited to celebrate all the ways that the Resurrection of Christ has given orientation to our lives.

COLOSSIANS 3:1–4 OR 1 CORINTHIANS 5:6B–8 The short reading from Colossians offers the community strong encouragement to put their faith and the results of their Baptism into practice in every dimension of their everyday life and their patterns of thought. They are to "set their heart" on higher things; that is, to focus their whole being on Christ's reign. Telling them to "seek what is above" (v. 2), the author is urging them to let their attitude toward life spring from their conviction that they were given a new identity in Baptism. Their challenge is to recognize that

CONNECTIONS TO CHURCH TEACHING AND TRADITION

- "The joy of evangelizing always arises from grateful remembrance. . . . The apostles never forgot the moment when Jesus touched their hearts . . . this remembrance makes present to us 'a great cloud of witnesses' (Heb 12:1). . . . Some of them were ordinary people who . . . introduced us to the life of faith. . . . The believer is essentially 'one who remembers'" (EG, 13).

- "The disciple is ready to put his or her whole life on the line, even to accepting martyrdom, in bearing witness to Jesus Christ, yet the goal is not to make enemies but to see God's word accepted . . . an evangelizing community is filled with joy. . . . It celebrates at every small victory, every step forward" (EG, 24).

because they are "with Christ in God" (v. 4) nothing will ever be the same.

First Corinthians challenges believers to "clear out the old yeast, so that you may become a fresh batch of dough." In the sacrificed and Risen Christ, we have been made "unleavened," clean and undefiled once more. In Christ, we have been forgiven and reconciled to God. Therefore, we are no longer to live in "malice and wickedness" but in "sincerity and truth." This is the core of our baptismal promises. In this manner, we intensify our witness, and continue the ministry of the Risen Lord.

SEQUENCE: VICTIMAE PASCHALI LAUDES Two themes stand out in the Easter sequence. The first is God's victory in Christ who redeems and reconciles humanity with God. The second is that of witness as it calls on Mary to proclaim the Resurrection by recounting her experience of the empty tomb. The song ends with the hopeful, joy-filled cry "Have mercy, victor King, ever reigning!"

JOHN 20:1–9 John's account of the empty tomb follows directly after the burial account. The burial took place on the sixth day, the day God completed the work of creation; the discovery of the empty tomb and the appearances occurred on the first day, the dawn of the new creation. In this reading we journey with the disciples in their sorrowful incredulity. Mary believes death has won and sees the empty tomb as a sign that "they" (v. 2) have further desecrated the body of the Lord. While it says that the Beloved Disciple "saw and believed" (v. 8), the text goes on to say that they did not understand. The disciples would need to encounter the Risen Christ before they could become faith-filled witnesses.

LUKE 24:13–35 In Luke's account of the Gospel, the Emmaus incident forms a bridge between the enigmatic accounts of the empty tomb and Jesus' appearance in the midst of his disciples. At first, we hear of two downhearted disciples retreating from Jerusalem who are unknowingly joined by Jesus. His question about their discussion stopped them in their tracks as they asked how he could not have heard about all that had happened from Jesus' ministry

- "God's presence accompanies the sincere efforts of individuals and groups to find encouragement and meaning in their lives. He dwells among them. . . . God does not hide himself from those who seek him with a sincere heart, even though they do so tentatively, in a vague and haphazard manner" (EG, 71).

through the women's discovery of the vacant tomb. He then reveals what they could not see. Luke has subtly designed this whole account to mirror the Eucharistic liturgy where the community finds Christ in their midst. It begins with an account of the apparent victory of evil, uses Scripture to reveal God's presence in the signs of the times, and ends with Christ's presence manifested among them in the breaking of the bread.

Easter Time

Overview of Easter Time

Although many are not aware of it, Easter Time is the longest liturgical season after Ordinary Time. Lasting a full fifty days, it is appropriately longer than the forty days of Lent or the flexible four weeks of Advent. The challenge for pastoral ministers is to help the congregation understand Easter Time as a real season, inviting celebration as conscious as Advent and Lent.

The life-transforming effect of the Resurrection is the core theme of the season. Our challenge is to make that real for ourselves and those with whom we worship. The season's readings are designed help us do that.

FIRST READINGS

All of the First Readings come from the Acts of the Apostles, the adventure novel of the New Testament. This cycle starts with Peter's preaching about Jesus' life, death, and Resurrection. We see how the disciples' mission caused conflict just as Jesus had. We are assured that discipleship involves sacrifice and suffering, even to the point of martyrdom. Finally, with the solemnities of the Ascension and Pentecost, we return to the origins of our mission with Jesus' ascent to the Father and the Spirit's empowerment of disciples until Christ's return.

RESPONSORIAL PSALMS

The psalms of Easter Time ring out with praise and joy remembering what God has done. They remind us that God is the God of all creation and nations, such that creation itself will join in praising the name and works of God.

SECOND READINGS

On Easter Sunday we hear from either Paul's Letter to the Colossians or his First Letter to the Corinthians. In each the message is clear that the Resurrection of Christ has changed reality and with God's grace our lives can reflect that truth. For the Second through Seventh Sundays our readings from the Book of Revelation are symbol-laden assurances that Christ has won the ultimate victory and God is with us. Because of that we will never have reason to fear anything. For the Solemnity of the Ascension of the Lord, Hebrews proclaims that Christ has opened the way for us. On the Solemnity of Pentecost, Paul's Letter to the Romans reminds us that while all creation awaits God's final revelation, our very spirit is already infused with the Spirit of God.

GOSPEL READINGS

During Easter Time, we hear more from the Gospel according to John than at any other time of year, with Gospel incidents chosen primarily from the Resurrection accounts and the Last Supper discourse. First, we watch Mary lead the disciples to the empty tomb; then we witness Jesus' appearance, assuring the disciples that he is truly risen, and blessing those who would believe without seeing him. On the Third Sunday, we stand with Peter learning that love of Christ will entail a loss of control over our own life. The selections from the last discourse reassure us as Jesus calls himself our shepherd and promises that God lives in those who love him. Because of that, we are empowered to love one another and become one among ourselves and with God. Luke's account of the Ascension portrays the Risen Christ's last act as one of blessing. Finally, in the Gospel account on Pentecost, Jesus offers himself to slake the thirst of the world, and he promises that the Spirit will give his disciples all the gifts they will need for their mission. As we celebrate this fifty-day feast of Easter, we are invited again and again to be so renewed that the Resurrection provides the key to our life. Christ has promised us the Spirit who makes that possible.

ACTS 5:12–16 The author of Luke and Acts created a two-part work with a specific purpose in mind. Just as the Gospel shows the Spirit of God directing the ministry of Jesus, Acts portrays the Spirit guiding the ministry of Jesus' disciples. The Apostles are now carrying on Christ's mission.

This connection is clear in today's passage. The sick are carried into the streets, and those who are infirm or possessed are brought from towns in the vicinity of Jerusalem to be healed by the Apostles. The passage records no specific miracle. It is instead a summary statement of the signs and wonders that flow from the Apostles' hands. Luke uses similar summary statements throughout his account to describe the miracles of Jesus (see Luke 4:40; 6:18–19). The Apostles are now doing what Jesus did, but they are even doing more. We are told that if the Apostles' shadow fell upon those who were afflicted, the sick were healed.

Nothing in the Gospel miracles comes close to this. Jesus routinely touches those he heals, but the Apostles do not need to touch the sick. They are acting in the power of the Risen Christ. The Apostles—and we who follow in their footsteps—are only servants of Christ, but the grace we offer is now that of the glorified Lord who sits at the right hand of God.

PSALM 118:2–4, 13–15, 22–24 (1)

Today's psalm is one of thanksgiving. It divides into two sections. The first section recounts a dangerous crisis that had threatened the psalmist. The second section requests permission to enter the Temple so that God may be glorified for saving the one who prays. Our liturgy has selected verses from both sections. Verses 13–15 describe the crisis: "I was hard pressed and was falling." Verses 22–24 are taken from the thanksgiving section. They employ a proverb to describe the psalmist's startling reversal of fortune. The rejected stone is now the cornerstone, which is the most important stone of all. It is the proverb that renders this psalm appropriate for Easter Time. Jesus quotes it in light of his own struggle (Mark 12:1–12), making it a fitting image to describe his passion. The psalmist's cry of thanksgiving that follows the proverb—"This is the day the Lord has made" (antiphon)—therefore becomes a joyous shout to express Christ's Resurrection.

CONNECTIONS TO CHURCH TEACHING AND TRADITION

- "The period, therefore, before the first and second coming of the Lord is the time of missionary activity, when, like the harvest, the church will be gathered from the four winds into the kingdom of God. For the gospel must be preached to everyone before the Lord comes (see Mark 13:10)" (AG, 9).

- "Evangelization takes place in obedience to the missionary mandate of Jesus: 'Go therefore and make disciples of all nations, baptizing them in the name of the Father and of the Son and of the Holy Spirit, teaching them to observe all that I have commanded you' (Mt 28:19–20). In these verses we see how the risen Christ sent his followers to preach the Gospel in every time and place, so that faith in him might spread to every corner of the earth" (EG, 19).

REVELATION 1:9–11A, 12–13, 17–19 This passage is from the inaugural vision that John of Patmos records in the Book of Revelation. It is appropriate for the Second Sunday of Easter because it is a vision of the Risen Christ. As powerful as the description of Christ is, his words are what ground the scene. Although once dead, he now lives forever. Yet his message is not only about him. It also points to "what will happen afterwards" (1:19). Jesus' Resurrection inaugurates the destruction of every evil, the end of Satan's kingdom, and the establishment of the kingdom of God. We are to join in this process. We are to carry on Jesus' work until he comes again.

JOHN 20:19–31 Preachers and catechists must be careful to understand the significance of the Jews in today's passage. The Jews in John's account of the Gospel is a technical and theological term used to identify those who are opposed to Christ's Gospel. "The Jews" cannot apply to all Jews in an ethnic sense. If the doors are locked to keep "the Jews" out, who is locked in? All the disciples (and Jesus) are Jewish. In this passage, "the Jews" are best understood as a reference to the Temple authorities.

The passage itself is widely recognized as the original ending of John's account of the Gospel. As such it focuses on the purpose of the Gospel—that we, the readers, may have faith that Jesus is the Christ. It is significant that this final scene is vague about who exactly is in the locked room. It mentions only the disciples and Thomas. This provides sufficient space for us to situate ourselves in the disciples' company. The blessing spoken to Thomas, "Blessed are those who have not seen and have believed" (20:29), is our blessing. We must come to faith without the benefit of touching the Risen Christ. Most importantly the commission to the disciples is our commission, "As the Father has sent me, so I send you" (20:21). We are to be the bearers of Christ's victory into our world. Here, the Gospel meshes with today's reading from Acts. Christ is risen, and we are sent to stand in his place, proclaiming the salvation of God.

Repent and Believe

ACTS 5:27–32, 40B–41 Despite the joyous Easter Time in which we stand, today's readings strike an ominous tone. Although Jesus has been raised from the dead, the full defeat of evil in the world has not yet been achieved. Therefore, those who follow Jesus must not only proclaim the triumph of the Resurrection but also contend with forces still opposed to God's will.

Today's passage from Acts asserts this truth forcibly. The Apostles are brought before the Sanhedrin because they continue to teach in Jesus' name. Although it would have been helpful for them to enjoy the support of the legitimate authorities in Jerusalem, the Apostles face opposition instead. Those who exercise human power are not in sync with God's plan. In fact, those authorities have given strict orders that the Apostles stop proclaiming the Good News. The Apostles find themselves in a conflict of commands. Human authorities demand that they remain silent, but God commands that they speak. Peter gives voice to their decision. They must follow God's authority. Even though Luke's concern is clearly the proclamation of Jesus' Resurrection, he is not afraid to associate the decision of the Apostles with the condition of all good men and women who must face opposition to the truth. Peter's words consciously echo those of Socrates before his accusers in Athens, "We must obey God rather than men" (5:29).

PSALM 30:2, 4, 5–6, 11–12, 13 (2A) Psalm 30 provides the reason we are able to face opposition—the Lord is with us. A prayer of thanksgiving, this psalm may have originally been composed to express gratitude after an escape from a fatal sickness. Death is certainly in view. The psalmist gives thanks that God's power has prevented him from sinking into the netherworld. The rescue is dramatic. The opening verse, "you drew me clear," is more accurately translated "you drew me up" (see verse 1) as if the psalmist had already been falling into the realm of death.

There is no indication of Resurrection in the original psalm, only the prevention of dying. Yet within the liturgical context a Christological dimension can be recognized. The same God who has the power to rescue the psalmist from death has also conquered death in Christ. This enlarged perspective gives courage to every disciple who

CONNECTIONS TO CHURCH TEACHING AND TRADITION

- "All Christians by the example of their lives and the witness of the word, wherever they live, have an obligation to manifest the new person which they put on in baptism, and to reveal the power of the holy Spirit by whom they were strengthened at confirmation, so that others, seeing their good works, might glorify the Father (see Matthew 5:16) and more perfectly perceive the true meaning of human life and the universal solidarity of humankind" (AG, 11).

- "The Christian is not to 'be ashamed then of testifying to our Lord.'[1] In situations that require witness to the faith, the Christian must profess it without equivocation, after the example of St. Paul before his judges" (CCC, 2471).

---

1. 2 Timothy 1:8.

must confront opposition. Through Christ, God has rescued us. We can be confident that our weeping will be changed to rejoicing and our mourning to dancing.

REVELATION 5:11–14 These verses conclude a vision of the worship that takes place continually before God's throne. The four creatures represent God's knowledge and care for the world. The elders (twenty-four in number—twelve for the Apostles and twelve for the tribes of Israel) stand for all the saints. All are united in praise of Jesus, who is the Lamb of God. The proclamation of all believers announces his Resurrection. His triumph gives power to continue that proclamation even when it is opposed.

JOHN 21:1–19 OR 21:1–14 This famous scene on the shore of the Sea of Tiberius contains many themes, but the narrative swiftly moves toward the dialogue between Jesus and Peter. This encounter is about reconciliation. Peter denied Jesus three times in the courtyard of the High Priest. Jesus questions Peter three times about his love, and each question is followed by a commission. Peter is now to feed Jesus' sheep. The text recognizes growth in Peter by contrasting his action when he was young to his action now that he is old. When he was young, Peter did what he wanted, and that led to his denial of Jesus. Now that he is old, he has witnessed his own failures and the power of the Resurrection. Now he is ready to follow Jesus. He is ready to become the shepherd Jesus is calling him to be. Of course, Jesus, as the Good Shepherd, is Peter's model. Peter must imitate Christ's love for the sheep and be ready to lay down his life as Jesus did.

By the time this passage was written, the knowledge of Peter's martyrdom was widely known. Even though the significance of Peter stretching out his hands is debated, the text clearly associates it with the death by which Peter would glorify God. Perhaps the best way to interpret Peter's gesture is as one of acceptance, embracing with open arms all that shepherding and discipleship entail. Significant forces opposed to the Gospel continue in our world. If we wish to be disciples, we must be ready for opposition, prepared to suffer, and confident that God's power will save us.

The Lord Has Rescued Us

ACTS 13:14, 43–52 This Sunday's readings are all about the Good Shepherd and the sheep's victory in Christ. In this selection from the Acts of the Apostles, we hear Paul preaching to Jews and Gentiles who enthusiastically listened to his message about Jesus. Of course, there is also a strong note of conflict. In addition to the hearers of the Word, we see powerful leaders who reject Paul's message and his acceptance of non-Jews. Almost as threatening to them as the message about Jesus, was the idea of accepting the participation of the uncircumcised in the People of God. Essentially, they refused to hear Paul as a spokesperson for God, and by their rejection of the Word of God, they excluded themselves from the life God offers in Christ. Paul replied to them, acknowledging the privilege of the Chosen People. However, he also reminded them that they were the first—but not the only—people chosen by God.

PSALM 100:1–2, 3, 5 (3C) Psalm 100 complements today's theme, calling us to rejoice in the fact that we are part of God's flock. In addition, it reinforces the theme of Paul's outreach to the Gentiles as it calls on the people of every land to sing to and serve the Lord. We too are invited to celebrate the fact that all of us, of every nation and people, are God's creation.

REVELATION 7:9, 14B–17 The Book of Revelation was written for a people undergoing persecution and needing assurance of God's loving care for them—despite all appearances. Thus, we hear of God's tender concern for the people of every race and tongue. This immense throng is promised the paradise of never knowing need of any sort because "the Lamb . . . will shepherd them . . . and God will wipe away every tear from their eyes" (v. 17).

When we ask whom this people comprises, we hear the enigmatic response, "they have washed their robes and made them white in the blood of the Lamb" (v. 14). That paradoxical symbolism offers immense comfort to people undergoing persecution. The "robe" (v. 14) is a metaphor for the person (clothing usually symbolizes something important about a person). Thus, washing one's robe in the blood of the Lamb means uniting one's very self to Christ's sacrifice in the total commitment of Baptism and especially

CONNECTIONS TO CHURCH TEACHING AND TRADITION

- "The church is, accordingly, a sheepfold, the sole and necessary entrance to which is Christ (see John 10:1–10). It is also a flock, of which God foretold that he would himself be the shepherd (see Isaiah 40:11; Ezekiel 34:11ff.), and whose sheep, although watched over by human shepherds, are nevertheless at all times led and brought to pasture by Christ himself, the Good Shepherd and prince of shepherds (see John 10:11; 1 Peter 5:4), who gave his life for his sheep (see John 10:11–15)" (LG, 6).

- "It is from God's love for all [humanity] that the Church in every age receives both the obligation and the vigor of her missionary dynamism, 'for the love of Christ urges us on'" (CCC, 851).

through martyrdom. We should note here that while the crucial sacrifice is that of Christ who offered his own blood, each person is responsible for washing his or her own robe, for their own participation with Christ. These are the ones who have joined themselves to Christ's victory, accepting even death without inflicting harm in return. The Lamb slain has been their true shepherd. Their lives attest that they have listened to his voice.

JOHN 10:27–30 On the Fourth Sunday of Easter, the Church reveres Christ under the title of the Good Shepherd. The shepherd is an ancient image of God, and God's people are represented as sheep no fewer than twenty times in the psalms and prophets.

Today's short selection from John's account of the Gospel comes from a larger context describing Christ as the Shepherd, but it can also stand on its own as a teaching of great depth. In context, Jesus' teaching takes place during the Feast of the Dedication (Hanukkah), a celebration instituted by Judas Maccabeus to commemorate the rededication of the Temple around 160 BC. Fittingly, at the time Jesus said these things, the people were celebrating God's victory over their enemies.

Our selection focuses on the sheep, the shepherd, and the Father. The sheep are those who listen to the voice of the shepherd. Lest that be confused with a passive hearing of words, Jesus specifies that those who truly listen also follow him. True hearing necessarily implies the commitment to go wherever the shepherd leads.

Interestingly, this selection does not focus on the sheep's knowledge of the shepherd, but on the fact that the shepherd knows them. One might think of Psalm 139: "Lord . . . you know me . . . / Behind and before you encircle me / and rest your hand upon me" (139:1, 5). Not only does the shepherd know the sheep, but Jesus describes them as a great gift from the Father and promises that nothing can snatch them out of God's loving care. This week's celebration invites us to gratefully choose to listen to and follow Christ. In return, we are promised the ongoing care of the one, truly Good Shepherd.

The Kingdom of God Is for All the Ages

ACTS 14:21–27 We are in an action-packed section of Acts. Between last week's reading and this, Paul and Barnabas carried on the mission in Iconium and then Lystra, where their cure of a crippled man caused the pagan crowds to acclaim them as gods. Even as they were trying to disabuse the people of that notion, enemies arrived and induced the crowds to stone Paul. After being left for dead, his disciples helped him recuperate and the missionaries preached in Derbe, and then retraced their steps. Paul's pastoral visit to Antioch focused on encouraging the disciples to persevere. Given all that Paul had been through, that was anything but an armchair pastor's advice. Paul believed that disciples would face what the Master had faced and that they would also share the joy of the Master. Thus, Paul interpreted persecutions as the "many hardships" (14:22) necessary for entry into the kingdom of God. The end of today's passage offers a vital clue to Paul's approach to ministry. When the Church gathered, he focused not on the persecutions (that is, on himself) but on all God had done and the growing faith of the Gentiles.

PSALM 145:8–9, 10–11, 12–13 (SEE 1) This psalm cannot get enough of singing about God. It praises God as kind, merciful, compassionate, and slow to anger—so unlike typical rulers. According to the psalmist, that is God's glory, and the reason that all peoples will rejoice in God's dominion.

REVELATION 21:1–5A The vision we hear from the Book of Revelation is the beginning of the longest description of heaven found in the Scriptures (see 21:1—22:5). Verses 1–5 provide a sufficient introduction; the rest simply adds detail.

These verses can aptly be described as the culmination of the entire Bible. Scripture began with the accounts of creation, the garden, the first humans, and the disruption caused by sin. Revelation envisions the end: a new heaven and earth, the New Jerusalem, where sin is overcome and all is as God intends and humanity has hoped it can be.

When we hear of "a new heaven and a new earth" (21:1), creation is not devalued; our physical-historical reality is not abolished, but rather redeemed. Its newness, the sign of redemption, is that God's presence permeates all of reality. There is no sea because there are no divisions, no borders or

CONNECTIONS TO CHURCH TEACHING AND TRADITION

- "The liturgy in its turn moves the faithful, filled with 'the paschal sacraments,' to be 'one in holiness'; it prays that 'they may hold fast in their lives to what they have grasped by their faith'; the renewal in the eucharist of the covenant between the Lord and his people draws the faithful into the compelling love of Christ and sets them on fire" (CSL, 10).

- "The Church's mission stands in continuity with the mission of Christ: 'As the Father has sent me, even so I send you' (John 20:21). From the perpetuation of the sacrifice of the Cross and her communion with the body and blood of Christ in the Eucharist, the Church draws the spiritual power needed to carry out her mission" (EE, 22).

- "To evangelize is to make the kingdom of God present in our world" (EG, 176).

boundaries separating people. This is where God dwells with all *peoples* (the original Greek word is plural). There is no need to remake countries or cultures into one image; God is in and with them all.

That very unity of people with one another and of peoples with God provides the "why" death, mourning, wailing, and despair will have passed away. This new creation fulfills God's every promise of life for all peoples and all ages.

JOHN 13:31–33A, 34–35 The command to love seems so familiar that we may miss much in this scene. First, because Jesus is announcing that he is going away, these words are his last testament and it consists in the "new" (13:34) commandment.

What is new about the command to love? Much more than we might think.

First, Jesus says that obeying this command verifies discipleship. He does not ask for loyalty to himself or worship of God: the mark of the disciple is to love others as Jesus himself has loved. (Note that, according to John 18:9, Jesus never ceased loving Judas.) He asks only that the love that comes from the Father continue, that it be expressed concretely as he is expressing it, from the washing of the feet to the giving of his life.

Second, biblical scholar Juan Mateos notes, John places the command to love between Judas' betrayal and the announcement of Peter's denials, the place where Matthew and Mark locate the institution of the Eucharist. Fulfilling the command is John's presentation of communion with Jesus, a reality already explained in John 6.

Third, the new commandment is indeed new. Jesus did not say "love God," as if that could be too susceptible to delusion. Neither are we told to love as we love ourselves: that makes us the measure. The new commandment is to love as Jesus loved, and it brings with it the promise of sharing in his glory—with all that entails.

ACTS 15:1–2, 22–29 Sometimes it takes a while for Church leaders to catch up with what God is doing among them. When it comes to a matter of great contention, even the saints may disagree about the details of what has happened. Thus, Luke's account of the Apostolic Council in Jerusalem in Acts 15:1–35 agrees only in part with Galatians 2:1–14, Paul's rendition of the same events. The narrative we hear today from Acts recounts what theologian Karl Rahner called one of the three key moments in the life of the Church. (The first was the events of the life, death, and Resurrection of Jesus, and the third was the Second Vatican Council, which, for the first time, brought representatives of the whole Catholic world together to discern authoritatively God's will for their times.)

Today's reading is actually an abbreviated account, stating the problem and its solution while skipping over the actual meeting at which it was debated and the gathered Church discerned the will of God. The problem was that "some," acting without the full backing of the community, demanded that converts become fully practicing Jews, expressed and symbolized by circumcision. The key to the solution was that the faithful gathered and listened to one another's experience of God working among them. Once they could appreciate God's presence in their diverse mission experiences, they could come to an agreement. They declared, "It is the decision of the Holy Spirit and of us." That is an astounding statement—either the product of unmitigated presumption or its opposite, a profound belief that God was showing them a way beyond their own opinions and preferences. This belief was based on the fact that they did not hide from conflict, that no one claimed absolute authority, and that they were willing to let their opinions be changed. Karl Rahner asserted that because they followed the lead of the Spirit, Christianity became a world religion instead of restricting itself to being a sect of first-century Judaism.

CONNECTIONS TO CHURCH TEACHING AND TRADITION

- "The immense importance of a culture marked by faith cannot be overlooked. . . . An evangelized culture . . . has many more resources than the mere sum total of believers. An evangelized popular culture contains values of faith and solidarity capable of encouraging the development of a more just and believing society" (EG, 68).

- "Acknowledgment of the living God is one path towards love, and the 'yes' of our will to his will unites our intellect, will and sentiments in the all-embracing act of love. But this process is always open-ended; love is never 'finished' and complete; throughout life, it changes and matures, and thus remains faithful to itself" (DCE, 17).

PSALM 67:2–3, 5, 6, 8 (4) The translation of this psalm found in the Lectionary asks for God's "pity," a phrase that others have translated as "May God be gracious to us" (v. 2). Both are legitimate translations, but "pity" (v. 2) may have unfortunate connotations in English. The import of the whole psalm, and especially the verses we sing, is a prayer that God's greatness be known throughout all the earth. In that sense, the psalm bridges our first two readings, underlining the universality of God's love and rejoicing that God's goodness has been revealed to the entire world.

REVELATION 21:10–14, 22–23 John describes the City that descends as having twelve gates and built on twelve foundation stones: respectively the tribes of Israel and the Apostles. God has built it through history, first with the Chosen People, and then through the people of the Lamb. Even though promised through the ages, the City of God is entirely new. Its twelve gates are not exits, but entrances, open to every area, every people, of the world. Most of all, and scandalous to some, the City has no Temple. As Jesus had announced in John 4:21, God's presence cannot be confined to any structure. Not only are the people who walked in darkness redeemed, but there is no need for created light. God's presence permeates everything and there is nothing to contrast with it. Now, God dwells among the people, with the Lamb illuminating everything.

JOHN 14:23–29 Today John repeats Jesus' assurance that those who follow his command of love, those who take up his mission, will know the love of the Father. God's own love will flow through them. That is what it means that the Father and Jesus will dwell in those disciples. To "keep" (v. 23) Jesus' word means to love as he did: to the end, displacing fear with trust in God. To live without fear is to know the peace of Christ. Just as Jesus spoke of his Father's love, not as something that singled him out, but rather as the source of his love for humanity, so too do we come to know the love of Christ and the Father by allowing God to live in us and love through us.

THE ASCENSION OF THE LORD
The Future, as the Past, Is in the Hands of God

ACTS 1:1–11 In the opening of Acts, Luke claims that he already "dealt with all that Jesus did and taught" (v. 1). While the other evangelists might beg to differ, Luke's point is that his account of the Gospel has set the scene for discipleship. All that is lacking is for disciples to carry Jesus' mission forward.

At this point, the disciples seem quite anxious for Jesus to complete his work, but Jesus counsels patience and expectation. While they look to him (are you at this time going to restore the kingdom to Israel?), he orients them to the Father and the Spirit. They cannot know the Father's plan; their role is to wait for the Holy Spirit to give them the power to continue the mission.

Then, because he has now said all that they need to hear, Jesus is taken up. As they watch, two mysterious figures call their attention back to earth. They are to wait for the Spirit; Jesus will return in God's good time.

PSALM 47:2–3, 6–7, 8–9 (6) This psalm, used by Israel to celebrate the ritual enthronement of God as Israel's king, does what background music does for a dramatic event; it permeates the atmosphere communicating the mood of all the action. Although the disciples may have been disconcerted at the thought that the Risen Lord would no longer appear to them as he had, the psalm interprets the Ascension as Christ taking the role of victorious King of all the earth. The psalm assures us that Christ reigns over all the nations. From that moment on, there is no such thing as a foreign territory; every place belongs to God's reign.

CONNECTIONS TO CHURCH TEACHING AND TRADITION

- "The people of God believes that it is led by the Spirit of the Lord who fills the whole world. Impelled by that faith, they try to discern the true signs of God's presence and purpose in the events, the needs and the desires which it shares with the rest of humanity today. For faith casts a new light on everything and makes known the full ideal which God has set for humanity, thus guiding the mind towards solutions that are fully human" (GS, 11).

- "Our age, more than any of the past, needs such wisdom if all humanity's discoveries are to be ennobled through human effort. Indeed the future of the world is in danger unless wiser people are forthcoming. It should also be pointed out that many nations which are poorer as far as material goods are concerned, yet richer in wisdom, can be of the greatest advantage to others. It is by the gift of the holy Spirit that humanity, through faith, comes to contemplate and savor the mystery of God's design" (GS, 15).

HEBREWS 9:24–28; 10:19–23 Surely, the Church chose to use this selection from Hebrews today because of its many connections with the solemnity of the Ascension. Its references to entering the sanctuary, to Christ's reappearance, and to the "new and living way he opened for us" (10:20) all call to mind the images of this day. Nevertheless, when writing this, the author of Hebrews probably did not have the Ascension in mind. The underlying message here, with all its allusions to the sanctuary and sacrifices, is that Christ's sacrifice accomplished the forgiveness of sin once and for all. There is no need of further sacrifice, Christ was "offered once to take away the sins of many" (9:28). Thus, what is left for us to do is to approach God with a sincere heart and be willing to confess the faith that gives us hope. As we ponder the last line of the reading, we might see that it describes Jesus' own faith and the faith we need to advance his mission. Nothing will impede us if we believe that "he who made the promise is trustworthy" (10:23).

LUKE 24:46–53 In this last scene of the Gospel, Luke summarizes it all in three statements about Christ: he had to suffer, he rose, and repentance and forgiveness would be preached in his name. Just to be sure the reader gets the message, this is the second time Luke summarizes the message this way, the first being in the conversation with the disciples on the way to Emmaus. Another note particular to Luke is that this scene takes place in Jerusalem, the center of Judaism. From there, the message will go forth to the ends of the earth, symbolized by Rome, where the Acts of the Apostles will come to a close. Luke closes his account with Jesus' Ascension into heaven and the Apostles' obedient return to Jerusalem where they prayed in the Temple and praised God as they awaited the coming of the Holy Spirit.

Seventh Sunday of Easter
Take Your Fingers out of Your Ears!

ACTS 7:55–60 Ears play an interesting role in this emotionally charged scene. Stephen has just finished a long homily outlining Israel's history of rejecting God's messengers, and he closes by indicting his accusers as "stiffnecked" (v. 51) and "uncircumcised in heart and ears" (v. 51). When Stephen said that, people well versed in the Scriptures immediately realized that he was quoting the prophet Jeremiah who said: "To whom shall I speak? / whom shall I warn, and be heard? / See! their ears are uncircumcised, / they cannot pay attention; / See, the word of the Lord has become for them / an object of scorn, for which they have no taste" (Acts 6:10).

As if to verify Stephen's accusation, his judges shouted and covered their ears as they threw him out of the city to stone him. Luke spared no detail: "they were infuriated, and they ground their teeth at him" (7:54).

Although the picture of religious leaders holding their fingers in their ears appears comical, it was also deadly serious. While many Jews were joining the Christian movement, the leaders judged the message and freedom of the disciples to be as threatening as Jesus had been. For whatever reasons, they felt the need to eliminate Stephen, taking the mob to come along for the ride. The tragedy here was the leaders' absolute refusal to listen to or hear anything that challenged their own position. Stephen's fate was clear; he had seen a vision of Christ, and he died imitating Christ's forgiveness. The leaders were the ones on the road to death.

Finally, a subtle note of hope appears in the mention of Saul, at whose feet they laid their cloaks. His eyes were eventually opened; the same could happen with their ears.

PSALM 97:1–2, 6–7, 9 (1A, 9A) This psalm, celebrating God's reign over all the earth, is both a call to praise and an indictment of anyone who refuses to recognize the Most High. Singing this psalm, we worship God as the ruler of the universe, remembering too that God is intimately involved in human history as the author of justice and its judge.

REVELATION 22:12–14, 16–17, 20 This selection from the epilogue to the Book of Revelation offers an interesting follow-up to our scene from Acts. In Acts, we witnessed the

CONNECTIONS TO CHURCH TEACHING AND TRADITION

- "There is one particular way of listening to what the Lord wishes to tell us . . . lectio divina. It consists of reading God's word in a moment of prayer and allowing it to enlighten and renew us. The spiritual reading of a text must start with its literal sense. Otherwise we can easily make the text say what we think is convenient" (EG, 152).

- "We need to practice the art of listening . . . an openness of heart which makes possible that closeness without which genuine spiritual encounter cannot occur. . . . Only through such . . . compassionate listening can we enter on the paths of true growth and awaken a yearning for the Christian ideal" (EG, 171).

conflict between the disciple and unbelievers. Now, in Revelation, we hear Christ promising to return soon. Here, Christ identifies himself as the Alpha and Omega. Now he is revealed, like the Father before him (1:8), as the beginning and the end, the eternal one, ever present and still coming.

This is beyond our understanding. Happily, full understanding is not what is asked of us. Our role is to take our place among the believers, to admit our thirst and to place ourselves among the hearers who say, "Come! Amen! Come Lord Jesus!"

JOHN 17:20–26 This passage speaks both to our mission and to the goal of our life. Jesus had told the disciples very clearly that he was going away and sending the Holy Spirit. Certain that his mission would continue, he prayed for all of us throughout history who would believe through the witness of his disciples.

This, the only prayer we hear Jesus pray for his disciples, presents an alternative to some popular piety picturing Jesus' knowledge of his future disciples. There are certain reflections on the crucifixion that propose that, while on the cross, Jesus contemplated all human sin. It is difficult to find any scriptural background to support that idea. On the other hand, Jesus' words in John's Last Supper discourse indicate that he did envision the future community of believers. His vision of our future showed forth the unity of disciples sharing in his glory.

Being in union with God and sharing the glory of the Father and Son describes the goal of human life in Christ. The Eastern Churches refer to this as *theosis*. Second Peter describes it saying, "he has bestowed on us the precious and very great promises, so that through them you may come to share in the divine nature" (2 Peter 1:4). We are called to more than the imitation of Christ. We are invited and empowered to enjoy union with him sharing his own oneness with the Father.

The sign of that union is God's love dwelling in us. Participating in God's loving activity is the sign of union with God. It is both a grace and a call, something of which we are incapable on our own, but which we can allow to become the core of our very lives.

- "Eucharistic communion also confirms the Church in her unity as the body of Christ. . . . Our union with Christ . . . makes it possible for us, in him, to share in the unity of his body. . . . The Eucharist reinforces the incorporation into Christ which took place in Baptism though the gift of the Spirit (cf. 1 Corinthians 12:13, 27)" (EE, 23).

The Firstfruits of the Spirit

GENESIS 11:1–9 This fascinating account from Genesis seeks first of all to explain the phenomenon of how different human languages and cultures arose from God's one creation. Seeing those differences as punishment and division, the account teaches that that the real unity of humanity comes, not through uniformity, but from accepting God as the one who gives humanity importance and leads us to justice.

EXODUS 19:3–8A, 16–20B Like the teaching of Genesis 11, this account reinforces the idea that real community is founded only in God. It also underlines God's fearsome transcendence, reminding the people that they and their petty projects will never prosper outside of the covenant.

EZEKIEL 37:1–14 This reading too underscores the futility of human projects that do not originate in the divine plan. Humanity and all of creation count for no more than deserted, dry bones when separated from the Spirit of God.

JOEL 3:1–5 As the Genesis reading emphasized, God's intention is for all peoples to be enlivened by the Spirit of God. No matter their age, gender, social status, or nationality, all flesh is destined to share in divine life.

PSALM 104:1–2, 24, 35, 27–28, 29, 30 (SEE 30) The verses we sing from Psalm 104 are a joyful plea for the active presence of God's Spirit among us. The first two stanzas chant unmitigated praise. The third and fourth recall our dependence on God as a blessing and the source of all life.

ROMANS 8:22–27 The firstfruits were the portion of the harvest gathered first and brought to be consecrated to God, honoring him as the author and source of life. We recognize the firstfruits as God's gift to us before we can ever consider returning them. God has bestowed grace on humanity as a foretaste of what will be, thus we are restless for the fullness of salvation. As the passage's opening line says, all of creation is groaning with humanity—what was set awry by sin has left all of creation yearning to be righted through the grace of God working in humanity.

Paul interprets the groaning we share with creation as hope. Those who believe have begun to experience the

CONNECTIONS TO CHURCH TEACHING AND TRADITION

- "The Spirit dwells in the church and in the hearts of the faithful, . . . prays and bears witness in them that they are his adopted children (see Galatians 4:6, Romans 8:15–16 and 26)" (LG, 4).

- "The Eucharist is a straining towards the goal, a foretaste of the fullness of joy promised by Christ (cf. John 15:11); it is in some way the anticipation of heaven, the 'pledge of future glory.' In the Eucharist, everything speaks of confident waiting 'in joyful hope for the coming of our Savior, Jesus Christ.' Those who feed on Christ in the Eucharist need not wait until the hereafter to receive eternal life: they already possess it on earth, as the first-fruits of a future fullness which will embrace man in his totality. For in the Eucharist we also receive the pledge of our bodily resurrection at the end of the world" (EE, 18).

freedom of being children of God, but our destiny, what it will all mean in the end, is truly unfathomable.

Finally, Paul assures us that the groaning, the yearning we share with creation, is itself a fruit of the Spirit. While the firstfruits create a deep desire in us, it is a desire for more than we can imagine. Thus, God's own Spirit prays in us, orienting us toward that future known fully only to God. Meanwhile, we tend toward it, drawn by a force stronger than gravity, yet one with which we must choose to collaborate by allowing God's Spirit free reign in our heart.

JOHN 7:37–39 John gives us an interesting context for these few lines when he names the day as the "last and greatest" of the festival. That phrase contains a double meaning: John is referring to the final day of the festivities, but also pointing to Jesus' last and greatest day as well. The feast of Tabernacles was the biggest agricultural feast of the Jewish calendar year, surprisingly outshining even the Passover celebration (see *Interpreter's Dictionary of the Bible*, volume 1, pp. 492–493). The tabernacles or booths the people erected symbolized the Israelites' sojourn in the desert. The feast also celebrated the rededication of the Temple, and water served as the key symbol for it all. On each day of the week-long feast, the people would process to the Temple with water to pour into wine-bearing vessels on the altar while singing, "You will draw water joyfully from the springs of salvation."

Seen within that context, Jesus' words contain definite messianic allusions. By inviting people "come to me" (7:37), he identifies himself as a replacement for the Temple, the place of encounter with divine life.

Jesus' message here is simple and earth-shaking: anyone who thirsts can drink of what he offers and be so filled with the divine Spirit that it will flow in and from them. This idea recalls Paul's words to the Romans when he said that those who have the "firstfruits" (Romans 8:23) of the Spirit continue to long for more. The only requirements Jesus presents for receiving the Spirit is thirst, or longing, and the turning to him for satisfaction. The offer is there for us, all we need do is allow ourselves to thirst and seek the one who offers full satisfaction.

Longing for the Spirit

ACTS 2:1–11 For Israel, Pentecost was the first agricultural feast of the year, highlighting the sacrifice of newborn lambs and leading flocks to summer pasture. The feast included a celebration of the reception of the Torah, which bound the people to God. Luke situated the Christian Pentecost by having Jesus tell the disciples to stay in Jerusalem to await "power" (Acts 1:8). That power came, most appropriately, when the entire group of 120 was gathered together as a believing, hoping, praying community.

The symbols of wind and fire recall Old Testament theophanies (see Exodus 19:16–19; 1 Kings 19:11–12; 2 Kings 2:11). The symbol of tongues has connections to what Paul talked about in 1 Corinthians 12, not in the sense of "speak[ing] in different tongues" (2:4), but as a reflection of Paul's teaching that God bestows every individual gift of the Spirit for the good of the whole community.

In the description of what happened at Pentecost, we see the gift of the Spirit in two dimensions. In one sense, the advent of the Holy Spirit completes the resurrection effect: the believers become a missionary community. The second, and perhaps more important, aspect of the gift was the ability to speak to people in their own languages. Much of the story of Jesus had been marked by others' refusal to move beyond their own fixed vision of faith, what we might call their own language. Now, the apostolic missionaries have received and exercise the power to speak other languages. In other words, they are now able to preach in ways that people of backgrounds different from their own can understand. Struggles over diversity would mark the early Church, but with the help of the Spirit they were able to overcome their ethnocentricity and embrace the universality of the Good News.

PSALM 104:1, 24, 29–30, 31, 24 (SEE 30) With the disciples waiting in Jerusalem, we beg God to send the Spirit because we and our earth are in need of renewal. As we pray, we remember God's works in our history, we happily admit our shared dependence on God and we pray that we and all of creation may be pleasing to God. Because of what we already know about God, we thirst ever more for the grace of the Spirit.

CONNECTIONS TO CHURCH TEACHING AND TRADITION

- "Cultural diversity is not a threat to Church unity. The Holy Spirit . . . transforms our hearts and enables us to enter into the perfect communion of the blessed Trinity, where all things find their unity. He builds up the communion and harmony of the people of God" (EG, 117).

- "With the command to evangelize which the Risen Lord left to his Church there goes the certitude, founded on his promise, that he continues to live and work among us: 'I am with you always, to the close of the age' (Matthew 28:20). The mysterious presence of Christ in his Church is the sure guarantee that the Church will succeed in accomplishing the task entrusted to her. At the same time, this presence enables us to encounter him, as the Son sent by the Father, as the Lord of Life who gives us his Spirit" (EIA, 7).

ROMANS 8:8–17 Just after we have asked that "the Lord be glad" in us, we hear Paul speak about how to please God. Yet Paul's message here is more about mysticism than morality; he is speaking to the source of our spirituality rather than prescribing specific activities. Paul's experience —and belief—is that, because the Spirit dwells in them, Christians live a new and different life. Paul and John coincide in their emphasis on our invitation to share the life of Christ in God. The way Paul speaks here, one would almost think that it has all been accomplished. There is a sense in which that is so, but Paul will also describe our longing for the fulfillment of the firstfruits we have received (see Romans 8:23).

SEQUENCE: VENI, SANCTE SPIRITUS Sequences originated as increasingly longer prolongations of the final "a" of the sung Alleluia, eventually acquiring poetic lyrics appropriate for the celebration of the day. The singing of the sequence was a precursor to congregational singing in the Liturgy. *Veni, Sancte Spiritus* emphasizes the themes we hear in our readings. As we celebrate this feast, we might fruitfully pick any phrase from the sequence for meditation and a spur to call upon the Holy Spirit.

JOHN 14:15–16, 23B–26 In his farewell discourse, Jesus promises to pray for those who live in him, those who share his life of love. Jesus promises that he and the Father will dwell in those believers and that the Advocate will teach and remind them of all they ever need to know.

Jesus goes on to promise an "Advocate" (14:16) from the Father, one who is "another Advocate to be with you always" (14:16). Jesus' hour of glory is coming, and that will bring an end to his incarnate presence among them. Now, the Father who sent him will bestow on them the Spirit who animated Jesus. This indwelling presence of God will provide them with all that they need in a way that no limited human being could. Thus, he told Mary Magdalene (see John 20:17) that she could not hold onto him.

As we celebrate the Solemnity of Pentecost, the Gospel reminds us that the coming of the Spirit was not a one-time event. Jesus promises the Spirit to everyone who loves him. Love of him, of course, implies that we love like he did. For that we must seek the aid of the Holy Spirit.

Ordinary Time

Overview of Ordinary Time

Ordinary Time focuses our attention on the mystery of Christ and our call to discipleship. Luke developed his "orderly sequence" (Luke 1:3) of Jesus for a patron named Theophilus, the "God-lover," a designation that fits any of us who desire to know Christ better so as to love him more. Throughout this year, Luke's account of the Gospel invites us to listen with our ears and heart tuned to hear the story of our beloved. In the earliest Sundays in Ordinary Time, we hear Luke's perspective on Jesus' public appearance and the beginnings of his ministry. In the later Sundays, we contemplate Christ's life, ministry, and the demands of discipleship as the portals to the fullness of life. As we in the northern hemisphere move through the seasons of summer growth and autumn harvest, we are invited to attend to our own growth as disciples, looking toward the culmination of our own life and the fulfillment of creation.

FIRST READINGS

Through this year, we will hear from eighteen of the forty-six books of the Old Testament, with selections in this season from prophets, historical books, and wisdom literature. The historical figures we meet include Melchizedek, David and Nathan, Elijah and Elisha, Moses, Abraham, Jeremiah, Naaman the Syrian, and the Maccabee brothers. Together, they comprise an inspiring procession of our ancestors in the faith with all their frailties and their faithfulness.

RESPONSORIAL PSALMS

Each of our psalms is chosen to help us digest and express our appreciation for what we have heard in the First Reading. They also give us the opportunity to prepare our hearts for hearing the Gospel message with intention and focus. The overwhelming theme of these psalms is joyful praise of God. Knowing that, we then sing these prayers proclaiming the reasons for our praise. We remind ourselves of God's special care for the poor and we plead for forgiveness. We recognize our hunger for God who is our help and beg God to teach us how to live, perhaps all best expressed in the petition "Teach us to count our days aright" (Psalm 90:12).

SECOND READINGS

The Second Readings, while not chosen to complement the Gospels and First Readings, provide us wisdom from the earliest days of the Church. The readings from the First Letter to the Corinthians stress that God calls us to live in community with such intensity and intention that we realize that we are part of one another, and thus need to learn to love one another as ourselves. The selections from Galatians emphasize freedom. We have the freedom of faith; we are free from prejudicial distinctions like race or gender. Thus, we have been made free to serve one another and, ultimately, to live as part of the new creation. Colossians reminds us of who Christ is and who we are therefore empowered to be. Selections from Hebrews teach about faith and God's Word at home in our heart. We could summarize the message of Second Timothy with Paul's injunction to "Stir into flame the gift of God" (1:6) in our hearts. Finally, the letters to the Colossians and Thessalonians remind us to pray for one another as we each seek the inheritance God offers us.

GOSPEL READINGS

The Gospels proclaimed during Ordinary Time in Year C begin with John's account of Jesus' self-manifestation at the wedding in Cana, and they continue through the year with Luke's presentation of Jesus' works and ministry. With Jesus' baptism in the Jordan River, Luke emphasizes that he is God's beloved Son. From there, we follow Jesus as he announces the keys to his ministry, meets his first rejection, calls disciples, and preaches the Sermon on the Plain. In the subsequent weeks, Luke notices women; beginning with a widow, he goes on to portray them as ideal disciples, a calling whose demands he emphasizes over and again. He shows Jesus as controversial because of his insistence on humility, on action over cultic worship, and forgiveness of all who seek it. Together, the Gospels of this longest season of the liturgical year call us to review and renew our life as disciples of Jesus, the Risen Lord.

Through Joys and Concerns

ISAIAH 62:1–5 Third Isaiah (chapters 56—66) continues the message of hope to the people in exile, which ended in 538 BC. The prophet speaks of the glorious future that God has in store for the city of Jerusalem: "liberty to the captives" (61:1), and a "year of the Lord's favor" (v. 2), jubilee year to restore all that was lost. Jerusalem felt like a spurned lover, cast aside even by God (60:15). The land that was "forsaken" and "desolate" is given a new name pronounced by the very "mouth of the Lord" (62:2). Jerusalem is a "crown of beauty . . . a royal diadem" (v. 3) held in the hand of God. As a young man calls his beloved "My Delight," (v. 4), so shall Jerusalem be the bride of God who is the city's "builder" and "bridegroom" (v. 5). All who despised the city of Jerusalem, especially those who destroyed it, will be forced to recognize her new status. Jerusalem, where God chooses to dwell in the Temple, will truly be "the city of God."

PSALM 96:1–2, 2–3, 7–8, 9–10 (3) Psalm 96 is found among the songs King David ordered to be sung when he brought the Ark of the Covenant to Jerusalem (1 Chronicles 16:7–36). The king invites all the people to sing the praises of God. The heavens and the earth join in the joyful chorus (Psalm 96:11). Unlike pagan gods, God sits alone on the throne of heaven. All peoples are commanded to "declare his glory among the nations" (v. 3). They are asked to abandon their false idols and worship the one true God in Jerusalem's sanctuary. God will rule all the earth and its peoples with "righteousness" and "truth" (v. 13).

1 CORINTHIANS 12:4–11 Paul writes to the gifted yet divided Corinthian Church that he helped establish. He appeals to the traditions he handed on to them (1 Corinthians 11:2), especially regarding the worship practices that created divisions among the members. Paul reminds the assembly that it has lost sight of the unity found in the body of Christ. Paul then addresses how the spiritual gifts are used in community. Apparently, a competition had arisen among them, with some people claiming that their gifts were more important, while others, who

CONNECTIONS TO CHURCH TEACHING AND TRADITION

- Our real home, our destination and meaning, are with Christ (NCD, 91).

- The desire for God is written on every human heart (GS, 19; CCC, 27–30).

- There are many ways of seeking home in this transitory world (CCC, 31ff.), but in the end we go home to God (CCC, 675–677).

thought they had few or no gifts, envied the rest. Paul states that there are "varieties of gifts . . . services . . . and activities," but their source is the "same Spirit . . . the same Lord . . . and . . . the same God who activates all of them in everyone" (12:4–6). The gifts God gives should be used to make them one, to build up the Church and not to tear it down.

JOHN 2:1–11 In the opening chapter of John's Gospel, he goes back to "the beginning," and the preexistent Christ who was "with God" and who "was God" (1:1). As in the Book of Genesis, John divides the time into seven days. This represents the new creation of God's self-manifestation through the coming of Christ. A "sign" (in Greek, *semeion*) in John's Gospel is a wondrous deed that reveals Jesus as the Messiah of Israel. The first sign is the transformation of water into wine at a wedding feast in Cana. The wedding is an image of God's covenant with Israel, and the abundance of wine suggests the beginning of the messianic age (Isaiah 25:6, 62:8–9). John says this occurred on the "third day" (John 2: 1). On the third day of creation, God gathered the "waters under the sky . . . into one place" (Genesis 1:9). When the wine runs out at the wedding (a symbol of the old age passing), Jesus' mother acts as intercessor. Her presence at this first "hour" of her son's glory looks ahead to the final "hour" of his passion and death (John 19:25). Mary's request to the servants (the Church) to "do whatever he tells you" (John 2:5) initiates her son's power even though the time for him to reveal his glory had not yet come. Jesus commands the servants to "fill the jars with water" (v. 7). The six stone jars (symbolizing the six days of creation) were used for purification purposes, and Jesus changes the water in them into wine. The people are enthralled at the new wine that pours out on their behalf. On the cross, Jesus will shed water and blood for their redemption, a sacramental sign of Baptism and Eucharist (see John 19:34).

Third Sunday in Ordinary Time
Baptized into One Body

NEHEMIAH 8:2–4A, 5–6, 8–10 Nehemiah was a servant of Artaxerxes, a Persian king. Having heard of terrible conditions in Jerusalem, Nehemiah asked and received permission around 450 BC to go there to restore the walls of the city and improve the social conditions of the people. According to his own account, his success was remarkable —he organized volunteers and accomplished the rebuilding task in a mere fifty-two days.

His concern for the people went beyond their physical well-being and thus, at the culmination of the restoration of the city, Nehemiah called the people to remember the law. As the author describes this ritual, we see what would later be done in the synagogue and in our own Liturgy of the Word. The reader goes to a designated space, opens the word, and announces the blessing/reading, and the people respond with their assent. When the reading of the word moved the people to recognize their need for conversion, the priest and Nehemiah explained that their response was a grace and that they should rejoice and feast because of what the Lord had done and would do for them.

PSALM 19:8, 9, 10, 15 (SEE JOHN 6:63C) The verses we hear from Psalm 19 give the response Nehemiah called for as the people were moved by hearing the reading of God's law. Nehemiah said, "rejoicing in the Lord must be your strength" (8:10), and our refrain declares that the Spirit comes to us and gives us life through the Word of the Lord. The viewpoint expressed in this hymn of praise for God's law is the opposite of a traditional legalistic outlook. It sees the decrees of the Lord as the only guide to happiness and fulfillment. This also tells us that God's will for us is fullness of life and a share in the Spirit.

1 CORINTHIANS 12:12–30 OR 12:12–14, 27 Livy, the Roman historian who died around AD 17, wrote a parable in which he compared the Plebian society to a human body whose members rebelled against one another. In this passage Paul goes further than Livy or other ancient writers because he talks not of a symbol, but rather asserts the reality that the community is indeed the very Body of Christ. That is the remarkable effect of Baptism: each is a part of the whole and the whole makes Christ present in the world.

CONNECTIONS TO CHURCH TEACHING AND TRADITION

- "Baptism is the sacrament of faith.[1] But faith needs the community. . . . It is only within the faith of the Church that each of the faithful can believe" (CCC, 1253).

- "In every liturgical action the Holy Spirit is sent in order to bring us into communion with Christ and so to form his Body. . . . [T]he Church is the great sacrament of divine communion. . . . Communion with the Holy Trinity and fraternal communion are inseparably the fruit of the Spirit in the liturgy[2]" (CCC, 1108).

- "Only from inside the Church's mystery of communion is the 'identity' of the lay faithful made known, and their fundamental dignity revealed. Only within the context of this dignity can their vocation and mission in the Church and in the world be defined" (CL, 8).

1. Cf. Mark 16:16.
2. Cf. 1 John 1:3–7.

That calls every member to an immense responsibility not only to foster unity in the community but also to fulfill every bit of their God-given potential.

LUKE 1:1–4; 4:14–21 As we saw in Advent, Year C of our cycle of readings features the Gospel according to Luke. Today's selection begins with Luke's introduction to his work. Luke is the only Gospel writer who explains why he is writing and for whom.

These four verses are filled with theological meaning. Luke promises an "orderly sequence" of events which were "fulfilled among us" (4:3, 4:1). Those phrases indicate that Luke is writing to illustrate how those events fit into the history of salvation. Theophilus, to whom Luke addresses himself here and at the beginning of his second volume, the Acts of the Apostles, was likely a real person but also represented the Christian community, the beloved of God, who would read the works.

From the opening lines of the Gospel, today's reading skips to Jesus' first ministry in the place where he grew up. Luke continues with his theme of "fulfillment" as Jesus begins a successful teaching ministry in Galilee under the power of the Holy Spirit. The first description of that teaching shows him in his hometown synagogue. As we noted with the First Reading, teaching in the synagogue is a formal activity. Jesus stood up, received the scroll, and read, after which he rolled the scroll again, returned it, and took the position of a teacher. Interestingly, what Jesus read cannot be found in that form in the prophet Isaiah. Jesus' words came from Isaiah 61:1–11 and 58:6, but Luke's focus here favors theology rather than historical detail. Under the influence of the Holy Spirit, Jesus is proclaiming the purpose of the ministry he is inaugurating. His will be a prophetic ministry because he has been anointed by the Spirit. Like the prophets before him, he will be the friend of the poor and outcast. As Luke said in his preface, the words of the prophet were fulfilled: Jesus had begun the ministry God had in mind for him.

• "Made in the image and likeness of God[3] . . . the human person is . . . called from the very beginning to life in society . . . , he can only grow and realize his vocation in relation with others[4]" (CSDC, 149).

---

3. Cf. Genesis 1:26.

4. Congregation for the Doctrine of the Faith, Instruction *Libertatis Conscientia*, 32: AAS, 79 (1987), 567.

Tell What I Command

JEREMIAH 1:4–5, 17–19 Prophets like Jeremiah were not only preachers of God's Word; they were also living examples of it. Their words and actions pointed to the Lord and the power of salvation he offered to his people if they would live their part of the covenant. In giving his warning cry to the people, the prophet Jeremiah reminded them when they missed the mark and that they needed to repent.

In the passage for this Sunday, we hear the Lord reassure Jeremiah that he was known and dedicated before he was even born. He is called to be a spokesman to tell the world what God has commanded despite his own shortcomings and fears, and without regard for the resistance that he might encounter. Jeremiah must stay steadfast even when he is rejected or scorned. The prophet's call is ours. We can almost hear the Word of God coming to us in a similar way: stand up. Speak what I tell you. No harm shall come to you. You are mine!

PSALM 71:1–2, 3–4, 5–6, 15, 17 The psalter contains more songs of lament than any other kind of psalm. The laments most often begin with a cry to God. In the opening lines of Psalm 71, the psalmist calls out to the Lord for refuge and safety. There is confidence and trust in the words of the psalmist that convey his dependence on the strength of God.

This psalm is written from the perspective of an elderly person, "I am old and gray" (v. 18). He has spent his entire life trusting in God from the moment within his mother's womb until death. We hear convincing images of the God who is worthy of such lifelong trust: "refuge," "safety," "rock," "stronghold," "fortress," and "hope." The psalmist has endured because of his trust in the Lord. He has sung the praises of God, who has been beside him all the days of his life. With the words of the psalm he promises to "sing," "declare," and "proclaim the glory of God." His words tell what God has done and they echo in our praise of God for his trustworthiness in our lives today.

CORINTHIANS 12:31—13:13 OR 13:4–13 Paul's Letter to the Corinthians is a powerful letter addressing the way a community of believers is to behave. While this Sunday's verses have often been used for celebrations of Christian marriage, the passage is more than a beautiful passage

CONNECTIONS TO CHURCH TEACHING AND TRADITION

- Disciples live the faith, profess it, witness to it, and spread it, following Christ along the way of the cross (CCC, 1816).

- Christ was baptized as a sign that we, too, must die to ourselves and follow the Father's will. A Christian disciple makes a conscious decision to follow Jesus despite the cost (USCCA, 184, 451).

- With our own gifts and responsibilities, we follow Christ by daily taking up the cross. This witness, empowered by the Spirit of God, is a sign to all of the love God bestows on the world (LG, 41).

- The Lord's disciples suffered martyrdom in testifying to the Gospel. Giving of one's life is an astonishing sign of the abundant fruit of the apostolic life and that God's Church is born of God's grace (CL, 39).

about only romantic or sentimental love. The call to act with these virtues and characteristics of love is an ethical challenge: How will believers in Jesus Christ act toward one another? What kind of love will influence the way of life that they will practice? Will it have its roots in the love God has for his people? Will it be an example that follows the one that Christ gave in dying for sins of the world's people?

A community that lives by the characteristics of love that Paul names for the Corinthians is to be a community that is not a clashing cymbal or resounding noisy gong—without love—but rather is a living community that proclaims the love of God by its actions and words. This community tells the powerful truth of God's saving love and practices love as he commanded in Christ. This kind of community would announce and do what God commands.

LUKE 4:21–30 Today's Gospel passage continues the account, begun last Sunday, of Jesus speaking in the synagogue in his hometown. After proclaiming the words of jubilee from Isaiah, Jesus begins to teach those assembled, but the lesson is not necessarily a welcome one. Jesus' message makes it clear to his listeners that God's salvation is available to all people, not just the people of Israel.

Some listeners seem amazed by Jesus, while some seem inclined to reject him perhaps because he is the son of Joseph, the carpenter. Yet it is his proclamation of a loving God that does not fit the expectations of the crowd and that causes the most fury. Jesus proclaims a God who offers his saving power to all people of the earth. As is often the way of prophets who did not find acceptance in familiar settings but found rejection and persecution, Jesus begins his ministry with his own people in his hometown of Nazareth and is rejected. His mission, however, extends to a wider group. He offers everyone the grace and loving providence of the God with whom he is one. Through the love Jesus offers to all, the universal love of God is made present. Jesus, the Father's Son, is his instrument in proclaiming divine love to the world, despite the rejection that will ultimately lead to his suffering and death.

Go Catch Them

ISAIAH 6:1–2, 3–8 Isaiah's call to ministry is a vision, full of awe, wonder, and majesty. In his vision, Isaiah is brought into the very holy of holies in the Temple. Isaiah is naturally terrified. Scripture had taught him that no one could ever see God and live to tell about it (Genesis 35:18–20). Miraculously, Isaiah does not die. Instead, one of the seraphim attending God's throne touches Isaiah's lips with a coal, and he is purified. He hears the heavenly court considering who shall be God's spokesperson. "Here I am; send me!" Isaiah calls, which is exactly what God does. Isaiah's vision was an extraordinary event that came in the midst of a very ordinary time in the lives of his people. Uzziah was an especially weak king, and his reign was mediocre. Yet God chose to speak during Uzziah's reign. Isaiah's vision also came to a very ordinary person. By his own admission, Isaiah was nothing special. Indeed, he even calls himself "a man of unclean lips." Yet he was exactly the one God wanted.

PSALM 138:1–2, 2–3, 4–5, 7–8 (1C) This is another psalm of thanksgiving for deliverance from personal trouble. Like many such psalms, it begins with a declaration of praise. The psalmist calls on "the gods," presumably the gods of other nations, to listen while he sings the praises of the God of Israel. By convention, most psalms of this type speak of God in the third person. This psalmist, however, goes to the Temple to speak to God directly. He praises God's majesty, majesty that even the kings of the earth are constrained to admit. The psalmist praises God for having heard him and for preserving his life from his enemies. Most importantly, the psalmist praises God for giving his life a purpose and for enabling him to fulfill his purpose even in the midst of trouble and opposition from others.

CONNECTIONS TO CHURCH TEACHING AND TRADITION

- God calls, prepares, and sends prophets to God's people (CCC, 904, 942).

- God calls us. To understand the ways God calls us, we must know how God called Israel (CCC, 218).

- Christ died for our sins, rose from the dead, and appeared to his disciples (CCC, 615, 641–645).

- When Jesus calls we should forsake everything to follow him (EN, 80; CCC, 2544).

- Christians are called to evangelize others (EN, 21).

- Nothing is impossible with God (CCC, 274).

1 CORINTHIANS 15:1–11 OR 15:3–8, 11 Paul wrote this passage to the Corinthians some twenty years after the fact to reassure them that, yes, the Resurrection happened. Some were apparently unsure, and others may have denied the Resurrection altogether. It is interesting that Paul does not describe the Resurrection or give evidence for it. He simply lists all those, including himself, who saw the Risen Christ. God disclosed the Risen Christ to them, and for Paul, that was enough. Paul was called to ministry the day the Risen Christ came to him on the road to Damascus. What does this tell us about our ministry? It tells us that our ministry is always at God's initiative, not ours. It tells us that Christian ministry begins with a personal encounter with the Risen Christ and that effective ministry is grounded in the Resurrection.

LUKE 5:1–11 This passage reiterates the theme of Paul and Isaiah's call to ministry. Like Isaiah, Simon and his colleagues are awed by the power of the divine. In the presence of this power, they feel inadequate. After all, they are just ordinary fishermen with very little formal education or experience outside the world of their homes and nets. Jesus, however, told them not to be afraid. Ordinary people were exactly the kind of people he wanted.

Like the witnesses Paul mentions, the call of Jesus' first disciples came at God's initiative, not their own. In fact, being called by God was probably the furthest thing from their minds that day. They were out on the lake doing their job when Jesus came by.

Like Paul, once they encountered Jesus, Simon and the others were never the same again. Their call to ministry transformed their lives and altered their priorities dramatically. They dropped the nets that had been their livelihood for years. They left familiar people and places. They even left the security of their homes to follow Jesus.

SIXTH SUNDAY IN ORDINARY TIME
Sermon on the Plain

JEREMIAH 17:5–8 In this passage Jeremiah emphasizes the importance of trusting in God. Those who trust in human strength are likened to "a shrub in the desert," while those who trust in God "are like a tree planted by water." Both manage to survive under normal circumstances, but only the tree, whose roots go deep, will survive a drought. Like trees by a stream, those who trust in God have an abundance of life within that carries them through difficult times. Jeremiah's message was aimed primarily at Judah's leaders, who apparently loved to say, "In God we trust," but who always built armies and political alliances just in case. It will not work, Jeremiah warned. When the invasion came, Judah's allies fell apart, and its armies were thoroughly defeated. Sooner or later we catch ourselves doing what Judah's leaders did: valuing social approval more than God's approval, trusting in our investments more than we trust in God, and protecting our interests more than keeping our faith. In the end, however, lasting blessings come only when we "let go and let God."

PSALM 1:1–2, 3, 4, 6 (40:5A) This psalm, like the passage from Jeremiah, pictures the faithful as "trees planted by streams of water, which yield their fruit in its season." The wicked bear no fruit but are rather like chaff, ultimately insubstantial. God's law is as life-giving to the human spirit as water is to a tree. Knowing and delighting in God's law enables a person to follow God's way. Unlike Jeremiah, the psalmist is less concerned with the political implications of his message. He is more interested in the average person who daily faces choosing between the way of sinners and scoffers and the way of God as revealed in the Torah. For the psalmist there is no neutral ground; we must choose one path or the other. When we choose the path of the righteous, we can be assured that God will help, protect, and delight in us.

CONNECTIONS TO CHURCH TEACHING AND TRADITION

- We are called to trust God in all things. Trusting in God will help us through all forms of tribulation (CCC, 2115, 1717).

- Christ is our hope of resurrection and the center of our faith (CCC, 995, 1004).

- Bodily death is not the end for Christians but merely a transition (CCC, 996, 999).

- The faithful may endure trials in this life but will be ultimately blessed. Those who do not place their trust in Christ may seem to gain only to ultimately lose (CCC, 1716–1717, 2847).

- Material success may block spiritual growth (CCC, 2545).

- The poor are close to God's heart (CCC, 2547, 544).

1 CORINTHIANS 15:12,16–20 This week's reading leads to the heart of Paul's teaching about the Resurrection. Yet before he can reach a dramatic conclusion, he has to address the Corinthians' resistance. To many Corinthians the idea of a resurrected body was repugnant. In their minds the body was a prison that one sought to escape from, not live in forever. Paul responds that if there is no Resurrection, Jesus' preaching was in vain, the Corinthians' faith was in vain, and both are to be pitied for having been so deluded. Even the Corinthians, he argues, would not want that. Paul concludes that the Resurrection is true. Paul's reasoning gives us insight into what the early Christians taught about the Resurrection. First, Christ was raised from the dead by the power of God. Second, Christ's Resurrection ushered in a new creation, overturning the sin of Adam by which death had been introduced into the world. Third, because Christ was raised, those who are in Christ shall also rise.

LUKE 6:17, 2–26 This reading comes from the sermon on the plain, Luke's adaptation of Matthew's sermon on the mount. To present Jesus as the new Moses, Matthew wrote that Jesus spoke from a mountain. Luke, for whom mountains were special places for communing with God, places Jesus on a "level place." In every case he edits Matthew's words to be more concrete, immediate, and political. Matthew's "poor in spirit" become "you who are poor," and "those who hunger and thirst for righteousness" become, "you who are hungry now." Using several passages from Deuteronomy as his model, Luke then parallels each of his Beatitudes with a "woe" (called "curses" in Deuteronomy). Luke intended to show Jesus' teachings as the beginning of a new order, not just an expansion of the Torah as Matthew did. For Luke, Jesus' teachings were a challenge to conventional wisdom. He pronounces curses on what society often values most—wealth, security, pleasure, and social approval—and blesses that which society most often fears and ignores—poverty, hunger, sadness, and oppression.

How Should I Act?

1 SAMUEL 26:2, 7–9, 12–13, 22–23 When the people demand a king to govern them and fight their battles "like other nations" (1 Samuel 8:20), Samuel anoints Saul. Saul's reign turns out to be a tragic failure, thus preparing the way for David, his successor. David is a man of contradictions, a singer of songs and a wielder of swords. Yet despite his many faults, he is "a man after the Lord's own heart" (13:14), who was appointed to rule over the people. God's covenant with David is an eternal promise that his "throne shall be established forever" (2 Samuel 7:16). As David's talents as a leader rise, Saul's diminish, and the rejected king makes several attempts to kill his rival. Saul pursues David with three thousand soldiers, vastly outnumbering David's outlaw army of three hundred. When David learns where Saul is encamped, he goes there with Abishai, the brother of his lieutenant Joab. Although David could easily kill the sleeping king, he spares his life. David honors the sacredness of "the Lord's anointed" (1 Samuel 26:23; see the parallel account in 24:6), and leaves Saul's fate to God. The story ends with Saul's repentance and blessing of David who "will do many things and will succeed in them" (26:25).

PSALM 103:1–2, 3–4, 8, 10, 12–13 (8A) This psalm is sung on the holiest day of the Jewish year, the feast of the Atonement. It is a prayer of thanksgiving for forgiveness of sins and healing from sickness. The psalmist praises God's "vindication and justice for all who are oppressed" (v. 6) and celebrates the compassionate love and mercy of God toward all people. The psalm recounts God's willingness to pardon not only individual sin, but also the sins of the nation. God is acknowledged as one who is "merciful and gracious, slow to anger and abounding in steadfast love" (v. 8).

1 CORINTHIANS 15:45–49 Paul reaffirms his belief in the Resurrection of Christ (vv. 1–11), and its importance for our own bodily resurrection (vv. 13–14). Paul is concerned about the influence of Gnosticism (in Greek, *gnosis*, "knowledge"), with its dualistic view of salvation as an escape from the body, which is seen as evil, to some sort of spiritual realm. Paul affirms the goodness of the human body made in God's image (in Latin, *imago Dei*) and its ultimate union with Christ. Paul makes a comparison

CONNECTIONS TO CHURCH TEACHING AND TRADITION

- Our words and actions say who we are. We exhibit the quality of our reverence for human dignity (CCC, 1700) in these basic ways: preserving and cherishing the family as the original cell of social life (CCC, 2207); protecting human life (CCC, 2258); maintaining integrity in the powers of life and love planted in us (CCC, 2338); respecting and protecting creation (CA, 37–38; CCC, 2415); and living in truth and purity (CCC, 2465, 2517, 2535).

between Christ and Adam. God formed Adam "from the dust of the ground" and breathed "the breath of life" (Genesis 2:7) into him. Paul sees the Resurrection of Christ as a new creation. Unlike Adam, Christ did not come forth from the earth, but from heaven. Whereas all human beings bear a physical resemblance to Adam, a living being, they are destined to bear the glorious image of Christ's resurrected body in his heavenly existence.

LUKE 6:27–38 Luke continues his "sermon on the plain," which is the counterpart to Matthew's "sermon on the mount" (Matthew 5—7). In Matthew's Gospel, Jesus tells his followers they must be "perfect . . . as your heavenly Father is perfect" (Matthew 5:48). Characteristically, Luke stresses, "Be merciful, just as your Father is merciful" (Luke 6:36). As children of a compassionate Father who offers undeserved forgiveness, Jesus' disciples must show mercy in all their dealings with their brothers and sisters. Central to Jesus' ethical teaching is love of neighbor and forgiveness of one's enemies. He speaks out against vindictiveness because of mistreatment or injury. No matter what a person does to another—insults, ill-treatment, and even injury—Christians should seek nothing but the person's highest good. Jesus' commands are clear: Love must replace hatred, blessings should defeat curses, generosity ought to supplant selfishness, and forgiveness must overcome enmity. Above all, prayer should be offered for "those who abuse you" (v. 28). The Rabbi Hillel, a contemporary of Jesus, taught, "Do not do unto others what you would not want them to do to you; this is the whole law, and the rest is merely commentary" (Babylonian Talmud, Sabbath 31a). Jesus repeats this "golden rule" in a positive way: "Do to others as you would have them do to you" (v. 31). Jesus gives a final admonition to encourage his followers to overcome hatred and oppression just as he did through forgiveness and love, and ultimately, through his sacrificial death. If Christians pardon the wrongdoings of others, God will absolve their sins at the last judgment. God's provisions are limitless, and God's grace is endless. God will shower down immeasurable blessings on those who are gracious to others.

Living the Life

SIRACH 27:4–7 Like many biblical books, Sirach was written in the midst of crisis and great social upheaval. In it, Ben Sira addresses his people's dilemma by combining the teaching of Moses with the newer insights developed by Israel's Wisdom tradition. Today's reading comes from a collection of proverbs. These proverbs focus on integrity, or as our theme for today puts it, "how our words and actions say who we are."

Instead of just telling us about integrity, however, Ben Sira shows us by providing three rather vivid images: a sieve, a kiln, and the fruit of a tree. All three tell us that the sincerity of our faith is disclosed by the way we conduct ourselves in daily life. Like a sieve, our words and actions sift what is inside us and reveals it, both the good and the bad. Our words and actions are also like the heat of a kiln, which melts away pretensions. Most of all, our words and actions are like the fruit of a tree. People know what kind of person we are on the inside by the fruit they see on the outside.

PSALM 92:2–3, 13–14, 15–16 (SEE 2A) As its title indicates, this psalm is widely used in Jewish circles to welcome the Sabbath. Originally, the psalmist wrote these words to thank God for delivering him from the hands of his enemies. The reading begins with praise and ends with the psalmist glorying in the benefits that come to the righteous by virtue of their faith. How are the righteous to be recognized? How do we know who is "living the life" and who isn't? The righteous are known by their conduct. Their words and actions reveal an inner faithfulness.

CONNECTIONS TO CHURCH TEACHING AND TRADITION

- The duty of Christians to take part in the life of the Church impels them to act as witnesses of the Gospel and of the obligations that flow from it. This witness is a transmission of the faith in words and deeds. Witness is an act of justice that establishes the truth or makes it known[1] (CCC, 2472).

- In every circumstance, each one of us should hope, with the grace of God, to persevere "to the end"[2] and to obtain the joy of heaven, as God's eternal reward for the good works accomplished with the grace of Christ (CCC, 1821).

- By death the soul is separated from the body, but in the resurrection God will give incorruptible life to our body, transformed by reunion with our soul. Just as Christ is risen and lives for ever, so all of us will rise at the last day. Jesus conquered death once and for all time (CCC, 1016).

---

1. Cf. Matthew 18:16.
2. Matthew 10:22; cf. Council of Trent: DS, 1541.

1 CORINTHIANS 15:54–58 The reading today begins just as Paul is concluding his remarks on the Resurrection. To those who may be doubting the truth of the Resurrection, Paul says that just as Christ was raised, there will also be a resurrection for those who are in Christ. When that happens, the Corinthians will know for sure that the Resurrection is "for real." For then the promise of Scripture will have come true: "Death is swallowed up in victory" (Isaiah 25:8). Therefore (and for Paul there is always a "therefore"), "be steadfast, immovable, and abounding in the work of the Lord." Paul often connected his ethical reflections with his theological ones and this reading is a perfect example. For Paul, simply believing in the Resurrection is not enough. If we are truly resurrection people (and Paul assumes that we are), then we will act like it, too. Even our words will reflect our Easter faith.

LUKE 6:39–45 This reading is a continuation of Luke's Sermon on the Plain. The proverbs which make up this reading probably came from the same source as Matthew, but while Matthew scatters them throughout his Gospel, Luke puts them in his "sermon." The intent of the teaching is the same. "Do not be fooled," Jesus says. "Apples do not grow on thorn bushes, and grapes do not grow on the stems of weeds." If you want to know what kind of person someone is, look at his or her conduct. Look at the words he or she chooses. For what we say and do truly is a direct reflection of what is in our hearts.

God's Love Is for All

1 KINGS 8:41–43 King Solomon's lengthy prayer on the occasion of the dedication of the Temple recalls the Lord's faithfulness to the covenant of mercy and kindness the Lord made to his [Solomon's] father, David. Solomon prays for the Lord to fulfill his promise to extend David's lineage for years to come. Looking into the future, the king requests that the Lord listen to the people when they do sin and then repent of their evil ways. Solomon knows that true forgiveness comes from the Lord in his heavenly dwelling place. It is at this point in the prayer that the three short verses of today's First Reading come. In these verses, Solomon broadens his prayer request to include "the foreigner" who does not belong to the people of Israel but comes from a faraway land to worship the Lord. Hospitality is Solomon's wish; he wants the Lord to treat the stranger as he would someone from his own people and grant all the stranger asks. Nothing less than the same hospitality toward strangers and guests in God's household is required of those of us who identify as God's people.

PSALM 117:1, 2 (MARK 16:15) The two verses of Psalm 117 make it the shortest psalm in the psalter. This hymn of praise invites all the nations to praise the Lord. Praise is due the Lord for his faithfulness to his people and the constancy of his love. How fitting that this psalm follows upon the excerpt from Solomon's prayer at the dedication of the Temple in the First Reading, for Solomon, too, recognized the Lord's faithfulness. The refrain comes from what scholars recognize as the "longer ending" to the Gospel of Mark. After having reproached the remaining Eleven for their unbelief, Jesus commissions them to go out and proclaim the Gospel to the world echoing the theme of universality in Psalm 117: all are summoned to praise the Lord, and all are called to hear the good news of God's love.

CONNECTIONS TO CHURCH TEACHING AND TRADITION

- The Church, following the apostles, teaches that Christ died for all men without exception: "There is not, never has been, and never will be a single human being for whom Christ did not suffer"[1] (CCC, 605).

- From the Sermon on the Mount onwards, Jesus insists on conversion of heart: reconciliation with one's brother before presenting an offering on the altar, love of enemies, prayer for persecutors, prayer to the Father in secret, not heaping up empty phrases, prayerful forgiveness from the depths of the heart, purity of heart, and seeking the Kingdom before all else.[2] This filial conversion is entirely directed to the Father (CCC, 2608).

1. Council of Quiercy (853): DS, 624; cf. 2 Corinthians 5:15; 1 John 2:2.
2. Cf. Matthew 5:23–24, 44–45; 6:7, 14–15, 21, 25, 33.

GALATIANS 1:1–2, 6–10 Paul authenticates his call to preach the Gospel in his opening greeting to the pagan converts of Galatia. His apostleship comes through the Risen Christ and his Father. On the basis of the apostleship, Paul has the strength to hold the Galatians accountable to the Gospel of Jesus Christ they had accepted. At this point in a first-century letter, we would expect the author to include a thanksgiving. Instead we find Paul expressing his amazement and disappointment at finding the Galatians so readily swayed to another gospel and distorting the Gospel of Jesus Christ. Anyone—even Paul and his associates who preach the one, true Gospel—should be "accursed" (anathema) if they chose to preach another gospel. Paul's words of admonishment should in themselves be enough to answer his concluding rhetorical questions, which arise because his opponents think he manipulates both people and God to serve his needs. The Apostle, as he often does, describes himself as a "slave of Christ." He might have been other before his conversion, but now his sole mission is to preach Christ and his Gospel.

LUKE 7:1–10 One of the motifs of Luke's account of the Gospel is the universality of salvation in Jesus Christ. In this passage, which bears similarity to the conversion of Cornelius the centurion in Acts 10, the faith of a Gentile centurion, who describes himself as unworthy, amazes Jesus. Not even in Israel had Jesus found such faith. On the basis of the centurion's faith, Jesus heals his cherished slave. Not only did the centurion's words attest to his faith, but his action of sending Jewish elders to Jesus to request the healing of his slave also demonstrated his faith. Jesus never enters the officer's home to perform the healing, for Jewish law considered Gentile homes to be unclean. In fact, Luke does not tell us how the healing happens. We can surmise, however, that Jesus heals through his words that acclaim the centurion's faith. Jesus does indeed triumph over illness and death. In him, the officer recognizes, good health is available to all regardless of background and life situations. The fact that the elders of the Jews approached Jesus on the centurion's behalf shows that already they, too, recognized that the gift of God's love in Jesus was available to everyone.

Rescued by the Lord

1 KINGS 17:17–24 Chapter 17 in 1 Kings tells the story of Elijah and the widow who cares for him by sharing the last bit of flour and oil that stood between life and death for herself and her son. At Elijah's request, she shared what she had and was rewarded by God with food for a year. Today's account happens after that experience. Her son falls ill and stops breathing. Thinking God is punishing her because of her sinfulness, she calls out to the prophet, "Why have you done this to me, O man of God?" (17:18). Yet when Elijah asks, she hands over her son from her arms. Once again, Elijah's actions show her that she has not been forgotten by God. Trusting in God, she takes her son, the one she most loves and relies upon, and hands him over the prophet, the messenger of God. Once again, she chooses to trust in the power of God to act, and God hears her cry.

PSALM 30:2, 4, 5–6, 11, 12, 13 (2A) Deliverance from death might be a theme for all of today's readings. It seems appropriate that the psalm is one of thanksgiving by one who has been healed of a deathly illness. The psalmist gives direct credit to God: "I will extol you, O Lord, for you drew me clear" (Psalm 30:2). Weeping has turned to rejoicing and mourning has changed into dancing. Elijah and Jesus both brought life to a widow's son and changed their grief into new life. Paul was delivered by God from a life of hatred and oppression of Christians to begin a new life as a missionary of Christ. This is cause for hope and trust that God's power and salvation is indeed at work in all of history.

GALATIANS 1:11–19 If ever someone was rescued by the Lord, it was Paul! Paul tells the story himself to the Galatians "how I persecuted the church of God beyond measure and tried to destroy it" (Galatians 1:13). By the power of God, Paul was transformed from a Jewish zealot who hounded and imprisoned followers of Christ (remember his presence at Stephen's martyrdom in Acts 7:55–60, a passage we heard a few weeks ago) into a missionary intent on preaching the Good News of Jesus Christ. The Lord called out to Paul and his response was to give his life to God. His faithful missionary zeal toward many newly formed communities and his letters to those communities

CONNECTIONS TO CHURCH TEACHING AND TRADITION

- "The dark door of time, of the future, has been thrown open. The one who has hope lives differently; the one who hopes has been granted the gift of a new life" (SS, 2).

- "Jesus also prays for us—in our place and on our behalf. All our petitions were gathered up, once for all, in his cry on the cross and, in his Resurrection, heard by the Father. This is why he never ceases to intercede for us with the Father.[1] If our prayer is resolutely united with that of Jesus, in trust and boldness as children, we obtain all that we ask in his name, even more than any particular thing: the Holy Spirit himself, who contains all gifts" (CCC, 2741).

- "Christ, the great Prophet, who proclaimed the Kingdom of his Father both by the testimony of his life and the power of his words, continually fulfills his prophetic office until the complete manifestation of glory" (LG, 35).

---

1. 1 Cf. Hebrews 5:7; 7:25; 9:24.

about making a response in faith to Jesus Christ echo in all our churches today.

LUKE 7:11–17 This story of Jesus raising the son of the widow from Nain is found only in Luke's account of the Gospel. It echoes a familiar theme for Luke: the compassion and deep concern that Jesus showed for those who suffered, the disadvantaged and the poor and lowly who were often oppressed in his society. In Jesus' time, families depended on their male members. As a widow whose only son had died, this woman would have lost her family, protection, and means of support. She probably would have lost a place to live and might even have been reduced to begging in order to survive. There are similarities to the story of Elijah's raising of the widow's son, but Jesus healed not with a ritual of praying three times or stretching his body out over the son as Elijah did, but rather with a command: "Young man, I tell you, arise!" (Luke 7:14). The power for new life comes from Jesus at his authority. Just before this story in Luke 7, Jesus cures the servant of a centurion, a Roman officer. In that account (which is heard on the Ninth Sunday in Ordinary Time, Year C) the centurion tells Jesus that he is unworthy to have Jesus enter his house to be with the dying servant. Yet recognizing Jesus' power, he acknowledges that all Jesus has to do is to say the word. "Lord, do not trouble yourself, for I am not worthy to have you enter under my roof . . . but say the word and let my servant be healed" (Luke 7:6–7). Amazed, Jesus comments on the man's faith: "I tell you, not even in Israel have I found such faith" (Luke 7:9). The centurion has responded to the power that Jesus had demonstrated.

The crowd in Nain, too, reacts with awe and recognition of this powerful act by Jesus. "Fear seized them all, and they glorified God, exclaiming, 'A great prophet has arisen in our midst,' and 'God has visited his people'" (Luke 7:16). This is the Son of God, a great prophet. In Jesus' actions among those in need, we recognize God's saving power to rescue and give new life. In those who listened and followed Jesus, we see the trust of those who acknowledge that power and believe in the hope-filled possibility of new life.

▪ "The transmission of the Christian faith consists primarily in proclaiming Jesus Christ" (CCC, 425).

The Extravagant Love of God

2 SAMUEL 12:7–10, 13 In the words leading to this confrontation, Nathan tells David a story of a rich man who, instead of slaughtering one of his many lambs for a guest, stole one from a poor man. David, who as the king is sworn to protect the poor and oppressed, becomes enraged by the injustice and is ready to sentence the thief to death (2 Samuel 12:1–7). It is then that Nathan identifies David as the real thief for his betrayal and murder of one of the men of his own army in order to steal his wife. Upon hearing this, David immediately acknowledges his sin. According to the law, David's sin was punishable by death, but instead he is pardoned by God and offered life. It is a wonderful story of a powerful beloved king of the Israelites who has sinned terribly and yet is given forgiveness by his God. David experiences the extravagant, forgiving love of God and an opportunity for the new life proclaimed in the last verse of today's psalm: "Be glad in the Lord and rejoice, you just; / exult, all you upright of heart" (Psalm 32:11).

PSALM 32:1–2, 5, 7, 11 (SEE 5C) Psalm 32 is a psalm of thanksgiving for God's forgiveness. The words of it could echo throughout our Scripture stories today. David, in his terrible sin against Uriah, sinned against the very God in whom he had professed belief. The woman who washed Jesus' feet with ointment and tears prompted him to tell the story of two debtors. Faults and sins are acknowledged. Wrongs are confessed. Yet the rejoicing is clear because God shelters sinners who ask for forgiveness. In a verse from Psalm 32 that we don't hear today, we can be confident, for God says: "I will instruct you and show you the way you should walk, / give you counsel and watch over you" (Psalm 32:8).

GALATIANS 2:16, 19–21 The Law, or Torah, was given to the Israelites so they might live in the covenant of right relationships, or shalom, as the people of God. In observing the Torah, however, many fell into purely legal observances of it. Paul reminds the Galatians that it is not by works of the law they are justified, but by faith in Christ and his works. Following Christ means living the way of love beyond the call of the law. Otherwise, Paul says, Christ died in vain. Jesus reveals this to Simon in the Gospel. Jesus tells

CONNECTIONS TO CHURCH TEACHING AND TRADITION

- "David is par excellence the king 'after God's own heart,' the shepherd who prays for his people and prays in their name. His submission to the will of God, his praise, and his repentance, will be a model for the prayer of the people. His prayer, the prayer of God's Anointed, is a faithful adherence to the divine promise and expresses a loving and joyful trust in God, the only King and Lord[1]" (CCC, 2579).

- "Jesus acknowledged the Ten Commandments, but he also showed the power of the Spirit at work in their letter. He preached a 'righteousness [that] exceeds that of the scribes and Pharisees'[2] as well as that of the Gentiles.[3] He unfolded all the demands of the Commandments" (CCC, 2054).

---

1. Cf. 2 Samuel 7:18–29.
2. Matthew 5:20.
3. Cf. Matthew 5:46–47.

the woman she is forgiven and tells her to go in peace (in shalom). Like David, she has a new chance to go forward in living right relationships with new life. Paul, too, testifies to God's extravagance and his new life: "I live by faith in the Son of God who has loved me and given himself up for me" (Galatians 2:20).

LUKE 7:36—8:3 OR 7:36–50 In the Gospel we hear who the main characters are right at the beginning: a Pharisee named Simon, Jesus, and an unnamed sinful woman. All the rest, perhaps reclining at table with Jesus or observing from the outside, are simply witnesses to the exchange. The recognition of the need for forgiveness is central to the story. The woman understands her need, yet Simon is blind to it. Instead, Simon can only see to judge the woman's sin and what seems to be Jesus' shocking acceptance of her as a sinner. Simon suggests that Jesus could not be a true prophet if he does not see this. Yet earlier in Luke's account of the Gospel, Jesus told the Pharisees and scribes, "Those who are healthy do not need a physician, but the sick do" (Luke 5:31). Jesus proceeds to tell him a story of two debtors and asks him to judge for himself. Even Simon cannot ignore the right answer to Jesus' probing question of who would respond with more love. Scripture commentators suggest that we should pay attention to unnamed people in Scripture stories, as their stories serve as prototypes for us. That story could be ours. Are we able to see in the tearful, unnamed woman a child of God expressing undying gratitude and praise, or are we as blind to her as Simon was? Do we recognize the extravagant gift of salvation that is already ours from God? Toward the end of this passage, we are told that Jesus continues his journey of "preaching and proclaiming the good news of the kingdom of God" (Luke 8:1). With him were the very people to whom this was good news: women, the Apostles, those who had been healed, the disadvantaged, and the oppressed. Like the woman who washed Jesus' feet, they saw in Jesus a sign of God's extravagant love for humanity, and especially for the poor. Their response to that generosity and love was to walk with Jesus in faith. Now we must decide our response to this message of Good News!

- "The Church teaches that true peace is made possible only through forgiveness and reconciliation[4]" (CSDC, 517).

- "We have come to believe in God's love: in these words the Christian can express the fundamental decision of his life" (DCE, 1).

---

4. Cf. John Paul II, Message for the 2002 World Day of Peace, 9: AAS, 94 (2002), 136–137; John Paul II, Message for the 2004 World Day of Peace, 10: AAS, 96 (2004), 121.

Following the Path of Jesus

ZECHARIAH 12:10–11; 13:1 The Book of Zechariah is most likely the work of two prophets. The first was active soon after the return of Israel from captivity in Babylon, during the efforts to rebuild the Temple (520 BC). The second wrote about a century later. This passage derives from the later prophet who is frequently called "Second Zechariah." It is clear to him that although the Temple had been rebuilt and many exiles had returned, Judah would never regain political autonomy or a Davidic king. The prophet therefore turns his attention to the future. God will provide a glorious eschatological restoration of Jerusalem and extend his reign throughout the world. The words "I will pour out" (12:10) that begin the passage are a common expression to indicate God's future action. The prophet understands that Jerusalem must be purified "from sin and uncleanness" (13:1). He makes a daring move in visualizing how the purification will take place. The postexilic period was far from ideal. It was characterized by poverty and suffering. Second Zechariah announces that God will use the pain of Israel for cleansing. The character of "him who they have pierced" (12:10) serves to connect suffering with purification. The enigmatic nature of this character allowed the Gospel according to John to associate him with Christ, whose lifeless body was pierced with a lance (see 19:37).

PSALM 63:2, 3–4, 5–6, 8–9 (2B) This psalm is a prayer for help in time of danger. The need is powerfully captured in the image of thirst. The psalmist sees God as the one who meets his need and quenches his thirst. God's presence and kindness are so powerful that they become the goal of the prayer. In a remarkable line, they are said to be "a greater good than life" (63:4). Even though the psalmist desires to save his life, the presence of God is more important. This psalm asserts the truth that those who believe may indeed suffer, but the kindness of God's presence provides consolation and hope.

GALATIANS 3:26–29 After Paul established the Church in Galatia, other Christian missionaries came and challenged his teaching. They insisted that to become heirs of God's promises it was necessary for Gentiles to become children of Abraham and therefore undergo circumcision and

CONNECTIONS TO CHURCH TEACHING AND TRADITION

- "Likewise, the church, although it needs human resources to carry out its mission, is not set up to seek earthly glory, but to proclaim, and this by its own example, humility and self-denial" (LG, 8).

- "Even though enlightened by him in whom it believes, faith is often lived in darkness and can be put to the test. The world we live in often seems very far from the one promised us by faith. Our experiences of evil and suffering, injustice, and death, seem to contradict the Good News; they can shake our faith and become a temptation against it. It is then we must turn to the witnesses of faith: to Abraham, who 'in hope . . . believed against hope'[1]; to the Virgin Mary, who, in 'her pilgrimage of faith,' walked into the 'night of faith'[2] in sharing the darkness of her son's suffering and death" (CCC, 164–65).

---

1. Romans 4:18.
2. LG, 58; John Paul II, *Redemptoris Mater*, 18.

observe all the Jewish cultic practices. Paul agrees with their first assertion but objects to the second. Indeed, Gentiles must become Abraham's children, but they become so through faith and Baptism in Christ.

Paul quotes what is most likely an early baptismal formula, exalting the importance of incorporation into Christ. In Christ, all distinctions between Jews and Greeks, slaves and the free, males and females are overcome in the oneness that flows from faith. In accepting Christ, we receive all that God wishes to give us. We are saved. We are one. We are Abraham's children.

LUKE 9:18–24 Suffering and trials have always been a part of human life. This is one reason that three of the four Gospel accounts preserve the saying of Jesus that those who would follow him must take up the cross. The teaching can be easily misunderstood. Taking up the cross does not mean that we should seek pain and misery. The cross we carry is the cross we cannot escape, the difficulties and trials that are unavoidable in human existence. Loving people, doing what is right, dealing with the imperfections in the world and ourselves, often cause us hurt and sadness. Yet those burdens are worth bearing for the good that comes with them.

Like the belief of Zechariah that wounds can lead to purification and the faith of the psalmist who recognized the power that God's presence can bring, Jesus tells us that carrying our cross will lead to salvation. His point is clear. It is not about losing our life but saving it. Luke makes an instructive addition to Jesus' teaching. He alone among the evangelists adds the word "daily" (9:23). We are not simply to take up the cross but to take it up every day. Mark and Matthew stress the immediacy of Jesus' return in glory. Luke believes that Jesus will return, but he supposes it will take some time. As we wait, we must take up our cross time and again. After two thousand years, we still await Christ's glorious return. Luke's perspective, then, is helpful. Each day, as trouble and disappointment appear, we are called to bear them courageously. The crosses we bear are not for our destruction. With the kindness of God's presence and the example of Jesus, we carry our cross in hope.

Plowing a Straight Furrow

1 KINGS 19:16B, 19–21 The passage from 1 Kings relates the call of Elisha. Elijah chooses Elisha to succeed him as God's prophet. Accepting that call necessitates a choice—a choice not only to accept what was new but also to leave behind what was old. To become God's spokesperson, Elisha would have to leave his family and his life working on the land.

Elijah's response to Elisha's request to bid farewell to his family is ambiguous. "Have I done anything to you?" (19:20) can be interpreted as a genuine recognition of Elisha's freedom or as an expression of disappointment that the response was not immediate—"Do what you will!" However we read the statement, there can be no doubt about the completeness of Elisha's decision. The boiling of his oxen for food indicates that there will be no turning back. His life as a farmer is over. God's call is the higher claim. For now on, he is God's agent.

PSALM 16:1–2, 5, 7–8, 9–10, 11 (SEE 5A) Psalm 16 is a hymn of complete confidence in God. Almost every verse expresses how God fills the psalmist's life. God is everything to the one who prays. The most concrete image to demonstrate this connection is calling God "my allotted portion and my cup" (16:5). The vocabulary comes from the Book of Joshua. Tribes and individuals were given a portion of the Promised Land as their inheritance. These sections were determined by the casting of lots. The land was the foundational gift for Israel. It provided security and sustenance. To say that God is my land is to say that my relationship with God is more important than any material reality. In the liturgical context this psalm reflects the decision of Elisha in the First Reading. It is a blessing to plow the land, but to follow God's command is greater.

GALATIANS 5:1, 13–18 Paul uses certain terms in his letters that do not translate well into modern categories. He advises the Galatians that they should not use their freedom as "an opportunity for the flesh" (5:13). Because we associate "flesh" (5:13) with sexuality, it might seem that Paul is addressing an issue of sexual morality, but his meaning is much broader.

Paul understood the Gospel as an announcement of God's coming kingdom. The Resurrection of Jesus

CONNECTIONS TO CHURCH TEACHING AND TRADITION

- "The act of faith of its very nature is a free act. The human person, redeemed by Christ the Savior and called through Jesus Christ to be an adopted child of God, can assent to God's self-revelation only through being drawn to the Father and through submitting to God with a faith that is reasonable and free" (DH, 10).

- "[Humanity's dignity] therefore requires them to act out of conscious and free choice, as moved and drawn in a personal way from within, and not by their own blind impulses or by external constraint. People gain such dignity when, freeing themselves of all slavery to the passions, they press forward towards their goal by freely choosing what is good, and, by their diligence and skill, effectively secure for themselves the means suited to this end. Since human freedom is weakened by sin it is only by the help of God's grace that people can properly orient themselves towards God" (GS, 17).

inaugurated the establishment of that reign, but the kingdom would not be complete until Jesus returned in glory. Paul, therefore, saw himself positioned between two ages: the present age that was characterized by evil and the age to come that would fully actualize God's will on earth. "Flesh" (5:13) describes the entire human person as he or she lives in the present age, always tempted to turn against God's will. "Spirit" (5:16; 5:17; 5:18) in contrast is the gift of God that rules the age to come in which God will be all in all. Therefore, when Paul says the flesh and the Spirit are opposed to each other, he is not opposing the material to the spiritual or sexual immorality to purity. He is reminding the Galatians that they already possess the Spirit of God's coming kingdom, and they should follow its promptings in all areas of their lives.

LUKE 9:51–62 This selection from Luke contains several sayings of Jesus associated with discipleship. They converge in the conviction that following the Lord must be valued above any other good. When potential followers ask Jesus for permission to bury their fathers or say goodbye to their families, he does not display the ambiguity of Elijah. Family concerns must be set aside in light of the greater call of the Gospel.

The importance of the call is illustrated by plowing. In Jesus' time, a farmer's plow was connected to a horse or a cow, which pulled it forward. It was the responsibility of the farmer to guide the plow as it turned over the hardened earth. The farmer needed to be attentive, because the straighter the rows and the closer they were to one another, the more productive the field would be. Looking back on what was already plowed was not helpful. The attention of the farmer had to be focused on how the plow was breaking the earth now.

Jesus uses this agricultural image to stress that looking back does not build the kingdom. Who we used to be, what mistakes we may have made, what possibilities we never realized cannot claim us. Christ's call is most important, and it is in the present. The plow is moving forward. Looking back will only distract us. That is why anyone who looks back is not fit for the kingdom of God.

FOURTEENTH SUNDAY IN ORDINARY TIME
The Abundant Harvest

ISAIAH 66:10–14C This reading from the last chapter of the Book of Isaiah includes a message found repeatedly throughout the entire book: hope and rejoice in what the power of God can do, even when reality appears to be hopeless. The historical setting for today's reading was the return of the exiles to the ruins of the city of Jerusalem. Although the devastation they encountered moved them to mourn, the prophet promises that their sorrow will be turned to joy. In his attempt to reassure the people that they can have hope in their future, Isaiah reminds them that God loves them like a mother who comforts her child. Although the material prosperity promised to the people never came to be, the message of the reading is that God's loving presence provides comfort in any distress.

PSALM 66:1–3, 4–5, 6–7, 16, 20 Coincidentally, this psalm of magnificent praise goes well with the fireworks typical of the Fourth of July. It is as if the psalmist were saying that not even if all creation joined together in worship would it be enough to sing the glories due God's name. As the psalmist recalls God's mighty deeds for Israel, we too are invited to remember how God has blessed us individually and collectively.

GALATIANS 6:14–18 With this passage we come to the end of Paul's Letter to the Galatians. Having said all that he could to persuade them that the cross of Christ has freed them from the Law, Paul reminds the Galatians that because they are in Christ, they are a new creation (see also 2 Corinthians 5:17). All they need to do is to make that freedom and life in Christ a reality in their way of living.

CONNECTIONS TO CHURCH TEACHING AND TRADITION

- We see the dawning of a new missionary age which will bring an abundant harvest if all Christians "respond with generosity and holiness to the calls and challenges of our time" (RMI, 92).

- The time for missionary activity extends between the first coming of the Lord and the second, for the Gospel must be preached to all nations before the Lord comes again in glory (AG, 9).

- The Gospel must be proclaimed by Christians who "show their capacity for understanding and acceptance, their sharing of life and destiny with other people, their solidarity with the efforts of all for whatever is noble and good." This wordless witness "is already a silent proclamation of the Good News and a very powerful and effective one" (EN, 21).

LUKE 10:1–12, 17–20 OR 10:1–9 Today's reading from the Gospel begins where last Sunday's left off. Immediately after he apparently turned away three prospective disciples, Jesus appoints seventy-two more. In so doing, he does not minimize the harsh nature of their task. He assures them that they will be like lambs among wolves. Without money, they will be totally dependent on the people to whom they are sent. Interestingly, they are twice told to eat what they are offered. That could be a subtle reference to later crises when the community would have to decide if they could eat "unclean" foods (Acts 10:9–48), or it could simply be an admonition to accept whatever a peace-filled person offered them, food as well as shelter.

In addition to accepting hospitality, the disciples were also sent to heal the sick and announce the nearness of the kingdom of God. In short, like the twelve apostles sent out earlier (Luke 9:1–6), they were to do what Jesus did: share table fellowship with others, even sinners, and perform the signs that gave evidence about the nearness of the kingdom of God.

Jesus' use of the image of the harvest is more of a sign of urgency than of plenty. He tells the disciples that the harvest is abundant—so much so that the Twelve were not enough to complete its work. The appointment of the large number of additional evangelizers recalls the seventy-two elders who helped Moses (Numbers 11:16–30) as well as the purported number of the nations of the earth. By including the account of this mission in his narrative of the Gospel, Luke is advancing one of his key themes: the mission of the Christian community is universal, extending beyond the twelve tribes of Israel to Jews and Gentiles throughout the world.

Today's readings invite us to reflect on the urgency of our mission to spread the Gospel and give witness to God's kingdom in our midst. The promises of Isaiah remind us that God's nearness transforms everything. While the nations may be caught up in competition for the goods of the earth, we are invited to situate ourselves in the new creation where there is enough for everyone who is willing to share, and where people reach out to bring Christ's healing presence to one another. The mission of the seventy-two reminds us that the task of making the proclamation of the kingdom of God visible is not left only to the professionals—the clergy and lay ecclesial ministers—but belongs to every baptized person.

A Heart for the Needy

DEUTERONOMY 30:10–14 The word "Deuteronomy" signifies "second law" and denotes that this entire book is a recapitulation and explanation of the Law Moses received on Mount Sinai. The section we hear today is part of Moses' farewell speech to the Israelites before they entered into the Promised Land without him. The entire speech is well worth reading (Deuteronomy 29:1—30:20).

In today's selection, Moses assures the people that the Law of God is not a complicated formula designed to trip them up, but rather is well within their grasp. They have talked about it enough that it is "in their mouths." More than that, in their loving covenant with God, they are capable of guarding the Law "in their hearts." The final phrase of the reading moves what could have been a simple and lovely meditation to the demanding present: "you have only to carry it out." It is easy to talk and to feel sentimental about God's love, but talk and sentiments must prove themselves in action.

PSALM 69:14, 17, 30–31, 33–34, 36, 37 OR 19:8, 9, 10, 11 (9A) The shortened version of Psalm 69 we pray today moves through a progression. Beginning by calling on the goodness of the Lord, the psalmist recounts personal pain, then expresses faith before finally offering testimony to God's goodness. If we would read the entire prayer, we would see how ably the psalmist brings his distress to God. Like some of the prophets, the psalmists have been called the great complainers of the Bible. Perhaps we have something to learn from them, not just in their honest complaint, but more so because even their suffering and grumbling bring them closer to God.

Like Psalm 69, Psalm 19, a possible alternative for today, meditates on God's goodness. The Psalmist points out the glories of creation as manifestations of God's goodness, the same goodness that God conveys to us in his teaching and laws.

COLOSSIANS 1:15–20 This reading is the first of four selections we will be hearing from the Letter to the Colossians. Whether written by Saint Paul or one of his associates, the purpose of the letter was to keep the community from falling under the influence of false teachers who suggested that salvation in Christ was insufficient, claiming instead that the

CONNECTIONS TO CHURCH TEACHING AND TRADITION

- "Union with Christ is also union with all those to whom he gives himself. I cannot possess Christ just for myself; I can belong to him only in union with all those who have become, or who will become, his own. . . . We become 'one body.' . . . Love of God and love of neighbor are now truly united" (DCE, 14).

- Conversion leads to communion expressed through hospitality on the part of communities where migrants are arriving (SNL, 41).

- The poor deserve preferential attention because they have been made in the image and likeness of God and this image has been obscured and even violated. For this reason, God has become their defender and the Church, following the spirit of the Beatitudes, is called to be on their side (RMI, 60).

people should practice asceticism to placate other "principalities or powers."

Today's reading is a hymn that would have had a great influence on the people who heard or sang it regularly. The verses we hear sum up everything Paul wants to proclaim about Christ, making it clear that he is the only one who brings humanity into reconciliation with God. Christ Jesus not only reveals the image of God, but is the image of true humanity as well (Genesis 1:27).

LUKE 10:25–37 Just as Jesus would turn the tables on his companions at a meal (Luke 7:36), he could also elude lengthy theoretical debates by cutting to the heart of the matter with a story. In this incident, we hear that a "scholar" (probably a scribe) pushed Jesus to interpret the demands of Deuteronomy 6:4–9 and Leviticus 6:18. The Deuteronomy injunction to love God called for a dedication of intellect, emotion, and strength—one's whole person to love of God. In Leviticus, the law dealing with one's neighbor referred to people who shared a common heritage. Interestingly, the inquiring scholar did not seem to have any question about how to love God; his only doubt was who might count as his neighbor.

Luke tells us that the scholar pressed Jesus for more detail "because he wished to justify himself." In response, Jesus launched into the classic tale that invalidates every justifiable prejudice that Christians might want to defend. In short, there was a man who was a victim. Because he had apparently been traveling alone on a very dangerous road, he might have been much to blame for his troubles. Nevertheless, whether he was innocent, reckless, or ignorant, the key detail is that he was suffering, which is what brings the question of loving one's neighbor into clear focus.

In the end, Jesus responds to his questioner by posing a question himself. Jesus asks not only about who is a neighbor, but also who knows and loves God. Jesus and the scholar were both schooled in the psalms. They knew how frequently God is depicted as the one who hears the cry of the poor, the one who rescues the victim. Jesus' response to the scholar interpreted both parts of the "Great Commandment." He made it clear that those who love God with their whole being will demonstrate that love by caring for the poor and suffering, the ones God favors (Luke 1:50–53).

GENESIS 18:1–10A In the desert culture of Abraham and Sarah, hospitality was considered next to godliness. Some even considered it a reflection of divine nature itself. In this reading, the author emphasizes Abraham and Sarah's hospitality. Not only does Abraham welcome mysterious visitors into his home, but he also offers them exceptionally fine food, converses with them as they eat, and offers them shelter. Sarah quickly rises to what is a last-minute invitation and graciously prepares for the guests. At first, Abraham and Sarah do not grasp that their visitors are angels. Later they discover they "entertained angels without knowing it" (Hebrews 13:2), but Abraham and Sarah would have done as much regardless of their guests' identities. To a person of faith, every person is a potential messenger from God. Every person has a spark of divinity, an image of God within him or her. When we welcome others, we also welcome God, particularly when we welcome those who are in need. The story clearly illustrates how closely love for God and love for neighbor are related.

PSALM 15:2–3, 3–4, 5 (1A) This psalm may have originally been used in a liturgy as people entered the Temple. As the people approached, the priests asked them questions (for example, verse 1 says, "O Lord, who may abide in your tent?" and the approaching pilgrims would answer). Their responses combine to form a list of standards for those who are worthy to enter the Temple. It is significant that all the requirements for worthiness involve getting along with other people. Love for God and love for neighbor are once again linked. The psalmist implies that hospitality to others is the most important qualification for entering the worship of God. One cannot go to Mass on one day and then proceed to exclude others, mistreat them, or use them for personal gain the rest of the week.

CONNECTIONS TO CHURCH TEACHING AND TRADITION

- God calls us to a deep, personal, and loving relationship. Catholics deepen this relationship with God through prayer and reflection on Scripture, through participation in the sacramental life of the Church, and through the love and service of our neighbors (CCC, 2083–2086, 2424).

- God created people in God's own image and likeness (GS, 12).

- Human dignity is a fundamental right of every person (EJFA, 12–15).

- The path of charity is one of love for God and for neighbor. Charity respects others and their rights, requires the practice of justice, and inspires a life of self-giving (EJFA, 16; CCC, 1844).

COLOSSIANS 1:24–28 Paul (or someone writing in his name) continues to reflect on the work of Christ by reflecting on his own ministry, a ministry that meant great suffering. However, the author still rejoices, knowing his suffering is the same suffering that Christ endured. In fact, in verse 24 the author boldly maintains that his suffering completes Christ's suffering. The author describes himself as a servant of God called to make God's Word known, a Word that was hidden but is now revealed. What is this hidden Word for which the author is willing to suffer? Gentiles also received God's glory, "which is Christ in you" (v. 27). In the past, Gentiles, such as the Colossians, were always unwelcome among the people of God. By law and by tradition, they were always excluded from God's covenant promises. Through Christ God welcomes even Gentiles into the Church. In fact, the Colossians themselves are living proof of God's gracious hospitality.

LUKE 10:38–42 This reading continues Luke's commentary on the Great Commandment that began in the parable of the good Samaritan. In that parable Jesus lifted up the commandment to love our neighbors as ourselves. In this reading he takes up the commandment to love God. Of the two sisters, Martha seems to exemplify the teachings in the story of the good Samaritan better, but in this passage, the more contemplative Mary is extolled. It is as if Luke is purposefully trying to strike a balance between the commandments, extolling the Samaritan's active love of neighbor and then extolling Mary's more contemplative love of God. Other features are also of interest. First, Jesus practices a highly expansive act of hospitality, considering the time and place in which he lived. Not only does he accept the hospitality of single women, he also treats Mary with the respect usually reserved for a rabbi's prized (and always male) pupil. Second, the religious tradition of Jesus and his companions regarded hospitality as a sacred religious value. By extolling Mary, however, Jesus seems to say that hospitality is not enough. We must place God before all else.

SEVENTEENTH SUNDAY IN ORDINARY TIME
Pushing God

GENESIS 18:20–32 Today's passage from Genesis unfolds like a drama, perhaps even like an escalating comedy routine. Abraham beseeches God to spare Sodom, but he knows that there is little warrant for doing so. Sodom is thoroughly corrupt. Nevertheless, Abraham pushes God to extend mercy if there are fifty good people in the city and then barters his way down. He moves from fifty to forty-five, then forty, then thirty, then twenty, then ten. His boldness and his persistence are amazing. With each verse the tension rises. We think to ourselves, "Abraham, quit while you're ahead!" Still, Abraham forges on, until God agrees to save Sodom for only a handful of just people. Abraham is not afraid to ask God for what he wants. He does not hold back or stand on ceremony. He speaks to God with an aggressiveness that can only be compared to a customer arguing with a merchant in a Middle Eastern bazaar. His example shows us that it is more important to be honest than polite in prayer. Abraham's boldness is not an indication of disrespect but of intimacy. It is only when we are close to God and cherish that intimacy that we will pray how we really feel. We are polite to strangers. We are brutally honest with those on whom our survival depends. Prayer is not courteous chatter but utter honesty. "God, this is what I need. Give it to me!"

PSALM 138:1–2, 2–3, 6–7, 7–8 (3A) This psalm is one of thanksgiving because God has answered prayer. Although it was probably written in the postexilic period as a confession of the entire community, the voice of the prayer is that of a single individual. In this way God's action for the entire people is personalized. If God has answered Israel's prayer and saved his people from exile, God will also answer my prayer when I call. Liturgically, the statement of the psalmist who thanks God "with all my heart" (138:1a) echoes the prayer of Abraham who throws his self, heart and soul, into his intersession with God.

COLOSSIANS 2:12–14 It is generally accepted that a liturgical baptismal hymn lies behind these verses. The Colossians were baptized into Christ, and Paul wants them to understand how that experience has influenced their past and their present. Whatever past sins they may have committed

CONNECTIONS TO CHURCH TEACHING AND TRADITION

- "The spiritual life, however, is not limited solely to participation in the liturgy. Christians are indeed called to pray in union with each other, but they must also enter into their chamber to pray to the Father in secret; further, according to the teaching of the Apostle, they should pray without ceasing. We learn from the same Apostle that we must always bear about in our body the dying of Jesus, so that the life also of Jesus may be made manifest in our bodily frame" (SC, 12).

- "Nothing is equal to prayer; for what is impossible it makes possible, what is difficult, easy. . . . For it is impossible, utterly impossible, for the man who prays eagerly and invokes God ceaselessly ever to sin" (CCC, 2744, quoting St. John Chrysostom, *De Anna*, 4, 5: PG, 63, 585).

- "For prayer is nothing else than being on terms of friendship with God" (St. Teresa of Avila).

have been erased. In vivid imagery, Paul compares their past transgressions to a handwritten note of debt that has been paid by "nailing it to the cross" (2:14), but Baptism also provides a new present. Paul compares the going under the waters of Baptism to a burial. Because the Colossians have been so buried with Christ, they have also now been raised up with him by the power of God. Because they were Gentiles, their past condition was "uncircumcision" (2:13), but now they are alive in Christ.

LUKE 11:1–13 Luke has collected in this section of his Gospel several discreet sayings on prayer. The small parable of the neighbor at midnight clearly shows the importance of persistence in prayer. This neighbor in need echoes the determination of Abraham as he beseeches God in the Genesis reading. It is important, however, not to allegorize the parable. Not every detail is intended to reveal a truth. Although the neighbor in the parable may be seen to represent us in prayer, the sleeping man who will not be bothered is not a valid image for God. God does not need to be persuaded to help us. The repetition of our request is tied to our need, not God's disposition. We are to pray over and over not to rouse God from indifference but to ground ourselves in the confidence that God will help.

Luke's version of the Lord's Prayer in its own way reflects the value of persistence. We usually offer this prayer using Matthew's formulation (see 6:9–13), but Luke's version is substantially the same prayer, containing five of the six petitions of Matthew. All the petitions make the same request. The Lord's Prayer calls upon God to bring about the kingdom. This is most clear in the petition "your kingdom come," but the other petitions also refer to the coming reign of God. On that day when the kingdom comes, God's name will be hallowed, we will share in the final banquet of which our daily bread is only a foretaste, and we will depend on God's mercy to forgive our sins and save us from the final test. Jesus, like Abraham and the neighbor at midnight, spoke to God with boldness and persistence. In the one prayer that Jesus has left us, he asks his Father over and over again, "May your kingdom come."

Teach Us Wisdom of Heart

ECCLESIASTES 1:2; 2:21–23 Ecclesiastes, Greek for the Hebrew title Qoheleth, is a wisdom book that deals with the meaning of life and the significance of all created reality. The name means "one who gathers a community," thus one who teaches or preaches in a faith community. Wisdom books aim to teach lessons about life. Ecclesiastes' key lesson is that life is "vanity of vanities" (1:2)—transitory, like breath or vapor that does not endure but quickly dissipates. One labors diligently throughout life and upon death all goes to another who has not worked for it, with no guarantee that it will be appreciated or used well. Life's constant toil brings with it sleepless nights and much worry. All this is vanity. The important message for us is that we learn what is really important in life and not get lost in greed, gaining possessions that ultimately do not satisfy, or thinking that we will live forever. How can we learn the wisdom that truly matters as we journey through life? We are challenged to learn the wisdom that only faithful covenant love with God can bring.

PSALM 90:3–4, 5–6, 12–13, 14, 17 (8) Psalm 90 is a communal lament psalm containing strong wisdom elements. Lament psalms involve complaints to God about some dire situation in life. In the context of prayer, the situation is presented to God, ultimately leading to trust in God and to the affirmation that only God can save us in our distress. While lamenting the current situation, the psalmist is still connected to and ultimately relies on God. While the psalm's first two stanzas, like Ecclesiastes, stress the transitory nature of all life, the next two stanzas petition God for help and guidance: "Teach us to number our days aright, / that we may gain wisdom of heart" (90:12). To learn the ways of God, the very intention and purpose for which we were created, should be the lifelong curriculum of every human being. These are the riches that we must work diligently to accumulate. The psalmist asks God to "fill us . . . with your kindness," referring to the *hesed* or faithful covenant love that must become the motivation that drives all we do in life. Only in this context will the work of our hands truly prosper.

CONNECTIONS TO CHURCH TEACHING AND TRADITION

- "The sixth beatitude proclaims, 'Blessed are the pure in heart, for they shall see God.'[1] 'Pure in heart' refers to those who have attuned their intellects and wills to the demands of God's holiness" (CCC, 2518).

- "By freeing some individuals from the earthly evils of hunger, injustice, illness, and death,[2] Jesus performed messianic signs . . . to free men from . . . sin, which thwarts them in their vocation as God's sons and causes all forms of human bondage" (CCC, 549).

- "Man participates in the wisdom and goodness of the Creator . . . which enables man to discern by reason the good and the evil, the truth and the lie" (CCC, 1954).

- "The moral law is the work of divine Wisdom . . . defined as fatherly instruction, God's pedagogy. . . . It is at once firm in its precepts and, in its promises, worthy of love" (CCC, 1950).

1. Matthew 5:8.
2. Cf. John 6:5–15; Luke 19:8; Matthew 11:5.

COLOSSIANS 3:1–5, 9–11 Last week, Colossians stressed the reality that in Baptism, we die with Christ so that through faith in the power of God we are raised to new life in Christ. Today's reading specifies the implications of what it means to be raised with Christ. Consequently, we are to seek what is above, focusing on Christ and the wisdom that only Christ can teach us. The image of our lives being hidden with Christ in God is rich in communicating how Baptism bonds us so closely to Christ that it is no longer us, but Christ living in us.

Colossians advises that we continually put to death "the old self with its practices" (3:9), namely, all those things that prevent us from being in right relationship with one another. We are called to constant renewal in the image of the creator who made us. Because Christ is the very image of the invisible God, "Christ is all and in all" (3:11). We are firmly reminded that in Christ, nothing separates us from one another. We are one in Christ and our lives are to reflect that right relationship with all humanity.

LUKE 12:13–21 A key theme in Luke's account of the Gospel is the dangers that riches pose in establishing right relationship with God and others. Riches have the potential of derailing us from the wisdom that comes from God. The parable of the "rich fool," preceded by Jesus' warning against greed and the dangers of riches, captures this message well. We are advised to cultivate a lifestyle of riches that matter to God, and are connected with care, love, and concern for others. The rich man appears to be concerned only with himself and his possessions and seems to have no concern for anyone else. He claims what he has been given for himself only, strategizing how to best preserve all his possessions. His riches and greed blind him to the reality that life will end. When death comes, nothing of lasting value is left behind, except his possessions that will be enjoyed by another. Jesus warns that such will be the fate of all those "who stores up treasure for themselves but are not rich in what matters to God" (12:21). What matters to God are riches of the heart, manifested in care and concern for others. In sharing what we have been given with others, justice, right relationship, and love dominate our lives. Jesus came to teach us wisdom of heart.

WISDOM 18:6–9 This section from the Book of Wisdom is part of a longer narrative recounting how attentiveness to God's wisdom, which suffuses all creation, leads to safety and protection, while inattentiveness to God's wisdom leads to death and destruction. The backdrop is the last of the ten Exodus plagues, the death of the firstborn. God's wisdom usually operates in ways that are distinct from human reasoning and expectation.

The Egyptians had the power, and the Israelites were at their mercy. On this particular night, however, God reversed the roles. God instructed the people to celebrate Passover and to use the blood of the lamb to mark their doorposts so that their firstborn would be spared. The Egyptians, not attuned to God's wisdom, were not spared from anguish and death in their households. In this manner, God was made manifest to the Egyptians, while the Israelites were honored as God's chosen people. Faith and waiting upon the Lord led to courage and ultimate victory for God's people.

PSALM 33:1, 12, 18–19, 20–22 (12B) The psalm revels in the special covenant relationship that the chosen people have with God. Because of this special relationship, the people are blessed beyond expectation, resulting in exultation and praise of God. Through this enduring covenant and the fervent hope that springs from the relationship, the people are assured that "the eyes of the Lord are upon" his people, "to deliver them from death" (33:18, 19).

Because of the Lord's kindness (*hesed*), God's faithful and enduring covenant love, the people wait upon the Lord as their help and their shield. The psalm ends with a prayer addressed to God asking that "your kindness, Lord, / be upon us who have put our hope in you" (33:22). Trust in God enables us to wait on the Lord with patience and courage, knowing that the Lord is ever attentive to our needs.

HEBREWS 11:1–2, 8–19 OR 11:1–2, 8–12 Hebrews 11—12 lists people in the Old Testament who were considered exemplary models of faith. The author defines faith as "the realization of what is hoped for and evidence of things not seen" (11:1). Faith is an objective trust and reliance on God, most especially when things are unknown or seem to go

CONNECTIONS TO CHURCH TEACHING AND TRADITION

- "Faith is certain . . . because it is founded on the very word of God who cannot lie. . . . 'The certainty that the divine light gives is greater than that which the light of natural reason gives'[1]" (CCC, 157).

- "When God calls him, Abraham goes forth 'as the Lord had told him';[2] . . . Such attentiveness of the heart, whose decisions are made according to God's will, is essential to prayer. . . . [O]ne aspect of the drama of prayer appears from the beginning: the test of faith in the fidelity of God" (CCC, 2570).

- "Jesus prays to the Father and gives thanks . . . so he teaches us filial boldness. . . . Such is the power of prayer and of faith that does not doubt: 'all things are possible to him who believes'[3]" (CCC, 2610).

---

1. St. Thomas Aquinas, *Summa Theologica*, II–II, 171, obj. 3.
2. Genesis 12:4.
3. Mark 9:23.

contrary to rational thought and evidence. Abraham and Sarah are offered as models of faith that led them to act with trust and courage, despite all evidence to the contrary. Abraham and Sarah leave home trusting that God would lead them to a land yet unseen. They continue to trust God's promise that they would have descendants as numerous as the stars even though they are childless and beyond childbearing years. When God gifts them with Isaac, their faith is again stretched when God requests that they sacrifice their son, even though he is the only hope for fulfilling God's promise. Abraham and Sarah have the courage to trust that God could restore the dead to life, and so it happened. The Letter to the Hebrews desires to communicate to that Christian community and to ours the reality that we are called to be people of faith. We are called to trust God no matter the task confronting us, the evidence to the contrary, or the total lack of any evidence at all. Consistent exercise of faith in God builds trust and courage leading to righteous living.

- "Only faith can embrace the mysterious ways of God's almighty power. This faith glories in its weaknesses in order to draw to itself Christ's power[4]" (CCC, 273).

- "Nothing is more apt to confirm our faith and hope than holding it fixed in our minds that nothing is impossible with God"[5] (CCC, 274).

LUKE 12:32–48 OR 12:35–40 Jesus advises us to wait on the Lord in constant readiness, for we do not know the day or hour when the master will return. The advice is prefaced by the assurance that God desires to give us the riches of the kingdom. Our readiness to receive God's kingdom is manifested in our attempt to simplify our lives by taking only what we need for survival and giving the rest away. This ensures that we do not get caught up in the trappings of this world but focus on the "inexhaustible treasure in heaven" (12:33).

The parable of the servants who are ever ready to greet their master no matter the day or time of arrival is the pattern for all disciples. The reward for such vigilance is truly great: the master will have them recline at table and wait on them. The parable of the servants entrusted with much addresses the leadership responsibility disciples have for using their gifts for the service and care of others. Accountability will be demanded upon the master's return. Those who have been given much and abuse that trust will be punished more severely than the others. God's gifts are given so that others might be served. Anything less is an abuse and it will be held accountable.

4. 2 Corinthians 12:9; Phil 4:13.

5. *Roman Catechism*, I, 2, 13.

Twentieth Sunday in Ordinary Time
Set the Earth on Fire

JEREMIAH 38:4–6, 8–10 Jeremiah understood Israel's history through the prism of the covenant in which God had promised blessing for faithfulness and punishment for sin. Although the religious and political leaders insisted that God would never abandon the Temple or the royal family, Jeremiah preached otherwise, making him an adversary to priests and princes. Jeremiah's stay in the cistern was one of many times he suffered at the hands of his enemies. Before this incident, he had nearly been killed by the people of his hometown, he was put in stocks in the Temple, he was flogged, and he nearly died in a dungeon (11:18–23, 18:18, 19:14, 37:15–16). When Jeremiah received his prophetic call, God gave him fair warning saying, "I place my words in your mouth" (1:9), along with the promise that the message would lead some to "fight against you, but not prevail over you" (1:19).

PSALM 40:2, 3, 4, 18 (14B) What psalm could better remind us to imitate Jeremiah's faith in the face of persecution? One of the things this psalm makes clear is that the faithful are not commanded to suffer in silence. Rather, we are to cry out to God, making our needs known. We should also allow others to see what we have undergone and how God's saving action has led us to sing a new song.

HEBREWS 12:1–4 The passage we hear now from the Letter to the Hebrews follows a tribute to the faith of the ancestors, the "cloud of witnesses" (12:1) to whom the weary and suffering people can look for encouragement. The people addressed in this letter are suffering scorn and even the loss of property because of their faith. Under those circumstances, the author encourages them to look to Jesus. Jesus is the one who has reached the final goal: union with God. Keeping our eyes on him, we will appreciate what it means to despise the "shame" of the cross (12:2). We will evaluate everything differently, looking not to reputation or ownership, but to moving toward God as our hearts' one desire.

CONNECTIONS TO CHURCH TEACHING AND TRADITION

- "Christ, the great Prophet, who proclaimed the Kingdom of his Father . . . continually fulfills his prophetic office . . . not only through the hierarchy . . . but also through the laity whom he made his witnesses and to whom he gave understanding of the faith . . . so that the power of the Gospel might shine forth" (LG, 35).

- "With the command to evangelize which the Risen Lord left to his Church there goes the certitude . . . that he continues to live and work among us. . . . At the same time, this presence enables us to encounter him, as the Son sent by the Father, as the Lord of Life who gives us his Spirit. A fresh encounter with Jesus Christ will make all the members of the Church in America aware that they are called to continue the Redeemer's mission in their lands" (EIA, 7).

LUKE 12:49–53 What is happening when the Prince of Peace claims to bring fire and division? In considering the question we might well recall Simeon's words: "This child is destined for the fall and rise of many in Israel, and to be a sign that will be contradicted" (Luke 2:34). As he speaks of fire, when Jesus solemnly proclaims, "I have come," he is making a statement about his mission. Speaking of baptism, his use of the word "must" indicates that this is the plan of God for him. We have already heard the combination of the images of fire and Baptism when John the Baptist said that Jesus would baptize with fire and the Spirit (3:17). Scholars suggest that the fire of which he speaks is one of two things: it may be the fire of eschatological judgment or the fire of the Holy Spirit coming at Pentecost.

In this section of Luke's account of the Gospel, we meet the prophetic Jesus whose ministry demands a personal and radical response. Jeremiah quoted the Lord as speaking against false, comforting prophets saying, "Is not my word like fire, says the Lord, / like a hammer shattering rocks?" (Jeremiah 23:29). Like Jeremiah, Jesus will speak harsh truths that will cause division. Although this phrase about Baptism is unique to Luke, there is a parallel in Mark 10:38–40, where Jesus asks James and John if they can drink the cup he will drink and be baptized with the same baptism. As that is clearly a reference to his passion, so, too, is this baptism a reference to what he will undergo.

The division Jesus causes comes from different responses to his ministry. On the one hand, he attracted devoted followers, on the other, powerful people began plotting against him from the beginning of his ministry. In referring to family divisions, Jesus almost quotes the prophet Micah 7:5–7, speaking of sons who dishonor their fathers and daughters who rise up against their mothers and mothers-in-law. That passage ends saying, "But as for me, I will look to the Lord, / I will put my trust in God my savior" (Micah 7:7).

Taken together, today's readings call for the courage to set our hearts on God's will. To do so, we must keep our eyes fixed on Jesus and be prepared for the ongoing baptism that results from spreading the fire of the judgment of the Spirit of God on the world and its powers.

- "The Church as marked and sealed 'with Holy Spirit and fire,'[1] continues the work of the Messiah, opening the gates of salvation for the believer[2]" (*Aparecida*, 151).

---

1. Matthew 3:11.
2. Cf. 1 Corinthians 6:11.

All Are Welcome

ISAIAH 66:18–21 In addressing the returned Babylonian exiles who felt that separation from other nations made them more pure in their relationship to God, Isaiah challenges them with an extraordinary gathering of people who come from Gentile lands to Jerusalem. They are brought together by the Lord to experience God's light and glory. God will then commission some of these Gentiles to other lands who have not yet heard of the Lord, so that more people will come to know God's glory. All the nations will stream to Jerusalem by various means and join with the Israelites in making offerings to God in the Temple. The passage concludes with the astonishing statement that the Lord will choose priests and Levites from the Gentiles who have come to offer themselves to God.

Isaiah's inclusive vision of God must have challenged the people of his day, just as it challenges us today. What was to happen to ritual purity? How could priests and Levites be of Gentile origins? How could non-Jews regulate Temple worship and sacrifice? Today we ask: Can Muslims can be saved? Are Catholics the only people that God truly favors? Can people who do not believe in Jesus enter into full relationship with God? Very often, it is difficult for most people to imagine God as being radically inclusive of all, yet that is the challenge offered to us by both Isaiah and Jesus.

PSALM 117:1, 2 (MARK 16:15) Psalm 117, the shortest psalm in the psalter, consists of these two verses. It calls upon all the nations to praise and glorify the Lord who has manifested great love and mercy upon Israel. God's enduring faithful love showers upon Israel, assuring them that God is always faithful, never gives up on them, and is always abundant in mercy. These loving manifestations of God toward Israel are observed by all the nations, causing them to marvel at Israel's God and be drawn to praise of the Lord. God's choice of Israel is not exclusive of others, but rather Israel becomes the means through which all nations are blessed and brought to the Lord.

HEBREWS 12:5–7, 11–13 How to best understand and endure trials within a faith perspective seems to be the gist of this passage from Hebrews. The traditional understanding of trials and suffering as punishment for sin is rejected

CONNECTIONS TO CHURCH TEACHING AND TRADITION

- "Since the human race today is tending more and more towards civil, economic and social unity, it is all the more necessary that priests should unite their efforts and combine their resources under the leadership of their bishops and the Supreme Pontiff and thus eliminate division and dissension in every shape and form, so that all humanity may be led into the unity of the family of God" (LG, 28).

- "Each Christian and every community must discern the path that the Lord points out, but all of us are asked to obey his call to go forth from our own comfort zone in order to reach all the 'peripheries' in need of the light of the Gospel" (EG, 20).

in favor of seeing trials as "discipline" training (see verse 6). Trials provide the opportunity for disciplined training that enables those engaged in it to arrive at the "peaceful fruit of righteousness" (12:11). In our trials, God acts as a loving parent who provides the necessary conditions for us to grow into loving, mature human beings. While not inflicting trials upon us, God guides us through trials the way a loving parent guides and directs a child through the difficulties of life. Through these experiences, we are to be like athletes who, for the sake of the prize, build themselves up to endure whatever it takes to become people of God. This growth process involves having to learn and exercise discipline so that we can walk through trials with faith and confidence in our loving God.

LUKE 13:22–30 On his journey to Jerusalem, Jesus is asked the question of how many will be saved. Jesus' response focuses on what is required for salvation and not on how many are to be saved. Similar to the Old Testament text, Jesus asks all who would be saved to "strive" (13:24) for that heavenly prize. Similar to athletes, salvation requires that we strive to commit ourselves to living the values and life style that Jesus models. Halfway or lukewarm attempts at righteous living will not cut it. Wholehearted commitment to God's ways of acting and viewing things is essential. God's ways are different from our ways of thinking and acting, usually involving a reversal of our mindset and worldview. Such reversal requires a great deal of effort on our part, demanding a discipline that strives to know and carry out what God desires.

The passage ends with a familiar proverb emphasizing this kind of reversal: "some are last who will be first, and some are first who will be last" (13:30). We are warned against presuming that just because we have some familiarity with God, we are on safe ground. Jesus warns his disciples that this is not enough. If we do not strive continuously to take on the mind and heart of Jesus, we will be left outside, while those we least expected enter and join at the table festivities in the kingdom of God. God's love is not restricted to one ethnic group or nation but is available to all who strive to live as God desires.

Twenty-Second Sunday in Ordinary Time
God Provides

SIRACH 3:17–18, 20, 28–29 Sirach, a wisdom book written in the early part of the second century BC, is literature that typically uses the form of proverbs to instruct and exhort young and old alike on what is important on our faith journey through life. This passage focuses on humility as a virtue that is to be cultivated, and one that others appreciate more than generosity in giving. This is especially true for those in high places of wealth or power, for in humility they find favor with God. Sirach also advises that one become aware of one's limitations and not seek or search beyond one's capabilities, so as not to be frustrated or disillusioned. Wisdom is acquired by attentiveness to the wise, and learning from experience encapsulated in proverbs. Finally, Sirach advises that just as water quenches fire, so almsgiving —that is, concern for others in need—atones for both personal and communal sin. Humility, coupled with attentiveness to the needs of others, activates the wisdom orientation necessary for right relationship with God and others.

PSALM 68:4–5, 6–7, 10–11 (SEE 11B) The psalmist images God as the powerful caretaker of the people, who showers bountiful rain upon the land, restoring it to fertility so that it can provide for the needy. God's power is made manifest in attentiveness to the needs of the just, who rejoice and exult in the Lord's goodness toward all, especially the poor. God is proclaimed as the "father of orphans and the defender of widows" (68:6a). God's loving power provides "a home for the forsaken" (68:7a) and "leads forth prisoners to prosperity" (68:7b). God's ways are unlike the machinations of other gods or unlike the categories that most humans operate from. Power and might are to be used not for one's benefit but are to be placed at the service of others, most especially the needy and the forsaken. This is what makes Israel's God so different from all the other powers and authorities. For this reason, the psalmist calls upon all the people to "rejoice and exult" (68:4b) and to sing and "chant praise" (58:5a) before God, as we exercise the same attitude toward others that God exercises toward us.

HEBREWS 12:18–19, 22–24A This passage from Hebrews contrasts the previous covenants God made with the people, centered most especially on the covenant made with

CONNECTIONS TO CHURCH TEACHING AND TRADITION

- "To become a child in relation to God is the condition for entering the kingdom.[1] For this, we must humble ourselves and become little" (CCC, 526).

- "We have been made sharers in the divinity of Christ who humbled himself to share our humanity"[2] (CCC, 526).

- "The benevolence and mercy that inspire God's actions and provide the key for understanding them become so very much closer to man that they take on the traits of the man Jesus, the Word made flesh. . . . Jesus, in other words, is the tangible and definitive manifestation of how God acts towards men and women" (CSDC, 28).

- "Discussions on religious matters should be marked by clarity of expression as well as by humility and courtesy, so that truth may be combined with charity, and understanding with love" (CD, 13).

1. Cf. Matthew 18:3–4.
2. Liturgy of the Hours, Antiphon I for Evening Prayer for January 1.

Moses on Mount Sinai, and the final covenant that God has made with the people, accomplished through Jesus' "sprinkled blood that speaks more eloquently than that of Abel" (12:24). This final covenant will enable all to approach Mount Zion, the heavenly Jerusalem, in which all will rejoice and celebrate in full, intimate relationship with God, something not fully possible in the previous covenants made with the people. This final and complete covenantal gathering will include all the followers of Jesus, as well as all the just who have gone before us. Together, we will be united with God and Jesus in loving relationship for all time.

LUKE 14:1, 7–14 Meal scenes play a prominent role in Luke's account of the Gospel. Luke has Jesus use such rich occasions to teach the values of the reign of God that he consistently proclaims. This Sabbath meal at the home of "one of the leading Pharisees" (14:1) provides Jesus with the opportunity to highlight God's ways of thinking and acting in contrast to our own. Jesus' parable admonishes those who seek to be exalted and honored at the expense of others. Instead of exalting themselves, they should seek the lowest place in case someone more important comes, and they would be shamed into taking a lower place. From God's perspective, it is those who humble themselves that are exalted. This reversal of human ways of acting applies to all, especially those who consistently strive for honor, power, and prestige.

Such meals were also used to build up connections and prestige by inviting the most honored and respected people of society, with the expectation that they would invite and honor you in return. Such prestige pandering was done by carefully avoiding any association with those considered shameful—namely, the poor, the homeless, and the stranger. Jesus proclaims that such are not God's ways. God looks favorably on those who invite others who cannot return the favor. In this manner, concern for others supersedes concern for one's prestige and honor. God's reign does not operate according to our social categories but on prevailing concern for the poor and disenfranchised. These will be rewarded by God at the "resurrection of the righteous" (14:14) for this is how God models what it means to be a member of God's reign.

WISDOM 9:13–18B Some commentators call the prayer that is excerpted in this reading the high point of the Book of Wisdom. The whole of chapter 9 is King Solomon's prayer begging for wisdom. In the early part of the prayer, we find the affirmation that wisdom, portrayed as a feminine figure, was present with God at creation and is an attendant at God's throne. Prior to the selection we hear today, Solomon spoke of his responsibilities and his inability to complete his mission on his own. The prayer is full of modesty and hope. We hear words of striking humility as the King calls human efforts timid and unsure, recognizing that the body is little more than a weak shelter. The mind, too, he says, has difficulty learning about its own surroundings, much less things of heaven. Hope comes because all things are possible if God sends wisdom to aid us in our frailty.

PSALM 90:3–4, 5–6, 12–13, 14, 17 (1) The mood of the verses we sing today echoes the development of Solomon's prayer. In the beginning, we concentrate on the fragility of humanity, especially in the face of God's power. Our sojourn on earth seems almost tragically fleeting, especially when we contemplate the God who created time itself. With the third strophe, the tone of lament changes to hope. God can, indeed, teach us to number our days aright. With grace, the heart of everyone who seeks is capable of wisdom. Finally, using the limited time that we have, the Holy Spirit can lead us to know God's kindness and our work can have true meaning.

PHILEMON 9–10, 12–17 This letter is addressed to an individual, Philemon, the head of a house church in Colossae. The letter revolves around the fate of another individual, Onesimus, a slave who ran away from Philemon and became a convert and friend to Paul. The entire letter is only twenty-five verses long, 335 words in the original Greek. The point of the letter is to encourage Philemon to accept Onesimus as a brother in Christ. Although Paul insists that he could order Philemon to do what is right, he claims to prefer that he do it freely. Nevertheless, Philemon's freedom to act seems to have been more fiction than fact as Paul reminds him of how much Philemon owes him. There are not-so-subtle comparisons made between Paul, a

CONNECTIONS TO CHURCH TEACHING AND TRADITION

- "Inspired by no earthly ambition, the Church seeks but a solitary goal: to carry forward the work of Christ under the lead of the befriending Spirit" (GS, 3).

- "Love is . . . an ongoing exodus out of the closed inward-looking self towards its liberation through self-giving, and thus towards authentic self-discovery and indeed the discovery of God: 'Whoever seeks to gain his life will lose it. . . .'[1] In these words, Jesus portrays his own path, which leads through the Cross to the Resurrection" (DCE, 6).

- "This kingdom and this salvation . . . are available to every human being as grace and mercy, and yet at the same time each individual must gain them by force . . . , through toil and suffering, . . . through abnegation and the cross, through the spirit of the beatitudes. But above all . . . through a total interior renewal . . . a radical conversion, a profound change of mind and heart" (EN, 10).

---

1. Luke 17:33.

prisoner, and the slave Onesimus. Another element conditioning Philemon's freedom could have been Paul's request for a guest room. Paul would be checking up on Philemon's decision. The letter reveals Paul's tenderness and his theology of the Church as a community with no distinctions, as he said to the Galatians, "There is neither Jew nor Greek, there is neither slave nor free person, there is not male and female; for you are all one in Christ Jesus" (3:28). The fact that the letter survived for posterity offers testimony that Philemon did do the right thing: otherwise sharing the letter would have been too embarrassing.

LUKE 14:25–33 As Luke tells us that great crowds were accompanying Jesus, the implication seems to be that while all journeyed to Jerusalem, the crowds were not necessarily his followers. Jesus turns to them and utters some of the strongest, most confusing Words in Scripture: only those who hate family and even their own life can be counted as disciples.

We cannot interpret this from the context of our own culture in which we understand love and hate primarily as emotions. In Jesus' day, they were understood as the attitudes from which all action springs. To love someone meant to be loyal, to do the right thing for them, and to give them preference. Thus, in line with the message of other readings from Luke, to "hate" father and mother meant to choose the community of disciples and the poor as one's primary family rather than hold to ties of blood and place of origin. In talking about the cross, Luke again, as he did in 9:23, uses vocabulary that indicates that the disciple's cross is not a singular event, but a way of life. If we follow the crucified, we will share his cross.

Luke finishes this section indicating that discipleship is a costly matter. People should know what they are getting into before they accept the responsibility. Like the tower, it will be more expensive than we might think. It will demand that we renounce everything that prevents us from following wholeheartedly. It will not be possible without the grace of God's Spirit, but that is the one thing we are promised (Luke 11:13).

Christ Jesus Came into the World to Save Sinners

EXODUS 32:7–11, 13–14 This conversation between Moses and God happened at the end of the forty days that Moses spent on the mountain talking with God. The beginning of chapter 32 tells us that the people had prevailed upon Aaron to fashion an idol for them and to offer sacrifice and make a feast. God, of course, is aware of their infidelity and thus speaks to Moses. Notably, addressing Moses, the Lord calls the people "your people" whom "you" brought out of Egypt (32:7). From the divine viewpoint, they have ceased to be a people of God. They are so depraved that they should be destroyed, leaving Moses as the progenitor of a new covenant people. Moses will have nothing of it. He will not accept the idea that these are not God's people and, like Abraham pleading for the people of Sodom, Moses dares to argue with his Lord. He recalls all that God has done for the people from the time of Abraham to that very day. In the verse that today's reading skips, he even says that the destruction of the people would be evidence to the Egyptians that God had never cared for this people or had made a mistake in starting the Exodus. With that successful prayer, Moses proved himself a father to his own people while God's unrelenting faithfulness and mercy was revealed.

PSALM 51:3–4, 12–13, 17, 19 (LUKE 15:18) The title of this psalm indicates that it was David's prayer after being confronted by Nathan over his sin with Bathsheba and subsequent killing of Uriah. It is the classic prayer of confession and each line is worthy of meditation. With words repeated in every Eucharist, it recognizes that only with the grace of God can we have a clean heart. The final line reminds us of the most important sacrifice we can offer: a heart contrite and humbled.

1 TIMOTHY 1:12–17 Timothy was a third-generation Christian whose grandmother, Lois, and mother, Eunice, were among the people converted by Paul. He was also probably Paul's most cherished companion in mission and ministry. Paul wrote the letter so that Timothy would "know how to behave in the household of God, which is the church of the living God" (3:15). The passage we hear today contains the core of Paul's teaching: "Christ Jesus came into the world to save sinners" (1:15). Throughout his correspondence, Paul

CONNECTIONS TO CHURCH TEACHING AND TRADITION

- "Christ's call to conversion continues to resound in the lives of Christians. . . . [C]onversion is not just a human work. It is the movement of a 'contrite heart' drawn and moved by grace to respond to the merciful love of God [1]" (CCC, 1428).

- "Yet my encounter with God awakens my conscience in such a way that it no longer aims at self-justification, and is no longer a mere reflection of me . . . but it becomes a capacity for listening to the Good itself" (SS, 33).

- "God's passionate love for . . . humanity is at the same time a forgiving love. It is so great that it turns God against himself, his love against his justice . . . so great is God's love for man that by becoming man he follows him even into death, and so reconciles justice and love" (DCE, 10).

---

1. Psalm 51:17; cf. John 6:44; 12:32; 1 John 4:10.

will insist that it is faith in Jesus, not obedience to the law, which brings salvation. He gives profound witness to his own appreciation of that as he goes on to say that the enormity of his sin allowed for the immensity of Christ's patience to be revealed.

LUKE 15:1–32 OR 15:1–10 The Gospel writers did not divide their work into chapter and verse. That was done much later by scholars who wanted to create a common system of reference for use among the faithful. Therefore, it is often helpful to look at how a text fits into its context. In the case of today's Gospel. Luke is making a strong point by following Jesus' teaching about useless salt and the warning that "whoever has ears to hear ought to hear" (14:35) with the statement that it was tax collectors and sinners who were drawing near to listen to Jesus.

There are some details to Jesus' examples that might escape our notice. Jesus was addressing himself to the Pharisees, educated men who developed expertise in interpreting the Law. When Jesus addressed them as if they were lowly—and usually not law-abiding—shepherds, he was doing the equivalent of addressing physicians by saying, "which of you while driving your garbage truck . . ." Then, because he has used a masculine image he adds a feminine one in typical Lucan fashion. Each of the three parables contrasts the lost and found. In the case of the coin, it was probably worth about a day's wage—no great fortune, but still significant to the woman who lit her lamp, carefully swept her dirt floor, and then called in her friends to rejoice with her.

The parable of the lost son, perhaps the best known and loved of Jesus' parables, is the most pointed in response to the Pharisees. With all its details, including the revulsion they would feel at the thought of tending pigs and sharing their meal, the ultimate point is that the one who asks, who looks for grace and forgiveness, will receive it. The ones who righteously reject the sinner without admitting their own failings have excluded themselves from the feast.

- "Holy Communion separates us from sin. . . . The Eucharist cannot unite us to Christ without at the same time cleansing us from past sins and preserving us from future sins" (CCC, 1393).

TWENTY-FIFTH SUNDAY IN ORDINARY TIME
God's Accounting

AMOS 8:4–7 It was a time not unlike our own. For the "haves" of Israel, the eighth century BC was a time of great prosperity. Business was good. The market was booming. Profits were growing. In fact, the only thing holding the "haves" of Israel back was government regulations mandating Sabbath time and religious holidays for workers.

For the "have-nots," however, times were not so good, for underneath the booming economy of eighth-century Israel was an increasingly poorer lower class. Thousands were suffering from the unfair business practices and the bottom-line thinking that were making the "haves" so successful. Many were being forced out of their homes. Some even had to sell themselves into slavery just to keep food on the table.

Amos gives his people a reality check in no uncertain terms. Such an oppressive system, he says, cannot continue. God will not tolerate this continual buying and selling or this continual cheating of the poor. Make no mistake about it, Amos says, the judgment of God is coming and will overturn the whole oppressive system.

How are we as people of faith to respond to such a situation? Amos doesn't say in these verses, but elsewhere he is quite clear. He denounces religious communities that collude with the system just as surely as he denounces the system itself. Our calling, he says, is to be faithful to the God of peace and justice. We are first and foremost to be a prayerful community, a community that listens to God and acts on God's message of justice for all.

PSALM 113:1–2, 4–6, 7–8 (SEE 1A, 7B) The psalmist praises God for helping the weak and needy. Using images reminiscent of Hannah's song in 2 Samuel, he celebrates God as a God of justice who does not tolerate inequality. Sooner or later, the psalmist says, God will right the scale, tossing those at the top of the ladder down from their positions of power and raising up those who have been oppressed and kept down.

The reality check that we are given here is twofold: First, the psalmist tells us that God is still God, no matter what it may look like in the political realm. Second, like Amos, the psalmist insists that the unjust social order we have become

CONNECTIONS TO CHURCH TEACHING AND TRADITION

- God's love and forgiveness is for all people.

- One of the implications of faith in one God is "knowing the unity and true dignity of all men: Everyone is made in the image and likeness of God[1]" (CCC, 225).

- God's fourth commandment also enjoins us to honor all who for our good have received authority in society from God. It clarifies the duties of those who exercise authority as well as those who benefit from it (CCC, 2234).

---

1. Genesis 1:26.

accustomed to will not last. In the end, those who are first will be last, and who are last will be first.

1 TIMOTHY 2:1–8 With this reading, the author of 1 Timothy begins to instruct his young colleague. The themes he highlights differ from anything Paul himself might have said but are very characteristic of the pastoral epistles—a concern for the social order, an emphasis on truth, and a faith that is more fidelity to orthodoxy than a way of life.

The author calls us to be a community of prayer that lifts its hands to not only pray for but also help others. That is our vocation as people of faith, he says. We are to pray and serve so that by our intercession, the whole world might come to know the love and justice of Jesus Christ.

LUKE 16:1–13 OR 16:10–13 The parable of the dishonest steward is certainly a strange one. Did Jesus really mean to commend the steward's cheating, or as many commentators suggest, did he mean something else, perhaps to commend the steward's bold action. The early Church clearly struggled with this story, for Luke himself gives three different interpretations of it right in the passage itself (vv. 8, 9, and 10–12).

When we look at this parable in the context of Luke's narrative, two possible interpretations present themselves. If we take the parable by itself and ignore the additions Luke made to it in verses 8 to 13, this story connects nicely to the parable of the prodigal son, which precedes it. Both parables are challenges to the Pharisees. In this case Jesus is saying that their stewardship of God's people is being called into account and they had better act quickly and boldly to get God's approval.

If, on the other hand, we follow Luke's lead, this parable could just as easily connect to the rest of chapter 16, all of which has to do with the faithful use of one's possessions. In that case, this story is like the parable of the rich man and Lazarus, which follows. Both are warnings to handle our possessions in ways that will gain us eternal life.

Woe to the Complacent!

AMOS 6:1A, 4–7 Today's reading from the prophet Amos follows the same lines as last week's, only with stronger language and the announcement of an unambiguous day of reckoning. In this passage Amos seems to be describing a celebration that included a feast. He could hardly do more to emphasize the luxury enjoyed by the wealthy participants. The beds (couches) on which they lounged had ivory inlay and their meat was the choicest, from calves that had been kept tethered so that they would be the fattest and juiciest. They even drank from the bowls reserved for sacrificial use, demonstrating the height of their arrogance. Their complacency had roots in a variety of circumstances. They were wealthy, their social status gave them a feeling of unique importance, and they felt that God's choice of Israel was irrevocable (see 5:14, 6:1).

The people at this feast supposed that their celebration made them closer to God, but it had the opposite effect. Earlier, Amos had condemned their sacrifices saying in the name of God, "I spurn your feasts / . . . Away with your noisy songs / . . . But if you would offer me holocausts, / then let justice surge like water / and goodness like an unfailing stream" (5:21–23). Because they did not do that, the self-satisfied revelers would soon be the first to go into exile.

PSALM 146:7, 8–9, 9–10 (1B) It may seem contradictory to follow God's guarantee of exile with praise of God's unwavering faithfulness, but as this psalm develops we come to understand more and more about what God's faithfulness entails. As we sang in last week's psalm, God is first and foremost faithful to the poor and the needy. Thus, we can also proclaim that the Lord loves the just. It is precisely that love for the little ones that leads God to thwart the way of the wicked. Only those who share God's care for the poor and pursue righteousness will rejoice in knowing that the Lord will reign forever.

1 TIMOTHY 6:11–16 Paul tells Timothy to pursue righteousness, and we could understand the next few verses as an explanation of what he meant. To be righteous entails many things. It begins with conducting oneself in a way that is pleasing to God and fulfilling the law. It also means meeting one's obligations to others. Thus, Paul follows the

CONNECTIONS TO CHURCH TEACHING AND TRADITION

- "Man, through a life of fidelity to the one God, comes to experience himself as loved by God, and discovers joy in truth and in righteousness— a joy in God which becomes his essential happiness: 'Whom do I have in heaven but you? And there is nothing upon earth that I desire besides you . . . for me it is good to be near God'[1]" (DCE, 10).

- "Love of preference for the poor, and the decisions which it inspires in us, cannot but embrace the immense multitudes of the hungry, the needy. . . . It is impossible not to take account of the existence of these realities. To ignore them would mean becoming like the 'rich man' who pretended not to know the beggar Lazarus lying at his gate[2]" (SRS, 42).

---

1. Psalm 73 (72):25, 28.
2. Luke 16:19–31.

injunction to pursue righteousness by mentioning "devotion" (6:11), or *piety*, a word which implies that one participates knowledgeably in worship and with the fear of the Lord that flows from awe at what God has wrought in creation and human history. *Faith*, as used here, involves two things: faithfulness to his vocation and the message he preaches, or the ongoing development of his own faith. In reality, the two are complementary: faithfulness to the mission will include growth in his own faith. Next, Paul uses the word *agape* for "love." That is a love that chooses to give preference to others; it is based in the will, not the emotions. Patience and gentleness also complement one another, as they are expressions of agape. Paul's injunction reminds Timothy that a man of God is one who continually pursues the fulfillment of his vocation to be pleasing to God. It is a reality and a process.

▪ "The education of conscience is a lifelong task. . . . Prudent education teaches virtue; it prevents or cures fear, selfishness and pride . . . and feelings of complacency, born of human weakness and faults" (CCC, 1784).

LUKE 16:19–31 In this parable, unique to the Luke's account of the Gospel, Jesus has Abraham remind the rich man, "They have Moses and the prophets. Let them listen to them" (16:29). Had the rich man paid attention to the prophet Amos? Had he prayed the psalms? Given his opulent life, what right did he have to call Abraham "Father"? There is an immense contrast between the two main characters here. The rich man is known only by his possessions while the poor man has a name—the only person to be named in any of Jesus' parables. While Lazarus lay outside, the rich man feasted in his own home. The rich man wore luxurious clothing and Lazarus was covered with sores. The rich man left scraps under his table while unclean dogs attended Lazarus. Death brought the reversal. The rich man simply died, and Lazarus is carried off by the angels. Lazarus is in the position of highest bliss while the rich man was confined to the place of the dead.

Jesus addressed this parable to the money-loving Pharisees who had mocked him for his teaching about the right use of material goods. He was critiquing their complacency in the face of the needs of others. The parable calls us, too, to consider how our own complacency might thwart our pursuit of righteousness.

Twenty-Seventh Sunday in Ordinary Time
God Hears and Responds

HABAKKUK 1:2–3; 2:2–4 Habakkuk cries out to the Lord for help, but the Lord appears not to pay attention and is not responding. Violence, ruin, misery, destruction, strife, and clamorous discord envelop Habakkuk and God's people, yet the Lord appears distant and uncaring. In times of crisis, we, like Habakkuk, cry out to the Lord in frustration at our inability to do much about what is happening. Crying out is a way of affirming and trusting that only the Lord's care and response will get us through the crisis. Habakkuk is assured in a vision that the Lord knows and cares for the people and is going to do something about it. However, the resolution will be accomplished on God's time frame, not ours. Meanwhile, we wait on the Lord for the promised vision to be fulfilled. The rash, who cannot wait on the Lord, lack faith, trust, and integrity. The just, those who have faith and trust and wait upon the Lord, shall live and experience God's power on behalf of the people. God's covenant love is ever faithful and trustworthy and will never disappoint. All who claim covenant relationship with God must trust and wait upon the Lord, always assured that God does hear and respond.

PSALM 95:1–2, 6–7, 8–9 (8) Psalm 95, which begins the morning office in the Liturgy of the Hours, contextualizes praise and worship of God within Temple liturgy, affirming God as "the Rock of our salvation" (95:1b), our creator and shepherd who protects and guides. With joyful songs of thanksgiving, the psalmist invites all to come into the Lord's presence, bow down, and kneel before our creator, shepherd, and Lord. Faithful covenant-love relationship demands that we attune ourselves to our shepherd who knows and guides us. The last stanza challenges all to pay attention to God's voice and not to harden hearts the way their ancestors did in the desert, even though God had done marvelous deeds on their behalf in liberating them from slavery in Egypt. The word "today" (95:7d) highlights the lived reality that God continues to do marvelous things today. We need to trust, wait on the Lord, and have attentive ears and open hearts. In this manner we will experience God's covenant love and see fruits of that love lived out in our everyday lives.

CONNECTIONS TO CHURCH TEACHING AND TRADITION

- "Certain constant characteristics appear throughout the Psalms: . . . the distraught . . . believer who, in his preferential love for the Lord, is exposed to a host of enemies and temptations, but who waits upon what the faithful God will do, in the certitude of his love and in submission to his will" (CCC, 2589).

- "All . . . disciples of Christ, persevering in prayer and praising God . . . , should present themselves as a sacrifice, living, holy and pleasing to God. . . . They should everywhere on earth bear witness to Christ and give an answer to everyone who asks a reason for their hope of eternal life" (LG, 10).

2 TIMOTHY 1:6–8, 13–14 The author, writing as if he were Paul, exhorts Timothy, a disciple commissioned for ministry, to "stir into flame" (1:6) the original fervor that was his when appointed "through the imposition of my hands" (1:6). Ministry is not to be done in a spirit of cowardice but rather through God's gift of "power and love and self-control" (1:7). Amid the difficulty and challenge of proclaiming God's countercultural message, Timothy is asked to bear the hardship of the Gospel proclamation with the "strength that comes from God" (1:8). The sound words that were handed on to him by Paul and others are to be guarded and cherished and, with the help of the Spirit, are to be creatively handed on to others so that others may experience that "faith and love that are in Christ Jesus" (1:13). The challenge of ministry is to know and trust that God is always with us, no matter how difficult the journey.

- "Until the arrival of the new heavens and the new earth in which justice dwells . . . the pilgrim church, in its sacraments and institutions, which belong to this present age, carries the mark of this world which will pass, and it takes its place among the creatures which groan and until now suffer the pains of childbirth and awaits the revelation of the children of God" (LG, 48).

LUKE 17:5–10 Luke's Jesus uses his journey to Jerusalem (9:51 to 19:28) as a curriculum for discipleship. In today's reading, Jesus responds to the disciples' request while providing another occasion for addressing different demands of discipleship. To the disciples' request to "increase our faith" (17:5), Jesus clarifies that having faith per se—and not its quantity—is what truly matters. If one truly believes, then faith as small as a mustard seed, the smallest of all seeds, will prove to be powerful enough to accomplish great or impossible things, like moving a large, strong-rooted tree into the sea.

The second instruction on discipleship is more involved but essentially examines the responsibilities of discipleship. Disciples called to serve others should not expect rewards or bonuses for doing what is required of them. The unsettling example of interaction between master and slave teaches that disciples do what is expected without seeking laurels. The expression at the end of the reading, "we are unprofitable servants" (17:10), is best translated as follows: "we are not owed anything; we have done what we were obliged to do." Like Habakkuk in the First Reading and Timothy in the Second Reading, discipleship demands faith and trust, waiting upon the Lord and knowing that God hears and responds, thus affecting the good work to which we have been called. We are owed nothing else.

God Offers Salvation to All

2 KINGS 5:14–17 Naaman, an Aramean general, a Gentile, and a leper, comes to the Israelite prophet Elisha requesting a cure. Elisha asks him to plunge into the Jordan River seven times. While initially refusing to humiliate himself by so doing, Naaman changes his mind and finds himself cured. In thanksgiving for his cure, he offers Elisha a gift that the prophet refuses. This long-distance miracle in which the prophet was not even present is due to God's graciousness and not Elisha's efforts. Naaman comes to believe in Israel's God as the only God "in all the earth" (5:15). Desiring to worship only Israel's God, Naaman asks for earth from the land so that when he returns home he will still be connected to and worship only the God of Israel, the only God in all the earth. Naaman's healing and conversion is a rich example of God's gracious offer of salvation to all, Jew and Gentile alike.

PSALM 98:1, 2–3, 3–4 (SEE 2B) This enthronement psalm, extolling the kingship of God over all creation, invites all to sing a new song to the Lord, who has done wonderful deeds and proved victorious over all the earth. Connecting it with both the First Reading's cure of the Gentile leper Naaman and the Gospel reading's cure of the ten lepers, including a Samaritan, the psalm proclaims that God has made salvation known in the sight of all the nations. God's covenant love, expressed as "kindness and . . . faithfulness" (98:3) toward Israel, is all-inclusive, enabling God's victory over chaos and disorder, and resulting in the establishment of justice and right relationship with all. God's graciousness toward Naaman is a manifestation to all the earth of God's saving power. Such deep and abiding covenant love for all humanity moves the psalmist to invite all to "sing joyfully to the Lord, all you lands" (98:4).

2 TIMOTHY 2:8–13 The author of 2 Timothy continues to exhort Timothy, the community's leader, to remember and thus make present in his ministry, the heart of the Gospel: that Jesus Christ, a descendant of David, is risen from the dead. The author refers to Paul's imprisonment on behalf of that Gospel, and to the "chains" (2:9) endured for the sake of proclaiming it, "But the word of God is not chained" (2:9). Therefore Timothy, in imitation of Paul, is exhorted to

CONNECTIONS TO CHURCH TEACHING AND TRADITION

- "Its [the Church's] joy in communicating Jesus Christ is expressed both by a concern to preach him to areas in greater need and in constantly going forth to the outskirts of its own territory or towards new sociocultural settings" (EG, 30).

- "The salvation which God has wrought, and the Church joyfully proclaims, is for everyone. God has found a way to unite himself to every human being in every age. He has chosen to call them together as a people and not as isolated individuals" (EG, 113).

"bear with everything for the sake of those who are chosen, so that they too may obtain the salvation that is in Christ Jesus" (2:10). God's graciousness, so freely and abundantly gifted to us in Christ, is for all. The reading ends with a poetic hymn highlighting numerous baptismal themes. If we die with Christ we shall also live with him, and if we persevere in living the Gospel we shall reign with him. If we refuse to acknowledge the Lord, however, we cut ourselves off from covenant relationship always freely offered. Even when we are unfaithful, God's covenant love remains always faithful, enduring, and always welcoming.

LUKE 17:11–19 As Jesus continues his journey to Jerusalem, he travels through Samaria, where he encounters ten lepers. Lepers were to stay away from villages and were to warn people with bells and sounds to stay away. People were not to approach lepers. These ten outcasts risk approaching Jesus and ask for pity and compassion. Jesus risks approaching and speaking to them, telling them to go show themselves to the priests who would determine if they were clean of their leprosy and fit to join the community. On the way, they are cleansed of their leprosy. Only one returns, "glorifying God . . . , and he fell at the feet of Jesus and thanked him" (17:15). He was a Samaritan, a foreigner and an outcast. Jesus, commenting on the others who did not return to give thanks, acknowledges the foreigner and says, "Stand up and go; your faith has saved you" (17:19). Like Naaman, the Samaritan leper is cured physically but, in the process, comes to deeper faith and enters into covenant love with God.

For Luke, Jesus is the savior of all humanity breaking down boundaries and sharing God's graciousness with all, most especially the outcast, the foreigner, and the marginalized. Naaman the Aramean and the Samaritan leper, both foreigners and outcasts, become models of faith and thanksgiving in response to God's all-inclusive gracious covenant love, singing of God's saving power that they have seen and experienced. Jesus reached out to all, regardless of the risk. As disciples we too are called to risk reaching out to the marginalized and outcasts of our day manifesting God's gracious love for them in all our encounters.

- "Whether it aids the world or whether it benefits from it, the church has but one sole purpose—that the kingdom of God may come and the salvation of the human race may be accomplished. Every benefit the people of God can confer on humanity during its earthly pilgrimage is rooted in the church's being 'the universal sacrament of salvation,' at once manifesting and actualizing the mystery of God's love for humanity" (GS, 45).

Prayer Opens Us to God

EXODUS 17:8–13 Joshua, mentioned for the first time in the Torah, is designated by Moses as leader of the ensuing battle with the Amalekites, a nomadic tribe that controlled southern trade routes to and from Egypt. The dispute probably centered on land or water rights, things essential for desert survival. Moses with Aaron, his brother, and Hur situate themselves on a hill to oversee the battle. Moses displays the staff of God that aided the people in their liberation from Egypt, and extends hands in a typical prophetic manner, mediating God's favor on behalf of the people. Whenever he got tired and let down his hands, the battle favored Amalek, so Aaron and Hur assist Moses by providing a seated place and by supporting his hands. In this manner, victory by Joshua on behalf of God's people was assured. God's power mediated through Moses, not human machinations, brings about the victory that God desired.

PSALM 121:1–2, 3–4, 5–6, 7–8 (SEE 2) This psalm of trust and confidence in God's help assures the psalmist and the community that our creator God will never fail us. Amid dangerous travel through mountains or hills, our ever-attentive God will not cause our feet to slip. Our guardian God protects and shades us from the dangerous effects of both sun and moon, always at our right side and easily accessible. Our very life is in the hands of God, who will guard it always from evil and every other harm. Prayer enables us to develop a deeper knowledge of God, who initiates an eternal love relationship with us, and who is ever ready to be there in all our coming and going. Prayer also enables us to respond to that love invitation with mutual love that both satisfies and never ends.

2 TIMOTHY 3:14—4:2 Timothy is encouraged to "remain faithful" (3:14) to what he has heard and come to believe not only from people like Paul but also from his family. Such "wisdom for salvation" (3:15) comes from being immersed in the Sacred Scriptures, now linked to faith in Jesus Christ. "Sacred Scriptures" refers to the Old Testament for there was no New Testament. Some Christians tend to see little value in the Old Testament, focusing almost exclusively on the New Testament. This passage states clearly that "all Scripture is inspired by God" (3:16), and useful

CONNECTIONS TO CHURCH TEACHING AND TRADITION

- "We only devote periods of quiet time to the things or the people whom we love; and here we are speaking of the God whom we love, a God who wishes to speak to us. Because of this love, we can take as much time as we need, like every true disciple: 'Speak, Lord, for your servant is listening'" (EG, 146).

- "Praying 'our' Father opens to us the dimensions of his love revealed in Christ" (CCC, 2793).

- "Mother church never ceases to pray, hope and work . . . and she exhorts her children to purification and renewal so that the sign of Christ may shine more brightly over the face of the church" (LG, 15).

- "'The Lord's Prayer is truly the summary of the whole gospel,'[1] the 'most perfect of prayers.'[2] It is at the center of the Scriptures" (CCC, 2774).

---

1. Turtullian, *De orat.* 1: PL 1, 1251–1255.

2. St. Thomas Aquinas, *Summa Theologica*, II–II, 83, 9.

throughout life as a guide to come to know God and what God desires.

Like Timothy, we are charged with sharing the "wisdom for salvation" (3:15) gained from immersion in Scripture and through faith in Christ Jesus. Reflecting prayerfully on the Scriptures opens us up to God, enabling us to know God more deeply. We are to proclaim this wisdom "whether it is convenient or inconvenient" (4:2). Even when challenged, discouraged, opposed, or rejected, we are to carry on "through all patience and teaching" (4:2). All prayer should be rooted in Scripture, allowing its "wisdom for salvation" (3:15) to suffuse all our actions and relationships.

LUKE 18:1–8 Luke sets the parable of the widow and the unjust judge in the context of advising persistence in prayer. The parable characterizes the unjust judge as fearing neither God nor humans, and correspondingly devoid of feeling or compassion for anyone. The powerless widow who has been treated unjustly comes demanding justice. The uncaring judge delays judgment, but the widow's persistence breaks down the judge who finally relents and administers justice, ultimately fearing some retribution from the widow. Jesus uses the widow's persistent demand for justice as a model for a disciple's prayer posture toward an attentive and compassionate God.

Prayer opens us up to God, enabling us to turn with confidence to a loving and compassionate God who listens and responds. However, the response comes on God's timeline, not ours. We are asked to trust and know that God will respond, no matter how long the wait. The passage ends with an end-time question concerning faith. When Jesus returns, will the disciple's faith and trust still be evident? Or will the disciple have given up on faith, thinking that God does not care and will never respond? The parables encourages all disciples to pray and have faith in a loving and compassionate God who cares, listens, and always responds.

The Lord Hears the Cry of the Poor

SIRACH 35:12–14, 16–18 Sirach is part of Israel's wisdom literature dealing with the proper exercise of justice, or right relationship. Justice is an essential component of covenant relationship. God is just, impartially promoting right relationship with all. Those claiming to be in covenant relationships with God, both rich and poor, are called to act justly. The rich act justly when attuned to the needs of the poor and respond accordingly. The poor are to act justly as well. Keenly attuned to the demands of justice, God is biased in favor of those whose rights have been violated. This passage asserts that, though impartial toward all, God hears "the cry of the oppressed . . . [and] is not deaf to the wail of the orphan, / nor to the widow" (35:13, 14). Acting justly demands the recognition of one's humble status and dependence on God. Whoever does so will be heard when they cry out to God in need and God will respond speedily, judging justly and affirming the right. To be in covenant relationship is to be aware of God's justice demands toward all, and to know that God sees, hears, and responds to every demand for justice.

PSALM 34:2–3, 17–18, 19, 23 (7A) The antiphon for Psalm 34 sums up the psalm's principal focus, "the Lord hears the cry of the poor." Those who take refuge in the Lord, who acknowledge their dependence on God's mercy and justice will be heard when they cry out and God will rescue them "from all their distress" (34:18b). The psalmist invites all to bless and praise the Lord who is "close to the broken-hearted; and those who are crushed in spirit" (34:19). God reaches out and saves them, "redeem[ing] the lives of his servants" (34:23a), once again establishing right relationship with all. The evildoers, those who neither act justly nor work toward right relationship, are not heard, and remembrance of them is blotted out. Fitting praise is due to our merciful, just, and loving God, who cares for all, especially the poor and lowly.

2 TIMOTHY 4:6–8, 16–18 The author of 2 Timothy employs various images when speaking of Paul's approach to his imprisonment, trial, and coming death as a model for all disciples. Paul's suffering is first seen as a libation, a pouring out of his life in sacrificial offering for others, replicating the

CONNECTIONS TO CHURCH TEACHING AND TRADITION

- "Christ's disciples are called to renew ever more fully in themselves 'the awareness that the truth about God who saves, the truth about God who is the source of every gift, cannot be separated from the manifestation of his love of preference for the poor and humble, that love which, celebrated in the Magnificat, is later expressed in the words and works of Jesus'" (CSDC, 59).

- "The preferential love for the poor represents a fundamental choice for the Church, and she proposes it to all people of good will" (CSDC, 3).

- "In all places and circumstances, Christians, with the help of their pastors, are called to hear the cry of the poor. This has been eloquently stated by the bishops of Brazil: 'We wish to take up daily the joys and hopes, the difficulties and sorrows of the Brazilian people, especially of those living in the barrios and the countryside—landless, homeless, lacking food and health care—to the detriment of their rights'" (EG, 191).

pouring out of a sacrificial animal's blood offered to God. Using a sports image, the author affirms that Paul has competed well in life's race, has kept the faith and has been faithful to God to the end. Having given his life for the Lord, the author is certain that Paul's reward will be eternal life, along with all those who longed for the Lord's final appearance. Paul asks forgiveness for all those who deserted him during his trial, knowing that the Lord was with him, giving him strength to complete his mission, the spreading of the word to Gentiles. Paul is confident of the Lord's help in all his trials, trusting that the Lord will rescue him from all evil, and welcome him home. For all this, Paul humbly gives praise and glory to God.

LUKE 18:9–14 The context of Luke's parable of the Pharisee and the tax collector going up to the Temple to pray is crucial to the lesson Jesus wants to teach all disciples. The parable addresses those who are "convinced of their own righteousness and despised everyone else" (18:9). Righteousness can lead to arrogance, setting itself up as the criterion for justice and right relationship while despising all who think and act differently. In their arrogance, the self-righteous are convinced that their way of thinking and acting is God's way.

Jesus' parable reverses this very common way of thinking among righteous people. The Pharisee, beyond exemplary in all his actions, is so caught up with his own righteousness that he despises the tax collector. Convinced that God is pleased only with him and not the tax collector, the Pharisee violates the key covenant requirement of care and concern, justice and right relationship, with all of God's people. The tax collector, through humble words and posture, acknowledges his sinfulness and asks God for mercy. Jesus asserts that the tax collector went away justified, not the Pharisee. Such reversal must have shocked his audience, as it continues to shock all whose arrogance and righteousness blinds them to their own need for God. Blind also to the need of others, especially the poor and sinners, they violate their covenant responsibility to them as members of God's family. God hears the cry of the poor, the materially as well as the spiritually poor. Do we?

The Lord Is Gracious and Merciful

WISDOM 11:22—12:2 This passage from Wisdom, written during the first century BC, fuses both Greek and Jewish concepts of God, as it focuses on God's mercy and love of all creation. God, seen through Greek lenses, is all knowing, all powerful, and beyond all things. Yet the all-powerful God loves, cares for, and sustains all creation. God, whose "imperishable spirit is in all things" (11:26c), works in and through the created world. The all-powerful God is also full of mercy and compassion, "overlook[ing] people's sins that they may repent" (11:23b). God's love relationship with the world is exercised in sparing all things "because they are yours" (11:26a). It also leads God to "rebuke offenders little by little, / warn them and remind them . . . that they may abandon their wickedness" (12:2). Our all-powerful God is truly gracious and merciful, faithful to all creation, and compassionate toward all. God's love and compassion are made real and are experienced whenever we exercise the same love and compassion for all.

PSALM 145:1–2, 8–9, 10–11, 13, 14 (SEE 1) The psalmist extols, blesses, and praises God "forever and ever" (145:1c) because "the Lord is gracious and merciful, / slow to anger and of great kindness" (145:8–9). Both "gracious" and "kindness" translate the Hebrew word *hesed* meaning "ever-faithful," "enduring," and "all-giving" covenant love. For the psalmist, God's *hesed* or covenant love is manifested in the Lord being "good to all and compassionate towards all" (145:9c) of God's creation. In response, the psalmist calls upon all creation to thank the Lord. The "faithful ones" (145:10b) those who enter into covenant relationship with God, are also to thank and bless the Lord, and speak of God's power and might manifested in all creation. God is faithful and holy, lifting up "all who are falling / and raises up all who are bowed down" (145:14). God's faithful covenant love is good to all, especially those in distress, pain, or anguish. Let us thank, praise, and bless the Lord always.

2 THESSALONIANS 1:11—2:2 Paul prays for his Thessalonian community that God's grace active in them may "powerfully bring to fulfillment every good purpose and every effort of faith" (1:11). For Paul, it is God's grace and gift of faith that activates ethical living and all good

CONNECTIONS TO CHURCH TEACHING AND TRADITION

- "Fidelity to the Covenant represents not only the founding principle of Israel's social, political and economic life, but also the principle for dealing with questions concerning economic poverty and social injustices. This principle is invoked in order to transform, continuously and from within, the life of the people of the Covenant, so that this life will correspond to God's plan" (CSDC, 24).

- "I invite all Christians, everywhere, at this very moment, to a renewed personal encounter with Jesus Christ, or at least an openness to letting him encounter them; I ask all of you to do this unfailingly each day. . . . 'No one is excluded from the joy brought by the Lord'" (EG, 3).

works. Belief in God through Jesus is primary, and through that faith we are gifted with the power to live in fidelity to God's love and presence. In this manner, God is glorified in them as they become more closely bonded with God in Christ. Paul also addresses the distress that some seem to be experiencing over the imminent return of the Lord. Either by some proclamation through a "spirit" (12:2), or possibly a letter falsely attributed to Paul, some in the community believe that the Lord will soon return. Anxiety could have resulted from lack of readiness for some, or from a relaxation of the demands of discipleship, thus doing nothing until Christ returns. Paul says that neither stance is a fitting response for a believer. One is to continue trusting in the Lord and living ethically through God's grace, so that whenever the Lord returns, all will be ready and will have nothing to fear or be anxious about.

LUKE 19:1–10 The Zacchaeus narrative, unique to Luke, highlights a key element of Jesus' ministry, namely, to seek out and save the lost and marginalized, welcoming them to God's table of mercy and love. As chief tax collector, the wealthy Zacchaeus was despised by fellow Jews for cheating people, typical of tax collectors, and for collaborating with Roman occupiers. However, Zacchaeus' desire to connect with Jesus, even setting himself up for shame and ridicule by climbing a tree, causes Jesus to connect with him and to invite himself to Zacchaeus' house for dinner. "Today, I must stay at your house" (19:9) connotes a necessity on Jesus' part to seek the lost and welcome them back to God and community. God's covenant love is experienced in the person and ministry of Jesus.

Zacchaeus enthusiastically responds to Jesus' invitation to experience God's mercy and love by offering to give half his possessions to the poor and by restoring fourfold anyone he has cheated. Using the word "today" (19:9) a second time, Jesus affirms that Zacchaeus has taken advantage of his saving offer and reestablished himself as a "descendent of Abraham" (19:9). God's gracious and merciful love activated by Jesus has accomplished what Jesus was sent to do, "to seek and save what was lost" (19:10). As Jesus' disciples, we too are called to activate Jesus' covenant love in all our encounters.

2 MACCABEES 7:1–2, 9–14 The history of the mother and seven brothers who were martyred for refusing to betray their faith follows on the account of the willing martyrdom of the elderly Eleazar who refused even to pretend that he was eating pork and thereby abandoning the covenant. His reasoning was that feigning apostasy would scandalize the young, which to him was worse than death. The full martyrdom narrative is found in 6:18—7:42.

The word martyr comes from the Greek word for "bearing witness," and that is precisely what each of these nine people did, awakening both astonishment and wrath in the king. These faithful people witnessed to a faith that no threat, persecution, or even the sight of their loved ones being tortured could sway. As a matter of fact, the influence of seeing each brother tortured and killed only strengthened the resolve of the ones remaining near their mother. When the last brother's turn came, the king ordered the mother to advise him to avoid death. Instead, she encouraged him, reminding him of the power of the Creator who had given him life and would return him to her in the future. We see here the same dynamic that the Church Father, Tertullian, expressed when he said, "The blood of martyrs is the seed of the Church." God indeed gave them strength, not only in grace but also through each one's witness and encouragement.

PSALM 17:1, 5–6, 8, 15 (15B) Those who pray this psalm begin by maintaining the rightness of their cause. The parts we pray insist on that and also express resolute and persistent faith. Following the message of 2 Maccabees, we trust that, despite setbacks or persecution, we are destined to be in the eternal presence of God.

2 THESSALONIANS 2:16—3:5 The key concept in this selection is prayer. Paul begins with a prayer for the community that reminds them of God's love for them. As in last week's readings, this prayer reminds us that the Christian life is a process that depends on grace. Paul also asks the community to pray for him so that he may accomplish his mission. His desire for deliverance is not to save himself, but to be able to continue evangelizing. Finally, he stresses that no matter what, they can count on God's faithfulness,

CONNECTIONS TO CHURCH TEACHING AND TRADITION

- "But in truly great trials, where I must make a definitive decision to place the truth before my own welfare . . . we need witnesses—martyrs—who have given themselves totally, so as to show us the way—day after day. We need them if we are to prefer goodness to comfort, even in the little choices we face each day—knowing that this is how we live life to the full" (SS, 39).

- "The local Churches should do everything possible to ensure that the memory of those who have suffered martyrdom should be safeguarded[1]" (EIA, 15).

- "Christ will raise us up 'on the last day'; but it is also true that, in a certain way, we have already risen with Christ. For, by virtue of the Holy Spirit, Christian life is already now on earth a participation in the death and Resurrection of Christ" (CCC, 1002).

1. No. 37: AAS, 87 (1995), 29; cf. *Propositio*, 31.

even when they may be called to demonstrate the very "endurance of Christ" (3:5).

LUKE 20:27–38 OR 20:27, 34–38 This interaction between Jesus and the Sadducees can be read in several ways. On one hand, it is a critique of the idea that the value of a woman is determined by her childbearing, or by her providing descendants for husband, but that is only a side issue. Like the Pharisees who mocked Jesus for his attitude toward material goods (16:14), this group of Sadducees ridiculed the idea of eternal life. The sayings of Moses to which they refer are from Deuteronomy 25:5–10, which includes the precept that if a man refuses to marry his brother's widow, even after the elders have admonished him to do so, she has the right to strip him of his sandal and to spit in his face, thereby releasing herself from all obligation to the family and leaving him known as "the man stripped of his sandal" (25:10).

Nearing the climax of his mission, Jesus refused their bait and instead used their absurd example to speak of the resurrection of the dead as something that even Moses had tacitly acknowledged. In that, he used their own sources of authority to annul their argument. The key point here, as in the reading from 2 Maccabees, is the teaching about the Resurrection.

In Maccabees, the promise of eternal life supported the decision of the martyrs to face death rather than be unfaithful; they judged their present on the basis of their hope for the future. In this scene, Jesus describes the "children of this age" (20:34) as those whose sights are set on material and biological concerns. The others are those who live in such a way that it is the "coming age" (20:35) that determines their activity. The latter are the ones who recognize that all that they are comes from and will find fullness in the God of the living.

• "Those who die in God's grace . . . and are perfectly purified . . . are like God for ever for the 'see him as he is'[2]" (CCC, 1023).

---

2. 1 John 3:2; cf. 1 Corinthians 13:12; Revelation 22:4.

There Are Challenges of All Kinds in a Lifetime

MALACHI 3:19–20A To our ear, this passage, heard alongside the Gospel passage in which Jesus speaks of the end times to his disciples, may feel like a prediction or forecast. Yet the Old Testament does not work like a fortune teller predicting the future. Rather, the words that were often spoken by a prophet (like Malachi whose name translated from Hebrew means "my messenger") speak of the real-life situations that challenge God's people and stress the importance for them to be faithful once again to the covenant. Malachi presents a contrast between those who are proud evildoers and those who fear the Lord. Earlier in the chapter he cites particular evil ways the people have chosen to act: "I will be swift to bear witness / Against the sorcerers, adulterers, and perjurers, / those who defraud the hired man of his wages, / Against those who defraud widows and orphans; / those who turn aside the stranger, / and those who do not fear me, says the Lord of hosts" (3:5). God's prophet and messenger invites listeners to return to God. When they do, they will be blessed and prosperous, and "they shall be mine, says the Lord" (3:17). Destruction will come to the wicked and justice and healing will come to the faithful and righteous.

PSALM 98:5–6, 7–8, 9 (SEE 9) Psalm 98 is an enthronement psalm that celebrates God as the Lord of all creation. In fact, Psalms 86, 97, and 98 all celebrate rejoicing in the face of God's power and glory. Psalm 98 can be proclaimed because truly all the ends of the earth have seen God act to save his people. Therefore, all peoples as well as all of creation clap, sing, and shout with joy for God comes to rule with justice and equity. Next Sunday as we end our liturgical year on the Solemnity of Christ the King, we remember this psalm of praise for God's saving power that rescues the powerless of the world not only in the present moment but for all time to come.

2 THESSALONIANS 3:7–12 Often the epistles were written not only to teach about faith in Christ but also to correct misunderstandings. Paul writes to the community of Thessalonica, where some believed they did not need to work or plan for the future because they could simply wait for Christ to come again. This attitude had become a

CONNECTIONS TO CHURCH TEACHING AND TRADITION

- "Jesus venerated the Temple by going up to it for the Jewish feasts of pilgrimage, and with a jealous love he loved this dwelling of God among men. The Temple prefigures his own mystery. When he announces its destruction, it is as a manifestation of his own execution and of the entry into a new age in the history of salvation, when his Body would be the definitive Temple" (CCC, 593).

- "The Church is called the building of God. . . . On this foundation the Church is built by the apostles and from it the Church receives solidity and unity. This edifice has many names to describe it: the house of God in which his family dwells; the household of God in the Spirit; the dwelling-place of God among men; and, especially, the holy temple. This temple . . . is compared in the liturgy to the Holy City, the New Jerusalem" (CCC, 756).

burden on others in the community. In his letter, Paul reminds them that "we always pray for you, that our God may make you worthy of his calling and powerfully bring to fulfillment every good purpose and every effort of faith, that the name of our Lord Jesus may be glorified in you" (2 Thessalonians 1:11–12). There would be many challenges both for the community and for believers, but Paul prays that "the Lord of peace himself give you peace at all times and in every way" (2 Thessalonians 3:16). Their faithful perseverance to that message is what is required of disciples and would bring them peace.

- "Christ's disciples hope to render to others true witness of Christ, and to work for their salvation" (AG, 12).

LUKE 21:5–19 Like Malachi, Luke sets up a contrast for his readers. There will be those who will harm, persecute, and imprison disciples and there will be those who testify to their God. Those who give witness, though they may be hated and even killed, will not be harmed. Their perseverance, strength, and resolve will render their persecutors powerless in the face of God's power. This is Jesus' last appearance in the Temple. By setting this story in the Temple, which only Luke does, Luke reminds his community of the other times the Temple was significant in Jesus' life. He was presented to the Lord in the Temple and recognized by Simeon and Anna (2:22–38). He was found by his parents as he did his Father's bidding (2:49). He drove out the money changers and taught the Good News (19:45—20:1). After his Ascension, the disciples returned to the Temple to give praise (24:52–53). The destruction of the Temple will not matter, it is Jesus' words to his disciples that will. Their rootedness in Christ and their willingness to give testimony will be all that is necessary.

The disciples who followed Jesus would face many challenges as they stayed faithful to his teaching and instructions. However, they are deeply rooted in Jesus and therefore grounded in their inheritance as people of God's covenant. No matter the trials or tribulations that confronted them, no matter the persecutions or sufferings "by your perseverance you will secure your lives" (Luke 21:19).

2 SAMUEL 5:1–3 As we celebrate this last Sunday of the liturgical year, we focus on Jesus Christ as the King of the Universe, the Risen Lord who has conquered death and now lives in eternal union with the Father and Spirit. Christ's kingship as deliverer and shepherd of the whole universe is prefigured in the person of David, king of Israel's united kingdom and that of the holy city, Jerusalem. David's anointing by all the other tribes as king of Israel is actually David's third anointing. Samuel performed the first one while David was still a youth, setting God's approval on David as future king (1 Samuel 16:13). David's second anointing designates him king of Judah (2 Samuel 2:4). Here, all the tribes acknowledge their intimate kinship with David, "here we are, your bone and your flesh" (5:1); they are pleased with David's previous leadership under Saul. David's role as leader and shepherd of the people is God's doing, and the tribes fully approve and promise loyalty and fidelity. As king, David promises to care for God's people, exercising justice and right relationship, thus becoming the visible representative of God as shepherd of the people. Hence, David prefigures Christ's future kingdom and rule over all creation.

PSALM 122:1–2, 3–4, 4–5 (SEE 1) This pilgrimage psalm expresses the great joy of those who cherished the opportunity to go to the Temple, "the house of the Lord" (122:1) situated at the very pinnacle of Jerusalem, the holy city established by King David. Jerusalem, the focal worship center of all the tribes, was admired for its Temple, its beauty, and its adherence to the covenant promises and Torah regulations. Both king and city were understood to be the living embodiment of the Lord's intimate dwelling and covenant relationship with all the people. Thanksgiving to God for such marvels as the Temple and the city was the only fitting response any pilgrim could give. Thus Jerusalem, the Temple, and the unity therein expressed became a symbol for intimate covenant relationship with God for all time.

COLOSSIANS 1:12–20 The author of the Letter to the Colossians inserts a preexisting liturgical hymn at the beginning of the letter to exalt Christ's role as king over all

CONNECTIONS TO CHURCH TEACHING AND TRADITION

- "That messianic people has as its head Christ. . . . Its law is the new commandment to love as Christ loved us. . . . Its destiny is the kingdom of God . . . brought to perfection by him at the end of time when Christ our life . . . will appear and 'creation itself also will be delivered from its slavery to corruption into the freedom of the glory of the sons and daughters of God'" (LG, 9).

- "The goal of salvation, the Kingdom of God embraces all people and is fully realized beyond history, in God. The Church has received 'the mission of proclaiming and establishing among all peoples the Kingdom of Christ and of God, and she is, on earth, the seed and the beginning of that Kingdom'" (CSDC, 49).

- "Let us believe the Gospel . . . that the kingdom of God is already present in this world and is growing, here and there, and in different ways" (EG, 278).

creation. The author introduces the hymn by inviting disciples to offer praise and thanksgiving to God for the privilege "to share in the inheritance of the holy ones" (1:12). Through Christ's passion, death, and Resurrection, God has gifted us with redemption, the forgiveness of sin, and "delivered us from the power of darkness and transferred us to the kingdom of his beloved Son" (1:13). Jesus is praised and exalted above all creation—the "firstborn of all creation" (1:15) in whom all things were created. In Christ, "all things hold together" (1:17). He is "the head of the body, the church . . . in him all the fullness was pleased to dwell" (1:18). Through the blood of his cross, Christ reconciled all things, "making peace . . . whether those on earth or those in heaven" (1:20). Such high Christology exalting Christ as the reconciling king of the universe is a fitting hymn for this last Sunday of the liturgical year.

LUKE 23:35–43 Death by crucifixion is far removed from the human concept of kingship. Kings usually exercise power over others. Luke narrates this scene with irony and paradox, asserting that the world's ways are not God's ways. Jesus is the chosen one of God, the Christ (Messiah), the true king of the Jews in the line of David, who has come to establish God's kingdom, and through his self-gift on the cross is accomplishing his mission. However, the rulers, the soldiers, and one of the criminals crucified with him cannot understand the cosmic events happening before their eyes. Paradoxically, everything they are saying in mockery about him is true, which they fail to see. One of the crucified criminals does see. Luke uses him to assert Jesus' innocence and undeserved punishment. This crucified criminal also acknowledges Jesus' kingly status, humbly asking to be remembered by Jesus when "you come into your kingdom" (23:42). Jesus, eagerly welcoming the repentant sinner, "today" (23:43) welcomes this lost son into paradise with him. Luke's main Gospel themes manifest themselves. Jesus, the universal savior of all, shows special care and concern for the rejected and for all repentant sinners. As Davidic king, Jesus came to establish God's kingdom and to call all to repentance and mutual loving service. In so doing, we too can anticipate Jesus assurance that "today you will be with me in Paradise" (23:43).

Holydays, Solemnities, and Feasts

Throughout the liturgical year, the Church celebrates the mysteries, events in the life of Our Lord and his Blessed Mother, events in the life of the Church, saints, angels, and all the faithful departed with solemnities, feasts, commemorations, and memorials—optional or not. A few of these days are kept as holydays of obligation, to be celebrated by all in the territories where they have been so designated. Most of these days are celebrated on their appointed dates unless they fall on a Sunday or within the Sacred Triduum or the Octave of Easter. Two, the solemnities of the Most Holy Trinity and the Most Holy Body and Blood of Christ, are permanently affixed to the first two Sundays in Ordinary Time after Pentecost. A few others are deemed of such importance to the life and memory of the Church that when they fall on Sundays in Ordinary Time they supersede the Sunday.

This chapter offers Scripture backgrounds for the holydays of obligation for the United States and for those feasts and solemnities that occasionally are celebrated on Sundays in Ordinary Time.

MALACHI 3:1–4 The Book of Malachi is the last prophetic book. It was written by an anonymous prophet after the Babylonian exile and the rebuilding of the Temple (515 BC). The name Malachi means "my messenger" in Hebrew. After the rebuilding of the Temple, the practices of the priest and the community did not live up to the high standards of the covenant. In Malachi, the prophet denounces the priests and the worship as corrupt. He reproaches the people for having "wearied the Lord" (2: 17). God's response to this unfaithfulness is a day of the Lord unlike any imagined. The people thought that the day of the Lord would be a day of victory and rejoicing. The prophet assures them that this day will be a day of judgment. God will enter the Temple, just as they asked, but they may be unable to withstand the encounter. God will clean them with "lye" and refine them with "fire," reducing them to a pure and faithful community. These new people will then be able to offer sacrifices worthily, as they did in earlier days (v. 4).

PSALM 24:7, 8, 9, 10 (8) The psalm welcomes the coming of God into the city. The gates of the city (or Temple) are too low, they are to "lift up" (v. 9) so that God can enter. This psalm was sung during a procession, perhaps carrying the Ark of the Covenant through the city and back to the Temple. Unlike the mood of Malachi, here the presence of God brings rejoicing.

HEBREWS 2:14–18 The community that the Letter to the Hebrews addressed considered the daily and yearly sacrifices of the Temple to be the way to insure permanent reconciliation with God. In this letter, Christ is portrayed as the great High Priest who makes a permanent and lasting offering of himself through the cross. His obedience unto death is the source of his perfection (5:7–10). In this letter, perfection means permanence and finality. Christ's death reconciles all of humanity to God once and for all, never to be repeated.

Obedience is an important theme in this letter; it implies choice and the ability to sin. Obedience is part of the human condition. In other words, Christ's death is not the death of a solely spiritual being who passes through the experience unscathed, but the real death of a real person who had to

CONNECTIONS TO CHURCH TEACHING AND TRADITION

- The Feast of the Presentation of the Lord celebrates and commemorates the fulfillment of Israel's expectation (CCC, 529). Jesus is revealed as the Messiah, the anointed one for whom Israel waits (CCC, 439).

- The feast illustrates the importance of the Temple in Jesus' early life and formative years (CCC, 583) and points toward God's sacrifice of the Son, and the Son's self-sacrifice (CCC, 614).

- The Presentation reveals to believers Jesus' identity as fully divine and fully human (CCC, 464–469, 480–482, 724).

struggle to remain faithful to God. Christ's obedience, his humanity, defeats death (sin) and restores creation to its original intent. Christ has forged ahead of us; he has made a path through the wilderness of temptation. We "descendants of Abraham" (v. 16) through faith can follow, knowing that he understands the trials and difficulties we face.

LUKE 2:22–40 Two representatives of the faithful Jews, Simeon and Anna, meet with Jesus and his parents. Simeon awaits the comfort of Israel (Isaiah 40:1), the day of salvation. He is described as "pious" and directed by the Holy Spirit (2:26). Three times Luke mentions the Spirit in connection with Simeon (vv. 25–27). Luke sees in the faithful and devout Jews the same Spirit present within the Christian community. Simeon's prayer reveals Jesus' identity. The comfort of Israel arrives in Jesus (v. 30).

The message is given for "all people" (Luke 2:30–31, Isaiah 52:7–10) and goes out to two groups, the Gentiles and the Israelites (v. 33). Christ is in continuity with his Jewish faith and yet extends God's salvation to the whole world as promised by the prophets (Isaiah 42:6). Simeon's song is followed by his prophecy to Mary that Jesus will aid some people and will cause others to fall. Just as the sword divides (Ezekiel 14:17) between the faithful and unfaithful, Mary will have her own heart tested. Later in the Gospel, Jesus describes his mission as dividing family members from one another (12:51–53). The words of Simeon to Mary connect well with the first reading. God's coming will be a day of joy and of judgment. Luke parallels the story of Simeon with Anna. She is also described as pious and faithful, and as a widow, one of the least important members of the community. Widows may have a special place in the Lukan community, and Anna is a model. She recognizes in Jesus the salvation of Israel. The passage concludes with the return to Nazareth, where Jesus grows in wisdom and understanding (vv. 39–40).

PROVERBS 8:22–31 Today's solemnity is doctrinal, and the doctrine is clear. We believe in one God in three divine persons: Father, Son, and Holy Spirit. After the writing of the New Testament, it took centuries for the Church to express clearly this belief in our Triune God. What we find in the Scripture readings today are the seeds of this doctrine, and each passage emphasizes a particular aspect of God's glory.

The passage from Proverbs has been chosen for today's solemnity because of the figure of Wisdom. God is wise and has knowledge of all that is. Yet what sets this passage from Proverbs apart is that God's wisdom is not presented as an attribute of God, but as a distinct character. The Old Testament texts are unanimous in the belief that God alone creates. Wisdom is present to God before the creation of the world and continues in a relationship with all God has made. Wisdom, then, is a mediating character through whom God interacts with creation. This mediation anticipates the role of Jesus who, like Wisdom, is said to have stood with God at creation (see John 1:3; Colossians 1:16).

But as Wisdom stands distinct from God, she reflects who God is. In this passage, she reflects God's love for the world. Her delight in humanity testifies to God's delight in humanity. Wisdom reveals that God is not only creator, but a creator who glories in the beauty of what has been made. The world God has made is good. It gives God joy.

PSALM 8:4–5, 6–7, 8–9 (2A) Psalm 8 also rejoices in creation. It begins with admiration for all that God has made. The heavens are the work of God's fingers. The moon and the stars are what God has set in place. Then, the psalm takes a dramatic turn. It focuses on humans and sees them not simply as objects of creation but as agents of God. Men and women are given authority over creation. They reflect God's glory. In a way similar to the mediation of Wisdom, they extend God's presence to the beasts of the field, the birds of the air, and the fishes of the sea. God not only delights in creation but invites us to delight as well.

ROMANS 5:1–5 Although Paul did not conceive of God with the specificity provided by the doctrine of the Trinity, he often mentions God, Christ, and the Spirit together. This

CONNECTIONS TO CHURCH TEACHING AND TRADITION

- "Christ has risen again, destroying death by his death, and has given life abundantly to us so that, becoming sons and daughters in the Son, we may cry out in the Spirit: Abba, Father!" (GS, 22).

- "The new evangelization calls for personal involvement on the part of each of the baptized. Every Christian is challenged, here and now, to be actively engaged in evangelization; indeed, anyone who has truly experienced God's saving love does not need much time or lengthy training to go out and proclaim that love. Every Christian is a missionary to the extent that he or she has encountered the love of God in Christ Jesus" (EG, 120).

passage from Romans illustrates how Paul relates these divine characters to each other. God is always the source of salvation for Paul. It is peace with God that is our goal, but that peace is attained through our Lord Jesus Christ. Christ is God's agent, the one through whom salvation comes. The sign of that salvation is the Holy Spirit, who has been poured into our hearts. God is always working through Christ and in the Spirit. There is then a unity of action, grounded in the one God.

Here, Paul also recognizes the power of God's action in times of affliction. Even when we must face difficulties and loss, God is at work through Christ and in the Spirit to sustain us. God's action gives us hope, a hope that will not disappoint.

JOHN 16:12–15 No Gospel account speaks of the connection between Jesus and the Father in stronger terms than John. Today's passage from the farewell discourse presents a stunning example of that closeness. The topic of the passage is truth, but the dynamic of the discussion is the relationship among the Father, Jesus, and the Holy Spirit. Jesus assures the disciples that he possesses all that the Father has and that it is the role of the Spirit to reveal the truth to them. The resulting picture is one of profound intimacy between Jesus, his Father, and the Spirit.

It is an intimacy in which we are called to participate. The truth that Jesus possesses from the Father and that the Spirit communicates is directed toward us. We are caught up in the give and take between these divine persons. We are surrounded by the source, expression, and empowerment of truth. It is God all around.

The God who surrounds us also calls us to act. We who are invited into the divine life are meant to proclaim the one who animates us. Like Wisdom, we are to tell others of our God who delights in the goodness of the world. Following Paul, we are to be the compassion of God to those who are afflicted, giving them a reason for hope. The psalmist assures us that we are God's agents in creation. As such it is not enough to be surrounded by God's love. We must also be committed to reveal God's glory.

The Bread of Justice

GENESIS 14:18–20 The Solemnity of the Most Holy Body and Blood of Christ (Corpus Christi) celebrates the Catholic belief that the bread and wine of the Eucharist are transformed into the real presence of Christ—Body, Blood, soul, and divinity. Our Scripture readings today can be effectively used to enrich the context and meaning of the Eucharist. Melchizedek is a strange figure in the Old Testament, appearing only twice. In this passage from Genesis, he appears suddenly to acknowledge Abraham's victory in battle, preparing a meal for him and blessing him in the name of God Most High. The passage was certainly selected for today's solemnity because Melchizedek's meal was one of bread and wine, but it is actually the titles of this unusual character that provide the most helpful context for the Eucharist. The name Melchizedek literally means "king of righteousness or justice." His position as "king of Salem" (14:18) means "king of peace." Here then is a figure who prepares a meal and by his person associates that meal with justice and peace. The very elusiveness of Melchizedek's identity opens his person to wide interpretation. That interpretation is further developed in today's psalm.

PSALM 110:1, 2, 3, 4 (4B) Psalm 110 contains the other reference to Melchizedek in the Old Testament. The psalm served as the text for the installation of the Jewish king. By proclaiming the king as one who reigns according to the order of Melchizedek, the psalmist asserts that the king is to be a ruler of justice and peace. That peace would be attained by the defeat of Israel's enemies. Their evil intentions would be undone, and they would become the king's footstool. Even by the time this hymn entered the psalter, the Jewish monarchy was no more. Yet Jews continued to pray this psalm, extending it to an eschatological future. The psalm became a vision of a messianic king who would bring justice and peace as part of God's coming kingdom. Early Christians applied this psalm extensively to Christ. It is the most used psalm in the New Testament. Jesus is now understood as God's Messiah who has inaugurated the kingdom through his death and Resurrection. When Paul describes God's plan of salvation, he says that Christ must reign until he has put all his enemies under his feet

CONNECTIONS TO CHURCH TEACHING AND TRADITION

- "Christ left to his followers a pledge of this hope and food for the journey in the sacrament of faith, in which natural elements, the fruits of human cultivation, are changed into his glorified Body and Blood, as a supper of brotherly and sisterly communion and a foretaste of the heavenly banquet" (GS, 38).

- "Reading the Scriptures also makes it clear that the Gospel is not merely about our personal relationship with God. Nor should our loving response to God be seen simply as an accumulation of small personal gestures to individuals in need, a kind of 'charity à la carte,' or a series of acts aimed solely at easing our conscience. The Gospel is about the kingdom of God" (EG, 180).

- "A Eucharist which does not pass over into the concrete practice of love is intrinsically fragmented" (DCE, 14).

(1 Corinthians 15:25). Paul had this psalm in mind. The enemies to be defeated are every evil opposed to God's will.

1 CORINTHIANS 11:23–26 This passage from 1 Corinthians is the earliest account of Jesus' action with bread and wine at the Last Supper. Paul's comment at the end of the passage helps develop our Eucharistic theme. Paul explains to the Corinthians that the purpose of the Eucharist is intimately connected to God's coming kingdom. Eating of the bread and drinking from the cup allows us to proclaim today the death of the Lord until he comes. In a fundamental way, therefore, the Eucharist is to be a sign of the coming kingdom, an action that points to God's reign of justice and peace.

SEQUENCE: LAUDA, SION St. Thomas Aquinas wrote this dogmatic poem, which is optional for today's liturgy, around 1264. Drawing upon scriptural images of Passover, it lays forth the scholastic understanding of the Eucharist—Christ's flesh and blood under the signs of bread and wine.

LUKE 9:11B–17 The key to understanding the miracle of the multiplication of the loaves and fishes is to see it as a response to real human hunger. The hunger is not that of an individual but that of a huge crowd. It is the hunger of the world, representing all the forces and structures of evil that militate against God's will and undercut justice and peace. Christ feeds the crowd as a sign of the coming banquet that will be shared when God's kingdom is established. This will occur when Christ returns in glory and, as Paul tells us, puts all of God's enemies under his feet. This miracle is a sign, like the Eucharist, of the final victory of God in Christ. Both point to the reign of God when every evil will be destroyed, when hunger, injustice, and violence will be no more. Each time, then, as we share in the Eucharist, we can validly rejoice in the real presence of Christ whom we receive. However, we should also see in the bread and wine that we share the promise of God to bring about a kingdom of justice and peace and our call to hasten its coming.

JEREMIAH 1:4–10 Jeremiah was destined to prophesy in Judah during one of the darkest periods in ancient Israel's history: the Babylonian crisis. Nearly one hundred years earlier, in 721 BC, the northern kingdom of Israel was captured by the Assyrian Empire. A century later, what remained of the once-powerful united monarchy was now facing annihilation by the growing military, economic, and political forces in Babylon. Jeremiah's challenge was to shepherd the people of Israel through this new reality with only the Lord's assurance: "Do not be afraid . . . for I am with you to deliver you."

Today's reading covers the first part of the call of Jeremiah, 1:4–10 (see 1:4–19 for the full call). The call itself is actually a dialogue between Jeremiah and the Lord. In this brief exchange, we learn two important lessons about Jeremiah. First, he was destined from the womb to be "a Prophet to the nations." Whether from humility or fear, Jeremiah had a sense of the gravity of the call at his young age: "Truly I do not know how to speak, for I am only a boy." Second, Jeremiah was empowered to speak with divine authority: "Now I [the Lord] have put my words in your mouth." In his call, Jeremiah learned he would both "destroy" and "build" nations and kingdoms.

PSALM 71:1–2, 3–4A, 5–6AB, 15AB, 17 (6) Psalm 71 seems appropriate to commemorate John the Baptist's mission and dedication to the Messiah who was to come after him. This psalm of lament is full of strong images for God: stronghold, refuge, rock, and fortress. From the very beginning in the womb, the psalmist is confident that God is worthy of this trust and hope; God is a shelter worthy of this dependence. It seems an appropriate psalm to link with this feast of John the Baptist, who also experienced God in his mother Elizabeth's womb when she was greeted by Mary carrying the Son of God. John has been blessed before birth to carry the message entrusted by God. He can be certain that God will give him strength for the journey.

1 PETER 1:8–12 The author of 1 Peter provides some interesting catechesis for his Gentile recipients. He connects their faith in Christ to Israel's storied past as well as the Christian present. For the author of 1 Peter, both the

CONNECTIONS TO CHURCH TEACHING AND TRADITION

- "Jesus came to set this fire upon the earth, until all is ablaze in the love of God. We pray this fire will come upon us as disciples as we, led by the Spirit, carry out Christ's great commission to go and make disciples of all the nations" (GMD, 69).

- "Of her very nature, the Church is missionary. This means her members are called by God to bring the Gospel by word and deed to all peoples and to every situation of work, education, culture, and communal life in which human beings find themselves" (USCCA, 501).

- "In [John the Baptist], the Holy Spirit concludes his speaking through the prophets. John completes the cycle of prophets begun by Elijah[1]" (CCC, 719).

---

1. Cf. Matthew 11:13–14.

prophets and the Apostles saw the Gentiles as part of their target audience for evangelization.

Herein lies an important connection to John the Baptist. One traditional view of John the Baptist is that he was the final Old Testament prophet announcing God's salvation to the world. He serves as the transitional figure between the Old and New Testament. Descriptions of him as going forth "with the spirit and power of Elijah" (as heard in the Gospel reading) certainly reinforced this image.

LUKE 1:5–17 Many of the details about John the Baptist are presented in Luke's infancy narrative, where he offers parallel stories about the annunciations and births of John and Jesus.

Before Gabriel's announcement, Luke spends a significant amount of time describing the parents of John the Baptist, Zechariah and Elizabeth. He wants to leave no doubt as to their Jewish origins: Zechariah was of "the priestly order of Abijah" and Elizabeth "was a descendant of Aaron." Because many likely viewed the childless state of the couple as somehow reflective of their sin or the sins of the ancestors, Luke offers the highest praise of Zechariah and Elizabeth: "Both of them were righteous before God, living blamelessly according to all the commandments and regulations of the Lord."

This characterization of John's parents is confirmed by the first words spoken by Gabriel: "Do not be afraid, Zechariah, for your prayer has been heard." It was widely attested in Jewish history and tradition that God only hears the prayers of the righteous. Zechariah prayed for a son, and Elizabeth was found to be with child. Gabriel then goes on to describe the son of Zechariah and Elizabeth. John "will be great in the sight of the Lord" and "be filled with the Holy Spirit" even before he is born. John will impact people in profound ways: "He will turn many of the people of Israel to the Lord their God," and he will "turn the hearts of parents to their children and the disobedient to the wisdom of the righteous."

Most significantly, John the Baptist is destined to fulfill his greatest role: "to make ready a people prepared for the Lord."

ISAIAH 49:1–6 The Book of Isaiah contains four "Servant of the Lord" oracles: Isaiah 42:1–4, 49:1–7, 50:4–11, and 52:13—53:12. Each of these servant songs is taken from Isaiah 40–55, the middle section of the Book of Isaiah, which mostly preserves the words from the unknown prophet ("Second Isaiah"), active toward the end of Israel's captivity in Babylon, around 550 BC. Today's reading is the second of the four oracles, and it is autobiographical.

In this oracle, Isaiah reveals to fellow captives in Babylon his own spiritual journey as a prophet. First, Isaiah came to realize he was destined to be a prophet since before his birth: "The Lord called me before I was born, while I was in my mother's womb he named me." Second, Isaiah learned over time both about his gifts and his dependency on God: "He made my mouth like a sharp sword, in the shadow of his hand he hid me; he made me a polished arrow, in his quiver he hid me away." Third, and perhaps most importantly, Isaiah accepted the call to be the Lord's "servant." In serving the Lord, Isaiah would show all people God's "glory."

As the Lord's servant, Isaiah would make known to the world God's plan to save not only his chosen people, the divided house of Israel and Jacob. He would also reveal God's plan to save all nations: "I will give you as a light to the nations that my salvation may reach to the end of the earth."

PSALM 139:1B–3, 13–14AB, 14C–15 (14) The psalm for today's celebration of the birth of John the Baptist speaks of God's intimate knowledge of us from the time we were formed in our mothers' wombs. The psalmist says that God so lovingly and tenderly probes, knows, and understands us that it is as if our very being was formed by God, knit together and wonderfully made. The final verses of the psalm, which we do not hear on this feast, speak of how fiercely we must be willing to do what God requires. "Do I not hate, Lord, those who hate you? / Those who rise against you, do I not loathe? / With fierce hatred I hate them, / enemies I count as my own" (Psalm 139:21–22). Our response to being so lovingly made is to defend our God with all the power we have within us. John the Baptist did just that with his preaching, witness, and eventual death at the hands of the enemies of God's Word and God's Son.

CONNECTIONS TO CHURCH TEACHING AND TRADITION

- John the Baptist prefigured what the Holy Spirit will achieve in and with Christ (CCC, 720).

- John bore witness to Christ in his preaching, his baptism of repentance, and his martyrdom (CCC, glossary).

- God knows and calls us even before the beginning of our being (CCC, 381). All life is sacred to God (CCC, 2258).

- Over the centuries Christian people organized the days, weeks, months, and seasons into a liturgical year or calendar (CCC, 1168–1171).

ACTS 13:22–26 This brief excerpt from Acts is taken from part of Paul's speech delivered in the synagogue at Antioch in Pisidia. Paul is attempting to convince fellow Jews and "others who fear God" (Gentiles) that in Jesus, God fulfills the covenant he established with David, Israel's greatest king.

Paul saw the baptism of repentance offered by John the Baptist—the forerunner to Christ—pivotal in fulfilling this covenantal promise. Paul's bold assertion here should not be taken lightly. God established his covenant with David while he ruled over the united monarchy from 1000 to 961 BC (see 2 Samuel 7:8–16 for the terms of the covenant). The people of Israel had been waiting for over a millennium to see the Davidic covenant come to fruition. Paul's position that God's "word of salvation has been sent" beginning with the preaching and baptism of John the Baptist likely raised both curiosity and concerns by the synagogue members that day.

LUKE 1:57–66, 80 While the Gospel reading for the vigil of this solemnity presented Gabriel's annunciation to Zechariah of the birth of John the Baptist, the Gospel reading for the day narrates the actual birth of John and the Jewish rites of his circumcision and naming.

Neighbors and relatives reacted in joy to the long-awaited birth of a son for Elizabeth and Zechariah. Fear came upon neighbors as they witnessed the miracle of Zechariah recovering his speech. As news of these events spread "throughout the entire hill country of Judea," many wondered of the newborn son: "What then will this child become?"

Outside the one-liner, "the child grew and became strong in spirit, and he was in the wilderness until the day he appeared publicly to Israel," Luke provides no further details about John the Baptist during his infancy, childhood, and formative years as a young man.

ACTS 3:1–10 After the descent of the Holy Spirit onto the Apostles (Acts 2:1–4), Peter delivers a speech on Pentecost in Jerusalem, officially launching their witness in Jerusalem. Shortly after this speech, Peter performs the miracle of healing the crippled beggar, today's reading.

First in speech, now in deed, Luke presents Peter in the Acts of the Apostles as a Spirit-filled man, leading the other Apostles in bearing witness to the power of the crucified and resurrected Messiah. Just as Jesus healed a paralytic man in the Gospel of Luke (5:17–26), so now Peter is associated with healing a crippled man from birth. In these otherwise parallel miracle stories, a subtle but significant detail is different. Whereas Jesus healed the paralytic man with his own power, Peter healed the crippled man in Jesus' name: "in the name of Jesus Christ of Nazareth, stand up and walk."

Furthermore, the man whom Peter healed neither asked nor anticipated in being healed when he was placed at the gate of the Temple by others. He came "so that he could ask for alms" from the people. It was not this man's faith in Christ that set him free; rather, it was Peter's compassion for the man and Peter's faith in Christ that cured the crippled man. In the early weeks and months of the Apostles' evangelization of Jerusalem, which included persuasive speeches and mighty deeds, many were "praising God" and coming to faith in Christ through the witness of Peter and the other Apostles.

PSALM 19:2–3, 4–5 (5) This short response is aimed at helping us appreciate the work of the disciples, whose message has gone through all the earth and across the ages. It also reminds us that, for those who do not hear the preaching of the Gospel, nature itself, the heavens, the earth, and day and night, reveal their Creator.

GALATIANS 1:11–20 Galatians 1:11–24, most of which is heard in this reading, presents us with six facts about Paul's life. Paul offers these details about his life as a means of demonstrating to the believers of Galatia his authority as an Apostle of Christ.

The first, and arguably most important detail from Paul's perspective, is that his "Gospel" (his preaching about

CONNECTIONS TO CHURCH TEACHING AND TRADITION

- "In reality it was Christ's own love, free and unsolicited, which gave rise to his question to Peter and to his act of entrusting 'his' sheep to Peter. Therefore, every ministerial action— while it leads to loving and serving the Church —provides an incentive to grow in ever greater love and service of Jesus Christ the head" (PDV, 25).

- "In our times, the Church . . . has come to a more lively awareness of her missionary nature. . . . Our pastoral service . . . requires proclaiming Jesus Christ and the Good News . . . denouncing sinful situations, structures of death . . . and fostering intercultural, interreligious and ecumenical dialogue" (*Aparecida*, 95).

- "You go too. The call is a concern not only of pastors, clergy, and men and women religious. The call is addressed to everyone: lay people as well are personally called by the Lord, from whom they receive a mission on behalf of the Church and the world" (CL, 2).

Jesus) comes "through a revelation of Jesus Christ." In other words, Paul asserts his preaching is of divine origin. Second, before his conversion, Paul was initially "violently persecuting the Church of God and was trying to destroy it." Paul clearly began as an enemy to believers in Christ. Next, he "advanced in Judaism beyond many among my people of the same age." Evidently, others saw Paul as a bright and accomplished young man. Fourth, Paul stopped persecuting the Church after he had an encounter with the risen Jesus: God "was pleased to reveal his Son to me." He interpreted this revelation as a call to "proclaim him among the Gentiles." Fifth, it took Paul three years to begin making sense of this call and develop some sense of next steps. Finally, before he began his mission to the Gentiles, Paul visited with Peter (Cephas) in Jerusalem for fifteen days. Unfortunately, Paul offers no insight as to what he and Peter discussed.

JOHN 21:15–19 Scholars have long suspected that John 21 was a later addition to the original ending of the Gospel, John 20. It appears that the Johannine community desired some clarification on the role of Peter and the beloved disciple in the life of the Church.

In today's reading, we hear Jesus' commission of Peter to lead his disciples.

Not surprisingly, John sets the stage for this dialogue between Jesus and Peter in the context of a meal. The Gospel narratives consistently present Jesus in table fellowship with others, conversing about matters ranging from the kingdom of God to the meaning of true discipleship.

The exchange between the risen Jesus and Peter leaves no doubt that Jesus is commissioning Peter to lead the community of believers once he has ascended into heaven. Words such as *feed, tend, sheep,* and *lambs* make it clear that Jesus is entrusting Peter with this new leadership role. Perhaps unsettling to Peter was Jesus' foreshadowing of his martyrdom: "Someone else will fasten a belt around you and take you where you do not wish to go." It is within this context of Peter's martyrdom that Jesus commands Peter, "Follow me." For just as Jesus' death glorified God, so, too, will Peter's death.

ACTS 12:1–11 Peter's miraculous escape from prison fits part of the larger subplot of the Acts of the Apostles: the persecution of believers. Luke presents numerous instances of the persecution of Jesus' followers by Jewish leaders.

Luke consistently tells us that despite the persecution, the early Church was not destroyed. Quite to the contrary, "the word of God continued to advance and gain adherents" (12:24).

Luke, informing us that James' death "pleased some of the people" offers us a hint into the widespread anger and distrust that the first generation of believers encountered. Peter's harsh treatment in prison ("bound with two chains" and positioned between two soldiers) reinforces the degree to which Agrippa desired to kill Peter.

Whether in his Spirit-filled speeches, his works of powerful deeds, or now in his miraculous escape from prison, Peter was clearly guided and protected by the presence of the Holy Spirit. This, too, is one of the subplots of Acts of the Apostles: the early Church was grounded and driven by the Spirit.

PSALM 34:2–3, 4–5, 6–7, 8–9 (5) This psalm is an alphabetic psalm, with each line beginning with a successive letter of the alphabet, and it is attributed to David. It addresses the just and encourages them to join the psalmist in praising the God who rescues them. Echoing the Acts reading, the psalmist acknowledges the "angel of the Lord [who] encamps around those who fear him, and delivers them" (v. 7). The psalmist calls upon the hearer to "taste and see," that is, experience the goodness of the Lord.

2 TIMOTHY 4:6–8, 17–18 Today's reading contains two basic parts. First, Paul is reflecting on his ministry at the end of his life, and second, Paul is offering advice on the proper disposition needed to face the ongoing struggles. The first half of the reading presents Paul's departing words to his trusted coworker, Timothy: "The time of my departure has come. I have fought the good fight, I have finished the race, I have kept the faith." This offered to the recipients of this letter a model testament from one who had reliably born witness to the faith. The second half of today's reading gives some guiding principles for perseverance in the faith:

CONNECTIONS TO CHURCH TEACHING AND TRADITION

- "A first essential setting for learning hope is prayer. When no one listens to me anymore, God still listens to me. When I can no longer talk to anyone . . . I can always talk to God. When there is no longer anyone to help me . . . he can help me" (SS, 32).

- "During thirteen years in jail, in a situation of seemingly utter hopelessness, the fact that [Cardinal Nguyen Van Thuan] could listen and speak to God became for him an increasing power of hope, which enabled him, after his release, to become for people all over the world a witness to hope—to that great hope which does not wane even in the nights of solitude" (SS, 32).

draw your strength from the Lord in being committed to your call, be assured that the Lord will rescue you in times of distress, and always give glory to God for the good work accomplished.

MATTHEW 16:13–19 Peter's profession of faith in Jesus ("You are the Messiah, the Son of the living God") is one of the high points in the Gospel narrative.

Jesus begins his inquiries about his identity by asking the disciples about the crowds following them: "Who do people say the Son of Man is?" In the disciples' response, it becomes clear that the crowds are not wrong about Jesus. Perceiving Jesus as a prophet of Israel would certainly be a logical conclusion. As significant as the prophets were to Israel's relationship with God, the crowd's insight reflects only a surface understanding of Jesus' true identity.

When Jesus probes a little further and asks his disciples, "But who do you say I am?" it is Peter who speaks for the others. Note the "you" in Jesus' question is second-person plural, literally "you all." Peter's decision to speak for the other disciples points to his leadership already established among the disciples. While Peter correctly answers the question of Jesus' identity—Jesus is the Christ and the Son of God—Jesus reacts to Peter with an important nuance. Jesus sees that Peter did not come to this insight on his own, it was "revealed" to him by "my Father in heaven." This divine revelation to Peter was significant for Jesus. It communicated to Jesus not only that Peter was "blessed" in a special way; it also revealed who the Father had chosen to lead the Church that Jesus was establishing: "I tell you that you are Peter, and on this rock I will build my church."

While Peter and the other disciples could now move forward knowing with certainty Jesus' identity as the Messiah and Son of God, they would soon discover that Jesus was destined to be the suffering Messiah. With the three predictions of the passion to be announced by Jesus as they begin their final descent to Jerusalem, Peter and the disciples will begin to see more deeply into Jesus' divine identity. Peter will follow the Son of God who suffers to save the world, and Peter will lead the Church that likewise suffers in its witness to the Good News of Jesus, the Messiah and Son of the living God.

- Therefore all the disciples of Christ, persevering in prayer and praising God,[1] should present themselves as a living sacrifice. . . . Everywhere on earth they must bear witness to Christ and give an answer to those who seek an account of that hope of eternal life which is in them"[2] (LG, 10).

- Moved by the grace of the Holy Spirit and drawn by the Father, we believe in Jesus and confess: "You are the Christ, the Son of the living God."[3] On the rock of this faith confessed by St. Peter, Christ built his Church[4] (CCC, 424).

---

1. Cf. Acts 2:42–47.
2. Cf. 1 Peter 3:15.
3. Matthew 16:16.
4. Cf. Matthew 16:18; St. Leo the Great, *Sermo* 4, 3: PL, 54, 150–152; 51, 1: PL, 54, 309B; 62, 2: PL, 54, 350–351; 83, 3: PL, 54, 431–432.

Dominion, Glory, and Kingship

DANIEL 7:9–10, 13–14 The Book of Daniel is named for the hero of the stories in its first six chapters. Daniel, who has a special gift of wisdom, has been chosen along with three other young Jewish exiles in Babylon to be educated and to serve in the court of the Babylonian king. There they face many trials, such as the famous fiery furnace and the lion's den. In each case, their steadfast faith in the Hebrew God wins the day. Beginning in chapter 7, from which today's reading comes, the book presents a series of Daniel's visions. These visions belong to the "apocalyptic" genre—a type of vivid, dramatic narrative written during times of persecution. Daniel's visions were composed in the second century BC, when Jews were being forced to adopt Greek culture and religious practices. They were intended to comfort the persecuted Jews, strengthen them in their faith, and assure them that justice will triumph in the end.

In this powerful vision, an enthroned figure, the Ancient One, with dazzling white clothing and hair, is worshipped by "thousands upon thousands." Verses omitted from today's reading describe this as a court of judgment in which terrible beasts who have exercised power over the world are condemned and removed from power. Today's reading picks up when a new figure enters the scene: "one like a Son of man," who arrives coming "on the clouds of heaven." He is presented to the enthroned figure and given "dominion, glory, and kingship." Through this vision, Jews drew strength from the Lord and the Messiah dispatching the evil forces. In later centuries, Christians were also comforted by this scene of heavenly justice, but they saw a prophecy of God the Father entrusting the world to the care of his Son, Jesus Christ. That interpretation makes this reading a particularly appropriate choice for the Feast of the Transfiguration of the Lord.

PSALM 97:1–2, 5–6, 9 (1A, 9A) Psalm 97 celebrates the reign of God over Israel. The people experience God as a mysterious force, like "clouds and thick darkness" (v. 2). God's reign is founded on justice (v. 2), and God's power is overwhelming. The highest points on earth dissolve in the presence of the mighty one (v. 5). The psalm proclaims that no god is greater than the God of Israel (v. 9).

CONNECTIONS TO CHURCH TEACHING AND TRADITION

- In the transfiguration Jesus' real nature is revealed to his followers and to us (CCC, 464–469, 480–482).

- Face-to-face with the mystery of Christ's dual nature, the apostles respond in wonder (CCC, 554–556, 568).

- The transfiguration is a preview of God's glory, visible only with the eyes of faith (CCC, 2809).

2 PETER 1:16–19 Today all three readings point to Christ as the one empowered and sent to us by the Father. This passage from the Second Letter of Peter takes up this theme with the same purpose as the author of the Book of Daniel: to encourage his audience to hold fast to their faith, in this case, faith in Jesus Christ. The author first reminds us of the Father's voice from heaven at Jesus' baptism: "This is my Son, my beloved, with whom I am well pleased." Then, as an eyewitness to the events reported in today's Gospel ("We ourselves heard . . ."), he refers to the voice of God again commending Jesus Christ to us. What stronger confirmation of the "prophetic message" about Christ's identity could we desire? He urges us to "be attentive" to it as if it were "a lamp shining in a dark place."

LUKE 9:28B–36 We heard this Gospel reading on the Second Sunday of Lent, but today we hear it in a different context—Ordinary Time, when the Scriptures have been chosen to help us understand the demands of discipleship.

Previous to today's Gospel reading, Jesus had presented major points of his teaching on a mountain, a setting that recalls God's gift of the Torah to Moses on Mount Sinai. Matthew thus portrays Jesus as true interpreter of the Mosaic law. In today's account of Jesus' Transfiguration, Matthew depicts Jesus as the one who fulfills the Law and the Prophets, symbolized by the figures of Moses, the Lawgiver, and Elijah, prominent among the great prophets of Israel. These figures appear with Jesus, but they fade into the background after the revelation of divine presence in Jesus.

The "bright cloud" reminds us of the guiding presence of God as a pillar of cloud in Israel's desert journey. The voice from the cloud describes Jesus as "beloved Son," recalling the divine voice heard at Jesus' baptism. On the mountain, God's voice adds the command to "listen to him." In the Old Testament, to hear and obey God's Word was the identifying mark of a genuine response to God. In the Transfiguration story, God calls all disciples to listen to his Son's teaching, in the words he speaks and in the self-giving death he will embrace.

1 CHRONICLES 15:3–4, 15–16; 16:1–2 This text, written during the Babylonian Exile, recounts how David assembles all the people to bring the Ark of the Lord, the key symbol of the Lord's presence with the people, to the tent that David had pitched for it in the holy city, Jerusalem. This idealized picture of David, eliminating all his negative qualities, was cultivated long after David's death and ascribed not only kingly but priestly roles to him. It is David who gathers the people, who offers sacrifice, and who blesses the people. All the people as well as the priests and Levites are active participants, as they process the Ark of the Lord to its honored place in the holy city.

The connection with the solemnity of Mary's Assumption centers on the image of the Ark. The Ark contained God's Word written by the finger of God on stone tablets given to the people through Moses. It was the ultimate expression of the presence of the Lord among the people. Mary is understood as the new Ark of the Lord, the one whose yes to God enabled God to take flesh in her in the person of Jesus. Mary heard God's Word in her life and, through that hearing, allowed God to become one of us, truly human. Today, we honor Mary as the living Ark of the Lord who brought the Word of God to live among us.

PSALM 132:6–7, 9–10, 13–14 (8) The probable backdrop for this psalm is a warrior's return from battle to his permanent abode. This backdrop provides the setting for the procession of Ark of the Lord to its dwelling place among the people. David is said to have discovered the Ark and to have pitched a tent fitting to house the Ark in Zion, the holy city Jerusalem, representing both the land and the people. The people and the priests are summoned to enter God's dwelling, to praise and sing joyfully to the Lord, and to pray for the king, God's anointed. Because God had chosen Zion and prefers to dwell with the people forever, there is much to rejoice about. Zion is God's chosen permanent abode. Such intimate connection with God can only result in blessings for the king, the land, and all the people. Symbolically, Mary is the new Ark of the Lord, through whom God, in the person of Jesus, "made his dwelling among us" (John 1:14).

CONNECTIONS TO CHURCH TEACHING AND TRADITION

- "The Most Blessed Virgin Mary, when the course of her earthly life was completed, was taken up body and soul into the glory of heaven, where she already shares in the glory of her Son's Resurrection, anticipating the resurrection of all members of his Body" (CCC, 974).

- "This maternity of Mary in the order of grace began with the consent which she gave in faith at the Annunciation and which she sustained without wavering beneath the cross, and lasts until the eternal fulfillment of all the elect" (LG, 62).

- "Holy Church honors with especial love the Blessed Mary, Mother of God, who is joined by an inseparable bond to the saving work of her Son. In her the Church . . . joyfully contemplates, as in a faultless image, that which she herself desires and hopes wholly to be" (SC, 103).

1 CORINTHIANS 15:54B–57 Paul continues his discussion of the meaning of the resurrection of the body. Paul, a good Pharisee, believes in the resurrection of the body as the final stage in our union with God. Paul grapples to understand and to explain what the resurrection of the body will entail. Here, he speaks in terms of the "mortal" being clothed "with immortality" (15:53). We will continue to be who we are, but we will be different. His strong belief in the continuation of life in God leads Paul to personify death and ridicule its arrogance in thinking that it has the final word on life. Rather, Paul knows that the "sting" of death (15:55), the result of sin and slavish adherence to the law, has been completely defeated by God in the victory that we have in Christ Jesus. Paul implies that by clothing ourselves with Christ, we are clothing ourselves with Christ's victory over sin and death as well. As he says elsewhere, if we are willing to die with Christ, a lifelong struggle, then through faith in the power of God that raised Christ, we too will be raised, or clothed with immortality. This is what Mary did with her whole life, and in this solemnity of the Assumption we celebrate her being clothed with immortality.

- "The Assumption of the Blessed Virgin is a singular participation in her Son's Resurrection and an anticipation of the resurrection of other Christians" (CCC, 966).

LUKE 11:27–28 A woman from the crowd, on hearing Jesus speak, blesses the "womb that carried [him] and the breasts at which [he] nursed" (11:27). The woman's obvious praise of Jesus is, for her, a reflection on his mother and family. Obviously, he was brought up well and it manifests itself in his life and speech. Jesus responds by not denying her blessing, but by bringing an added dimension to the qualities of being blessed. "Blessed are those who hear the word of God and observe it" (11:28). Jesus is affirming himself as doubly blessed in the person of his mother. Not only is Mary the woman who gave him birth, but Mary is also the one who taught him what it means to "hear the word of God and observe it." His own life and teachings are an outgrowth of her lifelong example of hearing God's Word and observing it. Jesus' ministry invites all disciples to live lives attuned to God's Word, and to manifest that Word in all they do. In so doing, we, like Mary, will share fullness of life with God.

REVELATION 11:19A; 12:1–6A, 10AB Several passages are combined to highlight the meaning of Mary's Assumption. Open access by all to God's temple and Ark is a vision of the end times when God will be accessible to and abide with all. Two signs follow: the woman who labors to give birth and the red dragon swollen with lust for domination. Ready to devour the child, the dragon is denied his prey, as God protects both the child and the woman. The last verses proclaim that with the birth of the child, God's anointed has arrived, with salvation and power, to establish the kingdom of God. While the vision and signs symbolize the struggle between the power of Rome (the dragon) and the Christian community (the woman), the child and the beginning and final acclamations proclaim ultimate victory over evil by Christ and his followers. Mary's Assumption into heaven is a direct result of her key role in making God's victory over evil possible by assenting to be the bearer of God. This solemnity celebrates the way in which God honors Mary with fullness of life for her role in cooperating with Christ to defeat sin and death. In Christ, we are called to the same role and, in expectant hope, to the same fullness of life.

PSALM 45:10, 11, 12, 16 (10BC) This royal psalm recounts a wedding celebration between a king and a bride from a foreign land. Already married, the queen takes her honored place at the king's right hand, arrayed in gold. She is counseled to forget her people and family since she is now her king's desire and resides with him. The verses end with the royal procession of the queen and her attendants into the king's palace. Liturgically, the psalm connects the queen's welcome to the king's palace and her honored place at his right hand to Mary's Assumption, her full welcome into God's palace and her honored place with her Son and Lord. After Christ, Mary is the first person to be granted such full access and communion with God. The Lord had done great things for Mary because of her willingness to cooperate fully with God's will and plan. Mary thus becomes the clearest model of discipleship and of the desired fullness of life with God for which all disciples yearn.

CONNECTIONS TO CHURCH TEACHING AND TRADITION

- "The most Blessed Virgin Mary . . . was always intimately united with her Son and in an entirely unique way cooperated in the work of the Savior" (AA, 4).

- "The Virgin Mary, who at the message of the angel received the Word of God in her heart and in her body and gave Life to the world, is acknowledged and honored as being truly the Mother of God and Mother of the Redeemer" (LG, 53).

- "Thus Mary, a daughter of Adam, consenting to the divine Word, became the mother of Jesus, the one and only Mediator. . . . She devoted herself totally as a handmaid of the Lord to the person and work of her Son . . . freely cooperating in the work of human salvation through faith and obedience. . . . For, as St. Irenaeus says, she 'being obedient, became the cause of salvation for herself and for the whole human race'" (LG, 56).

1 CORINTHIANS 15:20–27 Paul reflects on the Resurrection of Christ and its impact on all created reality from the moment of creation to the end of time. Death came into the world with the sin of Adam, representative of all humanity. Christ, representative of all humanity, was raised from the dead, bringing an end to the power of death. While in Adam we all die, in Christ, all are "brought to life" (15:22). Christ is the first full human being, the "firstfruits" (15:20), to experience resurrected life. Those who belong to Christ will also experience this newness of life. Christ will reign until everything opposed to God is defeated and death itself is destroyed. Then fullness of life in God will be experienced by all. Mary's Assumption celebrates the reality that she now experiences fullness of life with God. She is the first, after Christ, to experience the joy of resurrected life, body and soul, with God for all eternity. In living as disciples of Jesus, we, too, look forward in hope to the same fullness of life.

- "In the public life of Jesus, Mary makes significant appearances. . . . In the course of her Son's preaching . . . he declared blessed[1] those who heard and kept the word of God, as she was faithfully doing" (LG, 58).

LUKE 1:39–56 Mary visits her pregnant cousin Elizabeth soon after Mary assents to cooperate with God's plan of bringing salvation to the world through the birth of Jesus. This touching moment is rich with tenderness and full of praise for God and the special role that Mary will play in God's plan of salvation. Elizabeth blesses Mary and acknowledges that the child she is carrying is the Lord. Just as important is the fact that Mary believed God's Word and acted upon it without hesitation. In response Mary launches into her special praise of God with "the Almighty has done great things for me" (1:49). Mary sings of the wonderful things that God has done not just for her, a lowly servant, but for all humanity. In loving us so much to be willing to become one of us, God has remained faithful to the covenant promises. God has thus reversed the world's pattern of power and domination, by casting down the mighty and lifting up the lowly. God has sent the rich away empty while filling the hungry with good things. Because of her willingness to cooperate in bringing love into the world, "all generations will call [her] blessed" (1:48). Mary's Assumption is God's affirmation of the significant and world-changing role that Mary played in activating God's saving plan for the world.

---

1. Cf. Mark 3:35; Luke 11:27–28.

NUMBERS 21:4B–9 In the account we hear from the Book of Numbers, the Israelites continue their desert journey. By now, they are weary and untrusting of Moses and what he says about God's plan. Certainly, God has provided for them, not only in their escape, but also in giving them a new food to eat. Unfortunately, their response is to say that the manna is disgusting. Then, they are attacked by serpents, which kill many of them. With that, the people turned to Moses and admitted that they had sinned in complaining against the Lord and Moses. They were typical of people who repent when they see the negative consequences their actions bring on themselves. Nevertheless, Moses, the faithful, long-suffering leader, prayed for them and God offered him a solution. Moses was to fashion a bronze serpent and hold it up for the people to see. Those who looked at the raised serpent would live.

This might sound like magic, but in reality it is something entirely different. In holding up the serpent before them, Moses challenged the people to face their own pettiness and fears. They got themselves into trouble by forgetting the gratitude they owed their God. Then, they were afraid of the consequences of their actions. When Moses held up the serpent, they had to face those consequences; they had to face not only the result of their sin, but the fear they suffered. Through Moses, God brought the people into greater responsibility for their own lives, and to a greater trust in the One whose only desire was to bring them to salvation.

PSALM 78:1–2, 34–35, 36–37, 38 (SEE 7B) This psalm is a fitting reminder to people who find it easier to complain against God than to cherish and give thanks for all they have received. Praying this psalm invites us to remember the works of the Lord in our own lives, to test the sincerity of our praise and to trust in the God who will always forgive.

PHILIPPIANS 2:6–11 This hymn sings first of Christ's humility and humiliation and then of his exaltation and the homage due him. As it begins, Christ is at least subtly compared to Adam. Unlike Adam, Christ did not grasp at being or appearing godlike according to human standards. Rather, as the second person of the Holy Trinity, true God

CONNECTIONS TO CHURCH TEACHING AND TRADITION

- "Taking up St. John's expression, 'The Word became flesh,'[1] the Church calls 'Incarnation' the fact that the Son of God assumed a human nature in order to accomplish our salvation in it" (CCC, 461).

- "In the exercise of our freedom we sometimes reject . . . new life . . . or we do not persevere on the way. . . . Through sin, we choose a path of death. Hence, the proclamation of Jesus always calls to conversion, which makes us share in the triumph of the Risen One and begins a journey of transformation" (*Aparecida*, 351).

---

1. John 1:14.

and true man, he revealed an image of God as the one who will do anything, even suffer anything, in order to serve lost humanity. The hymn says that Christ was obedient, a concept that implies listening to God; God's will was Christ's only priority. While many of us seek our own exaltation, Christ obeyed rather than seek glory, and that attitude allowed God to exalt him. Because of that, every sentient creature is to bend the knee at his name and proclaim him as the Lord who gives glory to God.

JOHN 3:13–17 There is a Taizé hymn, sometimes sung on Good Friday that says, "All you who pass this way, look and see," based on Lamentations 1:12. That is an interesting injunction: not just to look, but to see, really see, what happened on the cross. The first part of today's selection from the Gospel according to John invites us to do just that. Jesus tells Nicodemus that, like the bronze serpent, he will be lifted up for all to see and believe. What are they to see and believe? They are to see that violence, oppression, and death are not the final answer. That is not how the universe really works. While we may carry on with our fears, our competitiveness, and our complaints against what God or fate have dealt us, the cross of Christ is there to say that there is no need to try to preserve our lives because we have already been promised eternal life.

Beyond the slogans flashed on the scoreboard about John 3:16, this teaching insists, like the previous readings, that God wills to save all people. Jesus became flesh, not to condemn, but to open our eyes and to offer an alternative possibility for how to live. As John's account of the Gospel proceeds, we will see that Jesus has no fear of death. He willingly and freely confronts death because he believes in the God of life who promises eternal life. Thus, on the cross, death and every death-dealing action are rendered impotent. When we realize that the cross was only a prelude to the Resurrection, we understand the meaning of this feast. Jesus' cross showed the utter futility of everything that has to do with death. Like Moses' serpent, the cross may be frightening if we only look. If we truly see, we realize that it is the greatest symbol of triumph in history.

• "For by his incarnation the Son of God has united himself in some fashion with every man. He worked with human hands, he thought with a human mind, acted by human choice,[2] and loved with a human heart. Born of the Virgin Mary, he has truly been made one of us, like us in all things except sin"[3] (GS, 22).

2. Cf. Third Council of Constantinople: "and so his human will, though deified, is not destroyed" (Denziger).

3. Cf. Hebrews 4:15.

REVELATION 7:2–4, 9–14 The Book of Revelation offers hope, courage, strength, and consolation to disciples who suffer persecution and death for fidelity to Jesus' values and lifestyle. Two vision scenes are pictured. The first addresses the disciples still struggling on earth as the angel seals the "foreheads of the servants of our God" (7:3). When destruction of their evil persecutors occurs according to God's plan, they will be marked with God's seal and be spared, for they belong to God. The symbolic number 144,000 represents the twelve tribes of Israel squared multiplied by the perfect number one thousand indicating an incalculable totality. The second vision recounts the heavenly liturgy of worship and honor given to God and the Lamb (John's symbol for the Risen Christ) by "a great multitude, which no one could count" (7:9). These are the ones who have remained faithful despite suffering persecution and death, those who remained pure and faithful even to death, modeling themselves on Christ who shed his blood on the cross for all.

Revelation richly expresses their identity as those who have "washed their robes and made them white in the Blood of the Lamb" (9:14). Their longing to see God's face motivated them to model themselves on Jesus, and to live the values of the Beatitudes proclaimed in today's Gospel.

PSALM 24:1–2, 3–4, 5–6 (SEE 6) The psalm's refrain captures well the Solemnity of All Saints as it invites us to acknowledge to God that "this is the people that longs to see your face." This Temple processional psalm declares that our God is the creator of the earth and all who dwell in it, establishing it by bringing order to the chaotic watery powers. Our powerful creator God who created and ordered the universe has chosen to enter into loving covenant relationship with us. The psalm's other verses use a dialogue question and answer method to acquaint the people to the demands of covenant relationship for anyone desiring to see the Lord's face, usually understood as experiencing the Lord's intimate presence in the Temple. Purity of heart and mind, and covenant love actualized in right relationship with all are the heart of covenant fidelity. These people do and will continue to experience God's intimate love relationship forever.

CONNECTIONS TO CHURCH TEACHING AND TRADITION

- "They are . . . to live 'as is fitting among saints,' (Ephesians 5:3), and 'as God's chosen ones, holy and beloved, to show compassion, kindness, lowliness, meekness, and patience' (Colossians 3:12) to have the fruits of the Spirit for their sanctification" (LG, 40).

- "All who in obedience to Christ seek first the kingdom of God will derive from it a stronger and purer motivation for helping all their brothers and sisters and for accomplishing the task of justice under the inspiration of charity" (GS, 72).

1 JOHN 3:1–3 John calls disciples "children of God," expressing the intimacy and the longing that covenant relationship through Jesus and the Holy Spirit engenders. However, fidelity to covenant living leads to rejection and persecution because covenant values challenge the typical manner of operating of the "world" (3:1). Just as the world rejected ("did not know" [3:1]) Jesus, so they reject and persecute his followers. Yet no matter what happens, we are beloved children of God here and now. What that love relationship will look like for all eternity in full intimacy with God we do not know. We do know that those who have "this hope" (3:3), this longing for full intimacy with God, strive to adhere faithfully to covenant love ("makes himself pure" [3:3]) modeled by Jesus, and will ultimately experience God's face and loving embrace for all eternity.

MATTHEW 5:1–12A The Beatitudes introduce Matthew's Sermon on the Mount, chapters 5 through 7. They are guidelines for disciples, encapsulating the values that Jesus came to proclaim both in his own life and in his preaching on the kingdom of God. On the Solemnity of All Saints, we claim that the lifestyle embedded in the Beatitudes is the essence of sainthood. The universal call to holiness in chapter 5 of *Lumen gentium* reminds us that all are called to sainthood. We accomplish this with the Spirit's help by taking on the mind and heart of Jesus as expressed in the Beatitudes' values.

These values form the core of right relationship with God and others, while challenging the ordinary patterns of people's lives. Can it be that the poor, the sorrowful, the meek, and those who hunger and thirst for righteousness are truly blessed? Do the merciful, the clean of heart, the peacemakers, and those persecuted for righteousness truly acquire blessedness in this world and the next? Often such a lifestyle leads not to blessedness but worries, troubles, and conflicts. Maybe that is why the Beatitudes end with a realistic assessment that such living results in insults and persecution.

Yet Jesus stresses that living these values brings about the kingdom of God on earth and results in eternal life with God. Longing to see God's face demands living out the Beatitudes daily, thus establishing right relationship with God and others that will last for all eternity.

- "All Christians in whatever state or walk in life are called to the fullness of Christian life and to the perfection of charity, and this holiness is conducive to a more human way of living even in society here on earth. In order to reach this perfection the faithful should use the strength dealt out to them by Christ's gift, so that, following in his footsteps and conformed to his image, doing the will of God in everything, they may wholeheartedly devote themselves to the glory of God and to the service of their neighbor" (LG, 40).

WISDOM 3:1–9 When the Book of Wisdom was written, many Jews in Alexandria were tempted to abandon the ethical standards of the Mosaic law. They were attracted by the philosophies of the Hellenist world, renowned for its libraries and scholars. The author of Wisdom, however, invites them to follow the example of Solomon, whose virtue was well-known and revered. The problem of suffering in the world—childlessness and early death—is also addressed by the author. Conventional wisdom viewed suffering as punishment from God, and those who suffered and died were considered foolish for following his ways. The afterlife was no more than the shadowy place of Sheol, where the wicked and righteous shared the same dismal end. In contrast, the author of Wisdom writes that unbelievers do not know "the secret purposes of God" (2:22), who destines the human soul for "immortality" (3:4). For the righteous, there is the reward of the life to come beyond the sufferings experienced in this world. They will be blessed with immortality and will judge nations and rule over peoples. They will be with their God for all eternity, for he will take them to himself.

PSALM 23:1–3A, 3B–4, 5–6 Though written in the first person singular, this psalm is a reflection on the Lord's loving care for his people on their journey to the Promised Land. The Lord is portrayed as a shepherd who guides his flock and as a host who sets a lavish banquet. In the Middle East, sheep are generally pastured on rocky and barren land. The well-watered land is reserved for growing crops. The Lord, though, both pastures his flock in "green pastures" and leads them "beside still waters" (Psalm 23:2). In "the darkest valley" (v. 4) of suffering, he is with them. Even in the presence of the enemy, his people can be assured of guidance.

ROMANS 5:5–11 Paul has been speaking about justification by faith. He assures the reader that if they persevere despite suffering, they can have confidence in God's love and mercy. The believer can have "hope of sharing the glory of God" (5:2). The basis of this hope is that "God's love has been poured into our hearts through the Holy Spirit" (v. 5). When people do nothing to deserve God's love, even when

CONNECTIONS TO CHURCH TEACHING AND TRADITION

- Death is the end of earthly life (CCC, 1006–1019), and in death, we are united with the death of Jesus.

- Death marks our entrance into everlasting life (CCC, 1020).

- We believe in the resurrection of the body (CCC, 988–1005).

- The Catholic tradition articulates beliefs in particular judgment (CCC, 1021–1022), heaven (CCC, 1023–1029), final purification or purgatory (CCC, 1030–1032), hell (CCC, 1033–1037), the last judgment (1038–1041), and in the hope of the new heaven and the new earth (CCC, 1042–1050).

they are his enemies, they still can trust in the certainty of his promise. This is not an abstract ideal. The death of his Son, Jesus, is the measure of his unconditional love. Few would consider dying for a good person, much less for one's adversaries as Jesus did. Because God can reconcile even his enemies to himself (v. 10), those who hope in him can trust and have confidence in his offer of salvation. If Christians hold fast to him despite their suffering, they will share in the risen life of Christ who reconciled them to God through his death.

JOHN 6:37–40 When the Hebrew people left Egypt, they suffered hunger in the desert. God sent manna from heaven to sustain them on their journey to the Promised Land. Those who ate this bread eventually died. Jesus comes as the "bread of life" (6:35) that lasts forever. Vast crowds follow Jesus in the wilderness because they saw the "signs that he was doing" (v. 2; "signs" is John's word for miracles). They were, however, not always aware of the signs of God's presence in the words of life Jesus spoke. Jesus is sent into the world to reveal God's wisdom and he teaches the people at length. The Wisdom tradition spoke of the "bread of learning" and "the water of wisdom" (Sirach 15:3). Unlike human wisdom, Jesus' truth lasts forever. When Jesus sees that the people have grown hungry, he takes ordinary barley bread, the food of the poor, and demonstrates that he is God's gift of life everlasting. God entrusts these souls to the care of Jesus; no one who comes to him in faith will perish. Everyone who believes in Jesus' revelation will share in the mystery of his death and Resurrection. Belief in Jesus Christ is the key to God's offer of salvation. Many find it difficult to accept that he is the one sent from God to give his body and blood for the life of the world. For believers, though, life is changed at death, not ended. The souls of the just will enjoy the fullness of life with Jesus, the Bread of Life, whose body and blood they have shared in the Eucharist during their life on earth.

EZEKIEL 47:1–2, 8–9, 12 The Lord called Ezekiel to be a prophet at a time of spiritual crisis during the Exile in Babylon (593 BC). In this reading water is a sign of hope in a time of defeat, the time of exile in a dry, desert land. The stream flowing from the Temple recalls the four rivers that issued from a single source in the Garden of Eden (Genesis 2:10–14). The four measurements in vv. 3–5 (not a part of today's reading) show the increasing depth of the water: ankle-high, knee-high, hip-high, and finally so deep you can only cross it only by swimming. Trees of every kind grow along the river. The fruit provides food, and the leaves serve as medicine for healing. The vision of the restored Temple is partially fulfilled when the exiles returned after 538 BC. Its full meaning awaits Jesus' inauguration of the heavenly Jerusalem. This reading provides the climax to which chapters 40 through 46 build. The life-giving water flowing out of the Temple symbolizes the power of God who can create life where none exists. God's love for his people is overflowing. For us today, its nature is such that the promise of life is fulfilled in we who hear his Word and participate in the Eucharist. His love in Jesus comes to us in our worship and flows out through the working of the Holy Spirit in us as we go forth from the Eucharistic liturgy.

PSALM 46:3, 4, 5–6, 8, 11 This psalm, which might have been written after one of David's many victories, encourages us to trust that God is with us in the worst of times. It is the first of the Zion Temple hymns, praising God for his presence to his people (Psalms 48, 76, 84, 87, 122). Though Jerusalem itself is not situated on a river, the psalmist uses the expression "a river whose streams" as a symbol of the divine presence as in today's First Reading (see also Isaiah 33:21; Ezekiel 47:1–12; Joel 4:18; Zechariah 14:8; Revelation 22:12). Because God is present, dwelling in Jerusalem, the city will be at peace, war will cease, and weapons will be destroyed. In its place, the stream of life-giving water will cause the city to rejoice. We today who are the "temple of the living God" can also rejoice because God is present with and in us.

1 CORINTHIANS 3:9C–11, 16–17 The Church of Corinth was blessed with numerous charisms, but they also

CONNECTIONS TO CHURCH TEACHING AND TRADITION

- The Church is the temple of the Holy Spirit (CCC, 797–798), as is the faithful (CCC, 1179), and as is the whole human person (CCC, 364–365).

- The Church building is a house of prayer and the house of God, and thus the proper place of worship (CCC, 1181–1186).

- In its churches, the Church offers public worship to the Holy Trinity (CCC, 1187–1199).

- In entering the Church, we pass from the world darkened by sin to the world of new Life (CCC, 1186).

- Worship is not tied to a particular place (CCC, 1179).

- The mission of Christ and the Holy Spirit are accomplished in and by the Church (CCC, 737, 778, 871–875).

experienced sharp divisions. Factions developed among the Corinthians because some of them were devoted to Apollos (a Jewish convert to Christianity who served the Church at Corinth), others to Cephas (Peter, Aramaic: "rock"), and still others to Paul himself (1:12). In his First Letter to the Corinthians, Paul urges them not to act out of rivalry, but to work in harmony with one another because they are "God's building" (v. 9). Paul founded the community "like a skilled master builder" (v. 10), and others have labored to construct it. However, the true foundation is Jesus Christ. One day God will test the quality of each one's work. Paul reminds the community that the Church is more than a building because "God's Spirit dwells" in each person as in a holy tabernacle (v. 16).

JOHN 2:13–22 Matthew, Mark, and Luke present the cleansing of the Temple at the close of Jesus' public ministry as the final act leading to Jesus' arrest and crucifixion. In contrast, John places the event at the beginning of his account of the Gospel. John locates the episode immediately after the wedding at Cana where Jesus changes water to wine (2:1–12), a sign of the messianic era. Cana is identified as a city of faith, because Jesus "revealed his glory; and his disciples believed in him" there (v. 11). In Jerusalem, by contrast, Jesus experiences rejection leading to his passion and death. Jesus goes to the Temple with his disciples to celebrate the Passover feast. Jesus' cleansing of the Temple resembles the symbolic deeds acted out by the prophets (see Jeremiah 7) and is a sign that the Temple needs purification because his Father's house has been made into a marketplace (John 2:16). The people demand a sign that Jesus is authorized to do such a thing. Jesus offers no proof, but foreshadows the destruction of his own body, the true Temple of God's presence. While the cleansing of the Temple points to Jesus' death and Resurrection, only people of faith truly understand the meaning of Jesus' actions in this reading from the Gospel, and their understanding comes only after he was raised from the dead. Though the Temple is destroyed in AD 70 by the Roman army under Titus, the risen body of Christ replaces it.

GENESIS 3:9–15, 20 Genesis 3 tries to explain humanity's first fall into mistrust of God. The lying tempter assured Adam and Eve that they could become like gods. Dazzled, they forgot that they were already created in the divine image; they took the bait and ate. Then, as soon as they faced God, they began the blame game, refusing responsibility for their actions.

If we pay careful attention to the way the Genesis author explains this incident, we may discover some subtle dimensions of its teaching. Eve understood God's plan and told the serpent that even touching that one tree was forbidden. God had said, "You shall not eat it . . . or else you will die" (3:3). When God sought out the couple and revealed their transgression, however, they were not slain on the spot, but told that they started something in motion that was going to make life difficult for everyone. Adam and Eve's original destiny was to live in God's world, but, influenced by the evil one, they chose another path; they chose to seek their own fortune rather than trust God as the ultimate giver of good. According to the story, when they disobeyed, what they learned about was fear and self-concern, and they passed that ego-protecting anxiety on to their children.

PSALM 98:1, 2–3, 3–4 (1) After the Genesis account of human frailty and arrogance, Psalm 98 reorients our gaze, focusing not on humanity, but on God and salvation. The psalm has close ties to the song of the Israelites when they were freed from fear of the Egyptians (see Exodus 15). Psalm 98 exhorts us to remember God's goodness and to rejoice in it. While the passage from Genesis reflects on the beginnings of human society and our broken relationship with God, the psalm presents a positive universal outlook: all nations can be witnesses to God's righteousness and justice. That justice, as we saw in Genesis, is always aimed at saving rather than punishing. That is an important message to remember as we praise God and live out the Christian commitment to justice.

CONNECTIONS TO CHURCH TEACHING AND TRADITION

- "The Church's devotion to the Blessed Virgin is an intrinsic element of Christian worship . . . from the blessing with which Elizabeth greeted Mary (cf. Luke 1:42–45) right up to the expressions of praise and petition used today" (MC, 56).

- "The Blessed Virgin's exemplary holiness encourages the faithful to 'raise their eyes to Mary. . . .' It is a question of solid, evangelical virtues: faith and the docile acceptance of the Word of God (cf. Luke 1:26–38, 1:45, 11:27–28; John 2:5); generous obedience (cf. Luke 1:38); genuine humility (cf. Luke 1:48); solicitous charity (cf. Luke 1:39–56)" (MC, 57).

EPHESIANS 1:3–6, 11–12 This selection from the opening of the Letter to the Ephesians is as dense with theology and spirituality as anyone could hope for. The first line we read recalls the connection of the followers of Christ with their Jewish brothers and sisters by using a traditional Jewish blessing and reformulating it to indicate that in Christ we experience the culmination of all God's blessings. One of most intense motifs of this short selection is the concept of election: we are the chosen ones. Here too, there is a connection with what went before. In the past, God prepared a chosen people, but that was not the end of the divine plan. We, those who came after, were also chosen from before the beginning of the world. That statement implies two things: the non-Jewish followers of Christ are just as much a chosen people as the Jews, and that choosing "before the foundation of the world" (1:4) has absolutely nothing to do with human activity. There is nothing that we did or can do to earn the blessings God bestows on us in Christ.

The concept of predestination should be understood in this context. It is God who has predestined humanity to be the recipient of divine life and love. This fact does not privilege a particular group, but rather underlines God's own "will" (1:5)—indeed, God's very "pleasure" that we all might praise God's glory by hoping in Christ.

LUKE 1:26–38 Luke's account of the Annunciation offers a wonderful culmination to the Scripture readings for this feast. Today we celebrate Mary, the "favored one" (1:28) of God. With that designation, as we have seen, she represents all of humanity as recipient of God's love. She also represents humankind in being offered the opportunity to collaborate with God in shaping history.

Our celebration of Mary calls us to imitate her faith and her readiness to let her entire life be defined by her desire to be the "handmaid of the Lord."

Key to Abbreviations for Church Documents

The following documents are referenced under the Connections to Church Teaching and Tradition sections that appear for each date. The full documents texts can be found in LTP's four-volume *Liturgy Documents* series; in *Vatican Council II: Constitutions, Decrees, Declarations; The Basic 16 Documents* translated by Austin Flannery, OP, published by Liturgical Press; on the Vatican website (www.vatican.va); on the United States Conference of Catholic Bishops website (www.usccb.org); or in other online locations, which can be located by searching the English or Latin title.

AA	*Apostolicam actuositatem*
AG	*Ad gentes divinitus*
Aparecida	*Documento Conclusivo de Aparecida*, Fifth General Conference of Latin Bishops (CELAM)
CA	*Centesimus annus*
CCC	*Catechism of the Catholic Church*
CD	*Christus Dominus*
CI	*Christian Initiation*, General Introduction
CL	*Christifideles laici*
CSL	*Communities of Salt and Light*
CSDC	*Compendium of the Social Doctrine of the Church*
CU	*Convenientes ex universo*
DCE	*Deus caritas est*
DH	*Dignitatus humanae*
DV	*Dei Verbum*
DVI	*Dominum et Vivificantem*
DPPL	*Directory on Popular Piety and the Liturgy*
EE	*Ecclesia de Eucharistia*
EG	*Evangelii gaudium*
EIA	*Ecclesia in America*
EJFA	*Economic Justice for All*
EN	*Evangelii nuntiandi*
GDC	*General Directory for Catechesis*

GMD	*Go and Make Disciples: A National Plan and Strategy for Catholic Evangelization in the United States*
CMEF	*God's Mercy Endures Forever*
GS	*Gaudium et spes*
LG	*Lumen gentium*
LMI	*Lectionary for Mass: Introduction*
MC	*Marialis cultus*
NA	*Nostra aetate*
NCD	*National Catechetical Directory for Catholics of the United States (Sharing the Light of Faith)*
OHWB	*Our Hearts Were Burning within Us*
PDV	*Pastores dabo vobis*
PO	*Presbyterorum ordinis*
PS	*Paschale solemnitatis*
RH	*Redemptor hominis*
RMI	*Redemptoris missio*
RP	*Reconciliatio et paenitentia*
SC	*Sacrosanctum concilium*
SNL	*Strangers No Longer: Together on the Journey of Hope*
SRS	*Sollicitudo rei socialis*
SS	*Spe salvi*
USCCA	*United States Catholic Catechism for Adults*